PageMaker® 5 for Windows

SELF-TEACHING GUIDE

PageMaker® 5 for Windows

SELF-TEACHING GUIDE

Kim Baker
Sunny Baker
Kyle Roth

John Wiley & Sons, Inc.
New York ▲ Chichester ▲ Brisbane ▲ Toronto ▲ Singapore

Associate Publisher: Katherine Schowalter
Editor: Tim Ryan
Managing Editor: Frank Grazioli
Editorial Production: Mary Ray Worley/Impressions, a Division of Edwards Brothers, Inc.

This text is printed on acid-free paper.

Library of Congress Cataloging-in-Publication Data:

Baker, Kim, 1935–
PageMaker 5 for Windows : self-teaching guide / by Kim Baker and Sunny Baker.
p. cm. -- (Wiley self-teaching guides)
Includes index.
ISBN 0-471-58953-5 (pbk. : alk. paper)
1. PageMaker for Windows. 2. Desktop publishing. I. Title. II. Series.
Z253.532.P333835 1993
686.2 ' 2544 ' 536--dc20 93-22644

Printed in the United States of America

Contents Overview

Contents

3 The PageMaker Toolbox, 55

4 PageMaker's Control Palette, 81

5 Text Processing with PageMaker, 97

13 Putting It All Together, 261

Glossary, 275

Index, 287

Introduction

Aldus Corporation's PageMaker 5.0 for Windows is the fifth version of the preeminent tool for PC desktop publishing. The term *desktop publishing* was coined by Paul Brainerd, founder and president of Aldus Corporation, as he saw the migration of page layout programs from expensive, dedicated computers to PCs. The initial release of PageMaker marked the beginning of PC-based page layout and design. First on the Macintosh and later on IBM-PC compatibles under Windows, PageMaker has consistently expanded and redefined the capabilities of the desktop designer.

On either the Macintosh or Windows platforms, PageMaker offers a unique and unmatched combination of power and ease-of-use. PageMaker goes beyond ordinary page layout capabilities in its typographic control and color standards. The product allows designers to create elaborate color page layouts right on the desktop, ready for output directly as film on an imagesetter. It also offers a wide range of streamlined functions for fast document assembly. In this introduction, we explain what PageMaker is and why you need this book to master its extensive range of features and capabilities.

Why You Should Learn PageMaker

For anyone involved creating documents, advertising, designs, or other publications on the IBM-PC and compatibles, PageMaker provides a powerful, full-featured tool. With version 5 of PageMaker, Aldus has incorporated more than 100 new features and enhancements. Therefore, anyone who wants to be on the cutting-edge of desktop publishing should learn PageMaker 5.

PageMaker 5.0 Provides Professional-Level Desktop Publishing Power

PageMaker 5.0 for Windows (which we'll refer to simply as *PageMaker* in this book) is a versatile, robust desktop publishing environment developed by Aldus, Inc. in Seattle, Washington. On the PC under Windows, PageMaker brings the full capabilities of professional-level type manipulation and design to the desktop. Using PageMaker, it is possible to assemble all kinds of projects from simple one-page black-and-white flyers to multicolor annual reports complete with photos and illustrations. And even though PageMaker provides enough power for professional publishing applications, the basic operations are easy to learn and use.

PageMaker 5 Fully Supports Color

Version 5 enhances PageMaker's extensive support of color. Until a few years ago, desktop publishing was a completely black and white world, but new technology has made color easier to use and more widely available. PageMaker provides professional-level color handling in an affordable product. This package provides complete control of color design on the desktop and allows desktop publishers to set up documents to print correctly on press.

PageMaker 5 supports a variety of color matching systems such as Pantone, Pantone Pro, Focoltone, and Trumatch. These color systems allow you to choose a color from a swatch book consisting of hundreds or thousands of colors and immediately apply that color to elements in your desktop design. These colors can then be matched on press exactly as specified in the design.

Workgroup Features

PageMaker 5 is a complete publishing workshop in one package. Initially, you may confine yourself to assembling documents on your own, and you may restrict yourself to simple designs containing only type and lines. But later you may want to work with multiple designers on complex projects. With PageMaker 5, the integration of work created with other programs by other people is relatively easy. For example, using the workgroup features of PageMaker 5, a group of desktop publishers can create a complete book project using PageMaker. While some members of the group write, structure, and lay out the text for the project, other members can use programs such as Aldus Persuasion or Aldus Freehand to create complex charts and graphics for integration into the document. Still others may scan in color photographs and edit them using Aldus Photostyler. Then the graphics and pictures can be imported into the PageMaker document and placed in the design along with the text. Once all elements are integrated, the book is ready to go to print in the form of a single document composed of components generated from different sources. PageMaker provides tools for the integration and production of the document as well as facilities for managing external files used to compose the document, such as scans of photos and illustrations produced with other products.

Why You Should Learn PageMaker

About This Book

This book is designed to help you learn PageMaker 5 quickly and effectively. The book introduces all of PageMaker's most important features, tools, and commands, and it is intended for people new to either PageMaker or desktop publishing in general. It does not, however, cover all of the features and options in PageMaker—that would take volumes. As a new user, you will be taken step by step through all the major functions of this feature-laden product. Because PageMaker is brimming with commands, functions, and dialog boxes, a large number of screen shots have been included to better explain the functions and to familiarize you with the flexibility and power of this product.

Assumptions

This book makes some basic assumptions about your system and your computer knowledge, which include:

▲ You have a hard disk with at least 10MB of free space, because PageMaker, its files, and the documents you create with

PageMaker take up a significant amount of disk space (approximately 10MB).

- ▲ You have at least 2 MB (4 MB or more is strongly recommended) of main memory (RAM) installed and your system is properly configured so that Windows applications can use this memory. (Check with your dealer if you are unsure whether your system has been set up correctly or if you don't know how to do this yourself.)
- ▲ You have a current version of Windows (3.0 or higher) correctly installed on your computer.
- ▲ You have installed PageMaker using its automatic installation routine on your hard disk.
- ▲ You are familiar with the basics of using Windows. If PageMaker is your first Windows-based product, get a copy of *Windows 3.1: Self-Teaching Guide,* written by Keith Weiskamp and published by John Wiley & Sons. It is a companion book for this one and will quickly bring you up to speed on installing and using Windows on your computer.
- ▲ You have a mouse. A mouse or similar pointing device is mandatory for using PageMaker effectively, even though it is not required for using Windows. PageMaker relies heavily on drop-down menus and control palettes that are easier to use with a mouse, and PageMaker's drawing tools require a mouse or other drawing device to select and draw elements on the screen.

Large Monitors and Desktop Design

Although a 14" VGA monitor with 640 by 480 pixel resolution on a PC is a very common configuration, to really get the most from PageMaker, a larger-format, higher-resolution monitor with a high-resolution card (SuperVGA or better) is highly recommended. A larger monitor allows you to see more of your document at one time, which makes design easier because you can visually compare larger sections of your document without scrolling. Although PageMaker allows you to zoom out to see large sections of your document at one time, with a small screen you lose detail. A large display with high resolution allows you to see bigger sections and more detail in illustrations, type, and colored objects.

Keep in mind that the interface for PageMaker and Windows takes up quite a bit of your monitor screen that then can't be used to display your documents. The Windows title bar for drop-down menus, PageMaker's window, which includes its title bar and scroll bars, plus PageMaker's floating control palettes, all take up room on the screen. In practice, you can only see about half of an 8 1/2" by 11" page on a standard 14" monitor if you view the page at 100 percent of the printed size. You can make the working area larger by putting away one or more of the useful palettes, but that forces you to use drop-down menus for control and substantially slows document assembly. You can also zoom out to see a reduced view of the document, but that means the detailed design elements are hard to see and type may become unreadable.

About This Book

Also be aware that higher resolution alone provides only marginal improvement. Windows screen type is sized in terms of pixels no matter what the size of the screen. The font on a high resolution 1024 by 768 pixel screen is approximately half the size of the same font on a standard VGA screen (640 by 480 pixels). The solution is to use a larger monitor as you move to higher resolutions. On a 14" monitor, SuperVGA (or simply SVGA), which is 800 by 600 pixels, is the maximum practical resolution. The next jump up in resolution is 1024 by 768 and this requires a 17" or greater monitor to be usable.

As you increase the resolution and/or the number of simultaneous colors of your display, the demand on the PC to move around all those pixels is also increased. Thus, at higher resolutions you will find that some operations take somewhat longer. Make sure that your PC is capable of handling a high-resolution card and monitor before you plunk down your money.

A last caveat: Before purchasing a large monitor and a display card to drive it, test the system thoroughly with all of the applications you plan to use. Even with Windows, incompatibilities do occur. We recommend taking some time to find a monitor/card combination that meets the size, performance, and resolution demands of desktop publishing. Remember that the advantages of a larger monitor, even with its higher price tag, make a big difference in your ability to design quality documents on the desktop. And, if you're new to desktop design and page layout, being able to see what your document looks like without scrolling and zooming will make learning PageMaker significantly easier than working with a small monitor.

PageMaker and Keyboard Commands

As you work through this book, you may notice that there is less emphasis on keyboard equivalents than in many books on DOS and Windows software products. The reason for this is simple: Although PageMaker offers many keyboard shortcuts, the interface emphasizes direct control via floating palettes and commands that open dialog boxes. PageMaker offers so many controls that there are not enough keyboard combinations available to offer memorable keyboard alternatives for every command. Instead, many control functions can be streamlined by using the floating palettes you will be introduced to in Chapters 1 and 2. Keyboard shortcuts, when available, are listed at the close of each section. Except for the most frequently used keyboard commands, you will probably find yourself using the mouse to open dialogs and set control parameters most of the time.

Defaults

A word you will see frequently in this book and in almost all computer books and manuals is *default*. A computer program's default settings are the ones that are used automatically every time the software is launched. For example, until you change the settings, each new PageMaker document is opened as letter-sized with 1" margins around the edge. These settings are the default settings and are set initially by the manufacturer because most users will want to start with letter-sized documents. The manufacturer-supplied defaults and preferences can be easily modified within PageMaker, and we'll show you how to do that in the book.

TIP

Italics are sometimes used in regular text paragraphs for emphasis or to indicate a new phrase or word. If a new word is used it will be defined or explained in the same paragraph where it appears in *italics* or in the glossary at the back of the book.

How to Use This Self-Teaching Guide

How to Use This Self-Teaching Guide

Self-Study Guides do more than present information—they help you learn it. The material in this book is presented in a sequence that promotes a gradual but steady increase of knowledge and skills. For example, by the end of Chapter 2, you will be familiar with PageMaker's menu and command interface and will know how to move around a PageMaker document with ease. By the end of Chapter 5, you will understand how to enter and manipulate text and type within PageMaker and will have covered the basics of assembling documents. The succeeding chapters continue to build your repertoire of PageMaker commands, options, and document design alternatives. Because typography is central to desktop publishing, Chapters 7 and 8 cover the basics of this vast subject and show how to specify type within PageMaker. Once you have mastered all of PageMaker's basics, Chapter 13 allows you to try out your skills assembling an actual publication. You will learn how to integrate the commands and steps you learned in previous chapters to create a complete newsletter from start to finish. In assembling this document, you will employ all of PageMaker's key features and will be able to show off your new skills.

Each chapter includes sections that cover specific topics and features. In addition, the following tools have been designed to make the most of your learning time:

CHECK YOURSELF

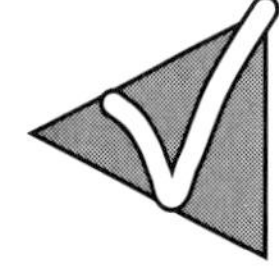

At the end of every major topic you'll see a Check Yourself section where you can bring together all the detailed steps you have learned into one smooth procedure.

PRACTICE WHAT YOU'VE LEARNED

Each chapter has one final Practice What You've Learned. This section lets you review and practice the procedures you have learned in the chapter. It also integrates separate topics from the chapter into meaningful procedures.

TIP

Tip sections appear throughout the book to draw your attention to special features and shortcuts. They also offer suggestions for using the features you learned about. Incorporating these tips into your normal routine enables you to work at the most productive level and shortens the time needed to perform tasks.

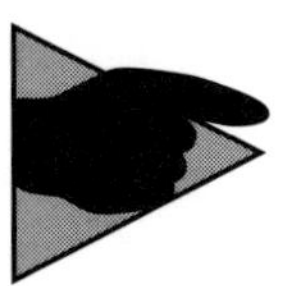

ALTERNATE METHOD

Throughout this book, this icon explains another way to accomplish the same process. PageMaker often has two ways of accomplishing the same objective. For example, type sizes can be changed from the **Type** menu, with a floating palette, or through the **Type Specifications** dialog box.

WARNING

Throughout this book, this icon signals a warning. Ignoring it could result in operational problems when using PageMaker or could damage the documents you create. Beware, and read these warnings carefully.

QUICK COMMAND SUMMARY

Quick Command Summaries fall at the end of each chapter and review any shortcut keys, tasks, and procedures covered in the chapter.

WHAT IF IT DOESN'T WORK?

After each Practice What You've Learned section, you'll find this icon. Explanations in this section will help you troubleshoot problems that may occur for particular steps in the practice session.

Ventura Publisher Users

If you are already an experienced user of Ventura Publisher, or another desktop publishing program, you may want to skip Chapter

1, which covers the basics of the Windows interface and using a mouse, and move quickly through Chapter 2 to learn how to manipulate pages and use PageMaker's powerful floating palettes. Then begin working seriously with the book at Chapter 3. This chapter shows how PageMaker places text and introduces the PageMaker Toolbox palette functions.

How to Use This Self-Teaching Guide

Guided Steps

As you work through this book, you'll encounter practice steps such as the ones that follow. The steps guide you in trying out each new procedure at your keyboard.

To follow these steps:

1. When you see guided steps, take the book to your computer and launch PageMaker (but not right now). Reading in front of your computer with PageMaker open is the easiest way to use this book, because not only can you follow the steps, but also you can instantly refer to PageMaker's menus, commands, and desktop should a question arise.
2. Do each step carefully. Read the entire step first, then try it.
3. If the results aren't what was described, restart the entire procedure. You might have missed or misread a step.

The guided steps take time and you may find that you want to skip them. You are encouraged not to skip them for three important reasons:

- ▲ There's less chance of your missing or misinterpreting something that's important.
- ▲ Your monitor will display the object being discussed so that you can see it as you read about it.
- ▲ PageMaker commands used in one procedure may duplicate a functionality found in other PageMaker commands used for other procedures; without actually working through the procedures demonstrated in the steps, you may become confused as to which command to use for what.

Getting Additional Help

As you work through the book, and especially when you've completed it and are using PageMaker on your own, you may find you need more help when creating a particular kind of document or when using PageMaker's most advanced type and color features. If you do need help on these questions, several resources are available. You might want to try them in the order shown:

1. This book: Try the glossary and the index.
2. The online help system built into PageMaker. We explain where to find it and how to use it in Chapter 1.
3. The PageMaker for Windows documentation.
4. A friend or colleague who knows PageMaker.
5. Your hardware or software dealer.
6. PageMaker technical support. Refer to your PageMaker documentation for the correct telephone number for the Windows version of the product. Should you need to contact PageMaker, Inc. for any reason, the main telephone number in Seattle, Washington, is (206) 622-5500.
7. Desktop publishing or PageMaker user groups that are springing up in most cities. You can find out about these by looking in desktop publishing magazines like *PC Publishing* or *Publish.*
8. Desktop publishing forums that exist in online services such as CompuServe and Genie. Aldus also maintains a forum on Compuserve. If you have a Compuserve account, type "GO ALDUS" after logging on.
9. Service bureaus who output PageMaker documents on their expensive imagesetters. These companies are described in Chapter 11.
10. Aldus Magazine—*Aldus Magazine* is published bimonthly and is free to registered Aldus users. Others may subscribe for $20 a year. Call (206) 628-2321.

PageMaker's Technical Support

Aldus Corporation's support center operates 24 hours a day, 7 days a week. Technical support is free for the first 90 days after you make your first phone call to the support department. Beyond that period, you may choose to either pay an annual fee for support, or forgo access to PageMaker's help line. If you plan to use PageMaker for complex projects involving large files and/or the inclusion of images and color, we recommend the annual support program. Contact Aldus Corporation for more information about support terms and pricing. If you are using PageMaker in a company with other users of Pagemaker or additional Aldus products, your "site" may be covered already.

PageMaker Operations

PageMaker has several command operations that you should be aware of as you work through this book and when you are using PageMaker to create documents.

OK — Clicking **OK** in a PageMaker dialog box works like dialog boxes do in most software products that use them. It closes the box and implements any changes that you made via the dialog.

Cancel — In most PageMaker dialogs, clicking **Cancel** puts the dialog away *without* implementing any changes made in it. In some applications, clicking **Cancel** is just a convenient method for putting dialog boxes away after making changes; in PageMaker it puts the dialog away as if it was never opened in the first place. All changes made in the dialog box are lost.

Commands

Commands are found in the PageMaker's drop-down menus. Rather than consisting of the kinds of command phrases you may be accustomed to under the DOS operating system, PageMaker's commands are descriptive and easy to evoke. You simply select the command and click the mouse. Within PageMaker, commands are shown in the drop-down menus and direct the program to carry out certain processes. Commands that are available appear in menus normally. Commands that are not currently available because they may be unsuitable for the operations currently in progress on the desktop appear as grayed out. Instead of appearing normally, their name appears as gray type. Should you attempt to choose a grayed-out command, PageMaker will simply pass the mouse over the command without any response. Command selection options will be explained more fully in Chapter 1.

Dialog Boxes

Dialog boxes are windows that open in response to a command in PageMaker's drop-down menus. Dialog boxes (or simply "dialogs") are used to carry out multiple functions. You know PageMaker will open a dialog box if a menu item ends with ellipses (. . .). Dialog boxes are used when more than one parameter must be set, values entered, files navigated, or selections made. For example, the menu item **Print...** opens the **Print** dialog box in which you set the parameters for printing a PageMaker document. **Character...** is another example of a command that will open the **Character** dialog box.

PageMaker Operations

Specification fields

Within many PageMaker dialog boxes and palettes there are specification fields. These are simply spaces in which you type information to tell PageMaker what to do. For example, in the **Character** dialog box, there is a field that allows you to type in the size of the type you want to use.

Double-Click

Some operations in PageMaker require two subsequent clicks of the mouse. For example, to close a floating palette requires double clicking on the **Control-menu** box. To double-click, click twice in rapid succession. If you're new to the operation of a mouse, this takes a little practice.

Shift-Click

To select multiple items in PageMaker, a procedure known as "shift-clicking" can save time. To select multiple objects, click on each object you want to choose (select) with the **Shift** key held down. If you pick up one you don't want, shift-clicking on it a second time will unselect it. For example, if you had a page layout in which you want to color several lines blue, shift-clicking on them one at a time will select them so you can change their color at the same time.

Submenus

Like all Windows products, PageMaker uses drop-down menus in place of the command-line commands common to applications that run under MS-DOS. Some of the menu commands will pop up in a submenu to the immediate right of the command after it is selected. These commands have an arrow shown on the right side of the menu to indicate that a submenu will be displayed.

Closing PageMaker Dialog Boxes

PageMaker has a couple of ways to close dialog boxes. First, most boxes can be closed by double clicking on Windows' standard **Close** command found in the **Control-menu** box. Second, depending on the dialog, you can choose from the **OK**, **Save**, or **Cancel** buttons to close the box.

Typographic Conventions

This book has a number of typographical conventions to make certain types of information clear.

Key+key	Two or more key names connected by a plus sign are meant to be pressed simultaneously, similar to a chord on a piano. Usually the first key is the shifting key (**Ctrl, Alt, or Shift**) and the other key is a function key or a character key such as **A, 1,** or *. For example, **Ctrl+S** means to hold down the **Ctrl** key while you press **S**.
Alt H→I	When a command is to be picked from a menu, the **Alt** key and a second key are first pressed simultaneously to drop down the menu. Then the key for the desired command is pressed.
Command	Commands to be selected from the drop-down menus are shown in bold.
Command...	Commands to be selected from the drop-down menus that will display dialog boxes are shown in bold with ellipses.

Now you should be ready to turn your computer on. While the computer is warming up, take a few minutes and just flip through the book to familiarize yourself with the organization of the chapters. You're about to enter a new world of professional desktop publishing possibilities. It's time to get started on your tour—we hope you have a good trip!

Desktop Publishing

By working through the exercises in this book you'll learn how to use PageMaker to produce professional-quality documents and designs right from your desktop computer. The PageMaker desktop, where documents are designed and modified, is actually a window that resembles a drafting board. PageMaker's electronic desktop has blank pages ready for the layout, a blank pasteboard area where type and photos can be placed temporarily before adding them to the layout, and palettes containing the tools to be used for creating the layout. These tool palettes replace the board-based publisher's coffee cups full of pens, pencils, X-acto knives, and other hand tools. In this chapter, you will learn how to:

- ▲ **Differentiate between desktop publishing and word processing**
- ▲ **Practice with the mouse**
- ▲ **Open a PageMaker document**
- ▲ **Tour PageMaker's desktop**
- ▲ **Get online help within PageMaker**

Desktop Publishing Versus Word Processing

In the past few years, word processors have become more like page layout programs. The line that once clearly divided word processing from desktop publishing is now difficult to identify. Advanced text and graphic capabilities are being added to popular word processing software. At the same time, page layout programs have become easier to use and in some cases provide speedy text entry and spell-checking functions that rival the best word processing products. There are, however, some major capabilities that, in most instances, differentiate word processing and desktop publishing from each other. These differences are especially important if you plan to have your desktop-created documents printed on a printing press or imagesetter. All of the following capabilities are available in PageMaker:

- The ability to extensively manipulate type. Type manipulation in a professional-quality page layout program extends beyond selecting a font or type size to the ability to make fine choices in leading, kerning, and tracking. (If you don't know what these things are, you'll learn about them later in the book.)
- The ability to move and resize objects, such as images and blocks of type, by simply clicking and dragging. This easy manipulation of diverse visual elements is not available in most word processing programs.
- The ability to link text along separate, independent paths so it can flow around objects and design elements.
- The ability to specify color, using standard specification systems such as the Pantone Matching System, to enable colors to be matched precisely by a printing press.
- The ability to predictably produce reliable high-resolution output suitable for reproduction at a print shop.
- The ability to integrate type and images, including photos and illustrations, in one document.

Desktop Publishing Versus Word Processing

In addition to these capabilities, a final point of distinction between word processors and page layout programs is based in the function the program was originally designed to handle. Word processors are by definition designed to handle words. Writing long documents in a page layout program is usually tedious, because key features—such as a thesaurus and the ability to split windows to see two different sections of a document—are missing or crippled. Page layout programs are designed to handle the design and look of a document. Therefore, even when some requisite page layout functions are available, the process is slow, limited, and cumbersome in most word processors. The tools for sophisticated page assembly are either missing, minimal, or awkward at best.

In this book, you will learn about the power of PageMaker for Windows. If you are already familiar with word processing, you will see that there really is no comparison between PageMaker and any word processor when it comes to developing sophisticated designs.

Using the Mouse

If you have recently added a mouse to your computer to better take advantage of Windows and, of course, PageMaker, read this section. If you are already an old hand at clicking and pointing with a mouse or another pointing device, skip to the next section.

Getting the Most from Your Mouse and PageMaker

To use PageMaker effectively, you need to master the use of the mouse. It is used for selecting objects, choosing commands, and is especially important for moving objects around on the desktop or resizing them (making them bigger or smaller). Your mouse is an important tool in desktop design and will ultimately become a necessary extension of your right (or left) hand.

To get the best from your mouse, you may want to alter its speed. To do this, double-click on the **Control Panel** icon (in the **Main** window). Then double-click on the **Mouse** icon. Experiment with different settings—when you have something that you're comfortable with, click **OK**. If the mouse is set to move the cursor too fast, you will have trouble accurately making minor adjustments to your page layout. If it moves too slowly, additional hand movement will be required as you move around on the desktop, and your hand may cramp up during a lengthy page layout session.

When the mouse fails to respond as intended to your hand movements, it can be extremely frustrating. The best way to work around this problem is to purchase a quality mouse rather than a cheap one. You should also purchase and use a large *mouse pad*, a specially designed surface for use with a mouse that is available from most computer stores. With the notable exception of mice that have a precision optical grid to ensure the accuracy of their movement, a mouse pad is essential to precision mouse operation. Before purchase, try the mouse out with the pad to ensure that they work well together.

Remember to clean the mouse's ball every few months, as well. Rubber cement thinner such as Bestine, found in every stationery and art supply store, works great for removing the black gunk that accumulates on mouse balls and the internal rollers that sense the ball's movement. Clean the mouse with cotton balls moistened with the solvent. Follow the cautions on the solvent's label carefully and never smoke near this product. If you keep your mouse clean, it will respond better.

Single-Clicking and Double-Clicking

As mentioned in the introduction, the difference between one click and two quick clicks is a very important distinction in making selections with a mouse. The left button on a typical two-button mouse is used for most functions in programs that work under Windows, including PageMaker. Clicking once selects an icon in a window or a drop-down menu item. Clicking once on a word or

Using the Mouse

sentence inside PageMaker inserts the cursor at that point just as in a word processor. Clicking twice on a program icon launches the program. Within PageMaker, clicking twice on a word of text selects the entire word. double-clicking takes a bit of practice. If you're too slow between clicks, the computer treats the clicking as a single-click. If you accidentally move the mouse while double-clicking, you may miss your target. You can adjust the double-click speed to your preference in the Windows Control Panel.

Dragging

The mouse is also used for moving objects around the screen. To *drag* an object, use the mouse to move the cursor onto the object. Now press the left-hand mouse button and hold it down. With the button still held down, move the mouse and the object will follow. When the object is where you want it, release the mouse button. The object will remain where it was dragged.

Mouse Practice

The best place initially to familiarize yourself with the mouse is inside Windows. Not only will you get lots of practice pointing and clicking, but you'll get a free tour of Windows functions as well! After practicing moving around on the screen with the mouse, practice pointing and (double) clicking by exploring the Windows Control Panel. Open the controls, experiment with the mouse settings in the Mouse Control Panel, and try different desktop configurations in the Desktop Control Panel. Try dragging icons around the window to rearrange them.

At first, the mouse will feel like a third hand would, if you were to suddenly acquire one. But within about an hour of use the mouse should begin to feel familiar; within a couple of days you'll wonder how you ever used a computer without one. In fact, if you begin working on a computer not equipped with a mouse, you'll find yourself unconsciously reaching for it!

Drop-Down Menus

If you're new to "mousing around," you will find the menus in Windows much easier to use with the mouse than with the keyboard equivalents that you may have been using.

To use the drop-down menus with a mouse:

1. Move the cursor (using the mouse) to the menu you want to use, then click on its name. This will display the menu items.
2. Using the mouse, move the cursor down the menu. Click to select the menu item under the cursor. The menu item will be briefly highlighted, then the command will execute.

Of course, you can still use the keyboard commands as you may have been doing before adding a mouse to your system, but the mouse is a much faster and more convenient way to take advantage of the drop-down menus in Windows and PageMaker. Single, repetitive commands such as **Save** may be executed faster by using the keyboard equivalent. (In PageMaker the keyboard equivalents for menu commands are listed next to the item in the drop-down menus. Check it out by pulling down some menus and seeing the equivalent commands.)

CHECK YOURSELF

Use the mouse to explore the Windows drop-down menus.

- ▲ Move the mouse around on the mouse pad and click on one of the menu items on the top bar of Windows. The drop-down menus will be displayed after clicking.

Take PageMaker for a Spin

Now that you've got the mouse under control, it's time to meet PageMaker for Windows and take a guided tour around the desktop. If you have not already installed PageMaker for Windows, do so now. PageMaker's manuals explain the installation process. Once installed, check that the PageMaker icon is present in the

Aldus window. If it is not displayed as shown in Figure 1.1, review your installation and setup procedures.

Take PageMaker for a Spin

Now double-click on the PageMaker icon to launch PageMaker for Windows. Depending on the speed of your machine's microprocessor and hard disk, PageMaker may take anywhere from 10 to 60 seconds to launch.

CHECK YOURSELF

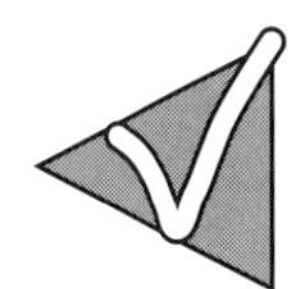

Launch PageMaker using the mouse and mouse buttons.

- ▲ Double-click on the PageMaker icon with the left button of your mouse. PageMaker will load, but you may have to wait for a minute to see the PageMaker menu bar displayed on your monitor.

Your screen should be blank, with a menu bar across the top as in Figure 1.2. Take a moment to investigate the menu titles on the

▼ ***Figure 1.1. The Windows Desktop***

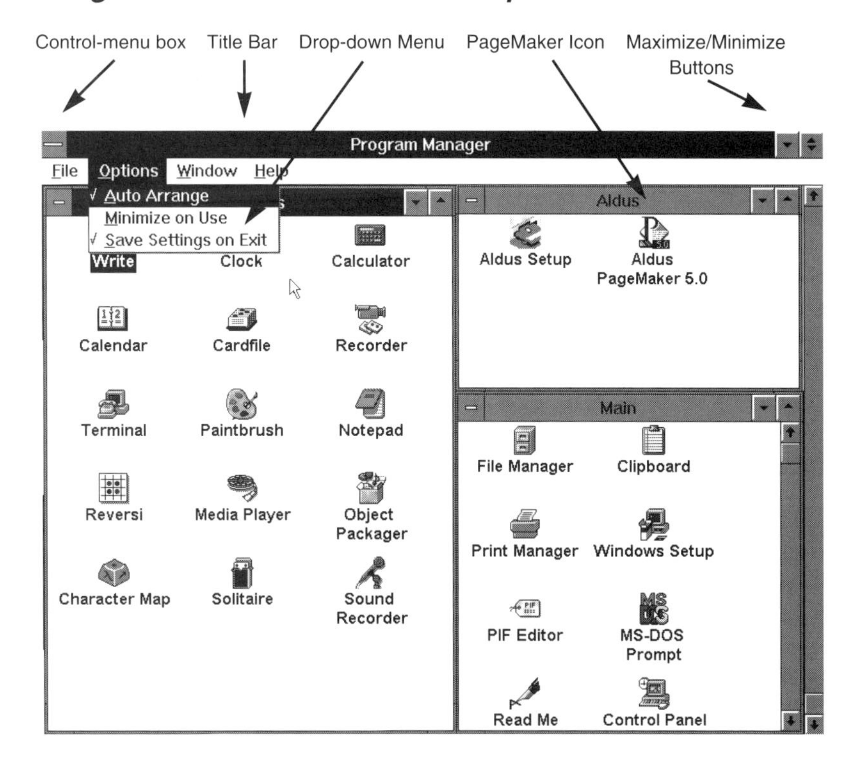

PageMaker menu bar. If you are experienced with Windows, some of them ("File," "Window," "Help") will be familiar. Use the mouse to click open each of the drop-down menus and examine their contents. Notice that some of the items in the menus are followed by ellipses (. . .) and some by a right-facing arrow (→). The ellipses indicate that clicking on that item will bring up a dialog box. An arrow shows that one or more submenus are available.

Now click on the **File** menu. Several of the menu items appear to be faded or "grayed out." These are commands that are not currently available. **Close** is not available now because you have no files open. The ability to gray out some menu choices allows PageMaker to cue you as to what operations are appropriate at any point in the program.

Other menu items have a carat (^) and a letter next to them. This represents the *shortcut key* for that operation. The carat is shorthand for the "Ctrl" key on the keyboard. For example, to open a new file you can either go to the **File** menu and click on **New. . .** or press the "Ctrl" and "N" keys simultaneously. Either operation will bring up the new publication dialog box. You'll find that as you work with PageMaker, many common operations can be performed quickly by using the shortcut keys.

The New Dialog Box

To begin a new publication, open the **File** menu and select **New. . . .** The dialog box shown in Figure 1.3 pops up. With this dialog, you establish the basic settings for your new PageMaker document. These settings can be a rough guess; later on you can use the **Page setup. . .** dialog from the **File** menu to change your initial settings.

First, choose the size of the pages that you will be using. PageMaker allows you to select from several standard sizes by

▼ ***Figure 1.2. The PageMaker Menu***

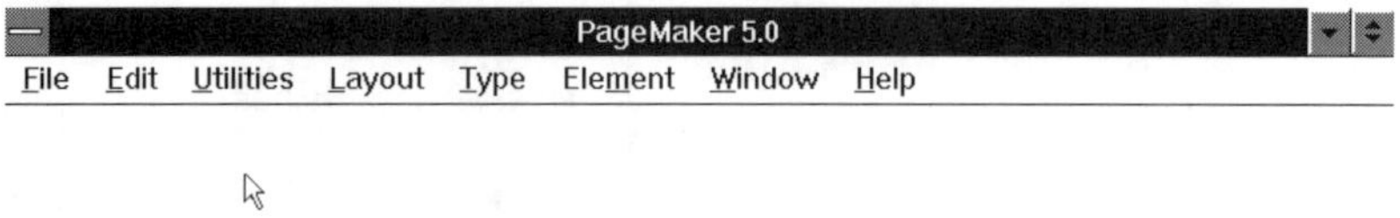

PageMaker 5.0
File Edit Utilities Layout Type Element Window Help

Take PageMaker for a Spin

▼ ***Figure 1.3. The New Dialog Box***

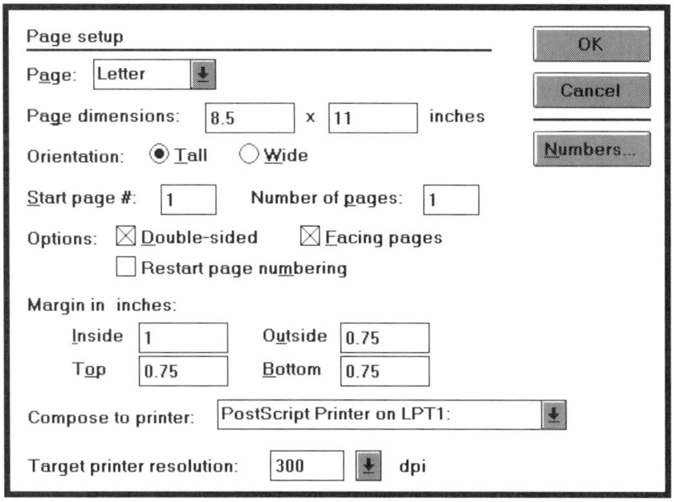

clicking on the arrow next to **Page:**. Alternatively, you may designate a custom page size by directly entering the dimensions in the **Page Dimensions:** boxes. Next, enter the orientation of your document; either tall (also known as "portrait") or wide ("landscape").

Now set the starting page number and the number of pages in your publication. If you are not sure of the number of pages in the final document, make a guess; you can later insert or remove pages through the **Insert** dialog. The **Numbers** button gives you access to a selection of page numbering styles for your publication.

Use the check boxes to indicate whether your document is to be single- or double-sided. If it is double-sided, PageMaker changes the side margins from "Left" and "Right" to "Inside" and "Outside" and gives you the option of working with the document using facing pages on your screen. You can then type in the publication's margins or leave them at the default. Be careful that your margins do not exceed the area that your printer is capable of handling. Many laser printers cannot print closer than .25 inch from the edge of the page. If you are unsure, check your printer's manual.

After setting the margins, move to **Compose to printer:** and specify your target printer and its resolution. Make sure the printer you select is the one you will be using for final production, not just for proofing. Your choice affects, among other things, which fonts will be available to you and whether you can utilize special effects such as text rotation.

CHECK YOURSELF

1. Start PageMaker and enlarge the PageMaker screen by clicking on the **Control-menu** box and selecting **Maximize.** Open the **File** menu and choose **New. . . .**
   ▲ The **New** dialog box appears.

2. Set the top, bottom, and outside margins to .75 inches and the inside margin to 1 inch. Set the number of pages to be 4. Check that **Compose to printer:** is set for your Windows printer. Finally, click on **OK.**
   ▲ A new PageMaker document opens with a blank first page. The margins are indicated by a dotted line. If they are not visible, select the **Layout** menu, click on **Guides and Rulers,** then click on **Guides**.

The PageMaker 5 Desktop

Figure 1.4 shows the PageMaker screen after completing the **New** dialog. In the middle is the first page of your publication. The dotted lines (colored blue on your screen) indicate the margin guides as specified in the dialog box. These help you place objects and text in your publication. They can be moved or additional guides can be added, as we will see in Chapter 3. Notice that on the right and bottom edges of the page the black lines are thicker. These form drop shadows to give you a visual cue that this is a right-hand page.

The Pasteboard

When designers manually lay out a publication, they tape down a specially manufactured piece of cardboard, called *illustration board,* to a drafting table. Design elements ready for use are tem-

Take PageMaker for a Spin

▼ *Figure 1.4. The PageMaker Desktop*

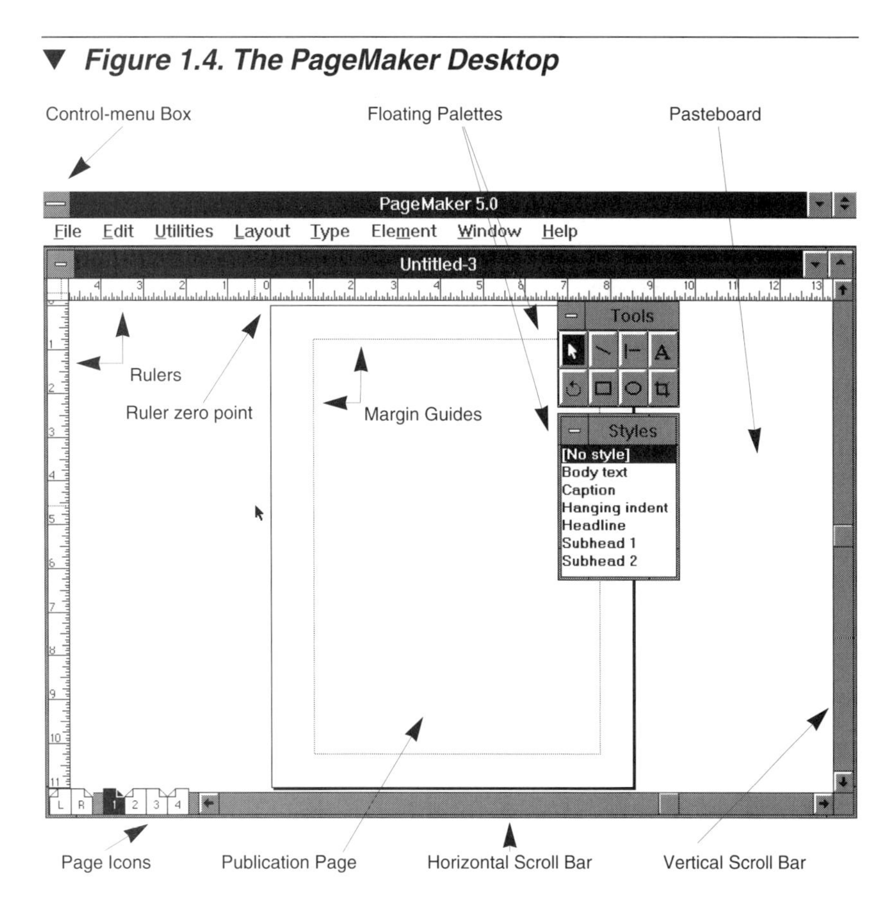

porarily placed on the surface of the drafting table before they are pasted down on the illustration board.

PageMaker simulates this design environment on-screen. The white space surrounding your page is the *pasteboard.* The pasteboard gives you an area in which to store text or pictures before adding them to your publication. You can also remove items from the publication and leave them on the pasteboard while you try out different layouts. Note that when you print a publication, the contents of the pasteboard do not print because they are not part of the layout.

Around the outside edges of the pasteboard are the horizontal and vertical rulers. They help you line up objects and text. As you move the mouse around, notice that dotted lines on both rulers track your motion. The origin, or *zero point*, of the two rulers falls at the upper left edge when looking at a single page, or at the upper intersection of the two pages in a facing-pages view.

The Floating Palettes

Also on your screen are the **Toolbox** and the **Styles** *palettes*. These palettes give you fast access to commonly used tools and commands without reverting to the drop-down menus. They can be repositioned to move them out of the way or to a more convenient spot (hence the term *floating* palettes). To move a palette, click on the palette's title bar and drag it to the new location. When you release the mouse button, the palette will stay where it was positioned. If you decide to close and then reopen a publication, the palettes will be where you last positioned them. You may also double-click on a palette's **Control-menu** box to remove it completely. This lets you put up only the palettes related to your current operations. To make a palette visible on your desktop, use the **Window** menu and click on the palettes you want visible. In addition to the Toolbox and the Styles palettes, which are displayed when you first start a new document, there are palettes for **Colors**, **Control**, and **Library**. We'll look at each of the palettes in more detail later in the book as we cover their functions.

In the lower left of your screen (if you did the last Check Yourself) are six *page icons*—labeled one through four and L and R. The two pages L and R are *master pages*. These allow you to set up style elements that run through the entire document. The pages one through four represent the pages of your production. Page one is highlighted to indicate that it is the page currently in your window. To make another current page, simply click on its icon.

View Size

When you open a new document in PageMaker, the entire first page is visible on-screen. This is a scaled-down picture of the actual document. You can control the size of the on-screen display from the **View** submenu of the **Layout** menu. The page on your screen can be adjusted to 25%, 50%, 75%, 100%, 200%, or 400% of the page's actual size. In addition, you can select **Fit to window** (the default), which will make the image just fill your current window. Smaller sizes allow you to get a feel for the overall "look" of a page or pages. Large sizes permit you to easily work on small details.

Take PageMaker for a Spin

The right-hand mouse button is handy for toggling between **Fit in window** view and **Actual size** view. While in **Fit in window**, position the pointer anywhere on the page and click the right mouse button. You'll now be in **Actual size** view. The section of the page where your pointer was originally positioned now lies in the center of the screen. Click the right-hand mouse button again and you're returned to **Fit in window** view.

The pasteboard area is actually quite large, providing room to store many pieces of text and graphics. It is easy to forget where a particular element was placed. The **Show pasteboard** command, available from the **View** submenu, brings the entire pasteboard into the current window, while shrinking the layout pages.

CHECK YOURSELF

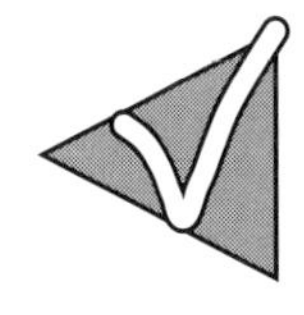

1. Using the publication from the last Check Yourself, double-click on the **Styles** Control-menu box.
   ▲ The **Styles** palette is removed from the screen.
2. Click on the title bar of the **Toolbox** and drag the menu to the left-hand side of the page.
   ▲ The menu stays in place when the mouse button is released.
3. Click on the icon labeled **3** in the lower left of the page.
   ▲ Two facing pages appear on the screen and the icons **2** and **3** are highlighted.
4. Select **View** from the **Layout** menu. Click on **25%**.
   ▲ The two facing pages shrink in size.
5. Select **View** again and click on **Show pasteboard**.
   ▲ The entire pasteboard is visible.
6. Go to the **View** menu and pick **Fit in window**.
   ▲ Pages 2 and 3 fill the window.

Getting Help with PageMaker

PageMaker has an online help facility that you can use any time you have the program open. This is a handy feature and may save you a trip to the PageMaker manuals if you can't remember a command or procedure. Operation of online help is consistent across most Windows programs. If you have used help before in Windows, PageMaker's help will feel familiar.

To get help in PageMaker, choose the **Help** drop-down menu and select either **Contents. . .** or **Search. . .** from the choices. Choosing **Contents. . .** opens a window with two sections: **How-to Information** and **Reference Information**. **How-to Information** includes step-by-step instructions for common PageMaker operations and an overview of using PageMaker's help facility. **Reference Information** allows you to look up commands, shortcuts, troubleshooting, and importing.

Choosing **Search. . .** allows you to choose from a list or search based on a topic name.

To get help using PageMaker for Windows:

1. Pull down on the **Help** menu and choose **Search. . . .**
2. Select one of the topic categories displayed or enter a topic name in the specification box.
3. Click on the **Show Topics** button or double-click on the desired topic.
4. If more than one subtopic shows in the box located under the **Go To** button, click on the one you want and then click the **Go To** button, or double-click on the subtopic you want.
5. When you are done getting help, double-click on the **Control-menu** box in the corner of the **Help** window or use the **Exit** command found under the **File** menu within the help facility.

CHECK YOURSELF

Using the document you opened in the last Check Yourself, use PageMaker's help facility to search for the entries under "Align."

▲ Leave the help function by choosing the **Exit** command from the **File** menu or double-clicking on the **Control-menu** box. You will be returned to your document. (Leave the document open for the next Check Yourself section.)

TIP

If you have room on your monitor, PageMaker's Help window can be left open to allow you to browse the topics as you work.

PageMaker and Windows

PageMaker supports the standard Windows drop-down menu controls, including tiling or cascading windows. The following are found under the **Window** drop-down menu: the **Tile** command, the **Cascade** command, the **Arrange Icons** command, which does not do anything useful in PageMaker, and a list of all PageMaker documents that are currently open.

PageMaker allows you to have several documents open simultaneously. You can use the **Window** drop-down menu to make any open document the active document. Just select the document name from the drop-down menu by clicking on it. You can also click on any window to bring it to the front and make it active. This is called *toggling* the open windows. If you are working on a monitor where the current window obscures the windows behind it, you can toggle the window to make the document you want to work on the active document.

You can also resize the windows for each open document by selecting a corner or edge of the document with the mouse. When you click the mouse, the cursor should change to a double-headed arrow. While holding the button down you can adjust the size of the window by moving the mouse in the direction desired. You can also arrange open document windows on your desktop manually by dragging them around with the mouse, or you can use the **Tile** or **Cascade** commands under the **Window** drop-down menu to arrange them on the desktop.

To view individual windows and show them as large as possible on your monitor:

1. Open the **Window** menu and choose **Cascade**.
2. To make the PageMaker document's window as large as possible, click on the **Maximize** button on the active window until it fills the screen. Or, drag the bottom corners of the window (Window corner) until it fills the screen.

Another function of the Window drop-down menu is to place all open PageMaker documents on-screen at one time. Instead of being stacked on top of each other, the individual document windows become tiles arranged next to each other. This allows to you to compare the contents of each document to the others and move objects from one layout to another simply by dragging them back and forth.

To create tiles of all open PageMaker documents:

1. Open the **Window** menu and choose **Tile**.
2. Arrange the tiles on your monitor any way you want by dragging them using the drag bar at the top of each window.

CHECK YOURSELF

1. Open a second letter-sized PageMaker document by choosing **New. . .** from the **File** drop-down menu. Open the **Window** menu and choose **Tile**. What happens?
   ▲ The two documents appear side by side as tiles.
2. Open the **Window** menu and choose **Cascade**. What happens? (Leave the document open for the next Check Yourself section.)
   ▲ The two windows appear on top of one another.

Saving Documents and Exiting PageMaker

To save a PageMaker document, open the **File** menu and select **Save. . . .** This brings up a **Save** dialog box where you name the

Saving Documents and Exiting PageMaker

document and tell PageMaker to finish the save by clicking on the **OK** button. As with all Windows and MS-DOS documents, the filename is limited to eight characters and a three-letter extension.

Until you click the **OK** button within the dialog box, the document is not yet safely saved on disk. If you are working with a document you have already saved and named, PageMaker saves the new version of the document on top of the old one, effectively replacing it. If you want to save the original file and the current file separately, save the new version as a separate file by choosing **Save As. . .** and give the document a new name to avoid writing over the last saved version. Selecting **Save As. . .** with a document not previously saved to disk has the same effect as choosing **Save. . . .**

Ending your PageMaker session is easy. Open the **File** menu and select **Exit**. PageMaker will ask you if you want to save the current document. Click on **Yes** to save the publication before exiting. If the document is already named, PageMaker will save it under the same name. If the publication has not been named, PageMaker will take you to the **Save** dialog box so that you can name it before quitting PageMaker.

Saving and Saving Yourself Trouble

When assembling documents, save your work frequently, because unexpected crashes do occur and any unsaved work is lost irretrievably. Just pull down the **File** menu and select **Save. . .**, or use the keyboard command **Ctrl+S.** Crashes may occur from a number of sources, ranging from conflicting software loaded into memory at start-up to problems with application software and memory partitioning. Because the Windows environment is in a state of continual evolution, which makes for incompatibilities on a number of fronts, frequent saving is your best defense against losing several hours of work. Get in the habit of using the keyboard command for save (**Ctrl+S**) every time you receive a phone call, toggle to another open program, get up from your desk, or sit back to think about your work. It's also a good idea to save before printing as well.

PageMaker is a very powerful program that pushes the capabilities of your PC and Windows to its limits. Occasionally it is possible to push too hard and crash your system. PageMaker documents can be incredibly large and complicated. A single document can contain a large number of typefaces, each containing elaborate formatting information. PageMaker documents may also contain black and white and/or color images saved in various formats and originating from several directories on disk. Such documents, standard in the publishing and printing world, tax a microcomputer, particularly one with too little internal memory. Fortunately, memory has become very inexpensive, so upgrading a machine from 2MB of RAM to 8MB is really not very expensive.

Until you work with PageMaker for a while and become confident that your system is stable, save frequently. Even if you think it is stable, still save your work frequently. Consider using a macro routine (available from most computer and software stores) to make your system save automatically every 30 minutes. If you have the macro set to save every half hour, the most you'll ever lose is half an hour's work.

WARNING

The worst kind of crash is one that occurs during a save operation. While this kind of crash is rare (fortunately), this usually renders PageMaker documents unopenable. You may be able to recover the text portion of the document through a word processor that can open any kind of file, but some of the information will still be lost or damaged.

CHECK YOURSELF

Exit PageMaker by opening the **File** menu and choosing **Exit**. What happens?

- ▲ You are prompted to save or discard changes, one file at a time, for open documents in which changes have been made. Click the **No** button to discard documents without saving them.

Understanding the Desktop Publishing Process

Understanding the Desktop Publishing Process

Now that you've learned to start PageMaker and open documents, you're ready to create documents. But, before we go on to talk about specific aspects of using PageMaker for this process, you should get an overview of the desktop publishing process in general.

The process of creating documents on the desktop with PageMaker usually follows a standard set of procedures. If your document will be completed on a laser printer or other computer-based printer, the steps are relatively brief. But if you plan to take your PageMaker-produced documents into print at a print shop, the steps are longer and a bit more complicated. With either process, it is important that you follow the standard steps or you may have to go back and make changes to your document, start over, or pay to reprint it after making corrections.

To avoid these time-consuming and potentially costly problems, always approach the process of creating documents as an orderly series of steps. Don't just jump in and start designing a document. If you do, you may end up with a mistake that won't become evident until the publication is on press—and then it is costly to repair. Use the following steps, which are summarized in Figure 1.5, for best results. Care must be exercised when creating documents either conventionally on a drafting board or with a sophisticated desktop publishing package such as PageMaker, because problems, like typographical errors and incorrect placement of images, can creep into designs through either method.

1. *Plan*: The first step in creating any document on the desktop, even a simple one, is to plan the process and select a physical format appropriate for the project. For example, if your project consists of a simple newsletter that you will design, but that someone else will write, work with the writer to select a format that is large enough to handle all of the publication's stories and pictures.
2. *Budget*: If the project will be reproduced at a print shop or in quantity at a copy center, get an estimate for the job before

▼ ***Figure 1.5. The Desktop Publishing Steps***

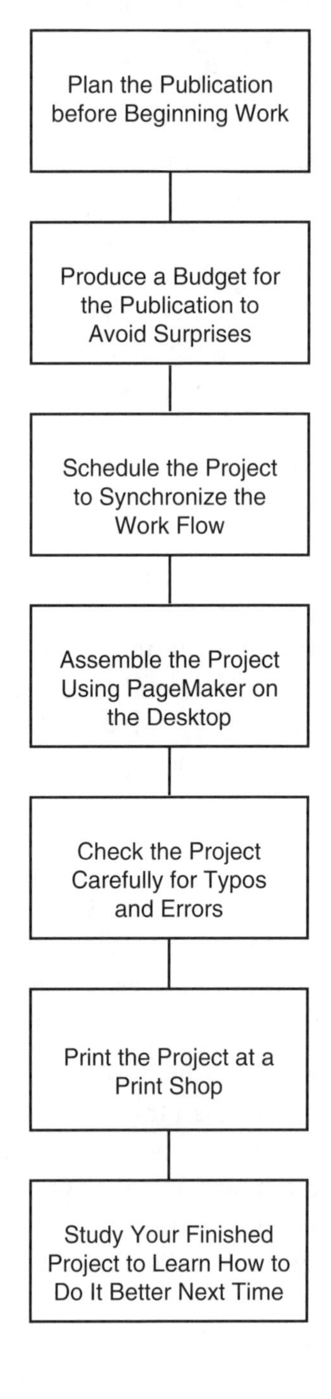

Understanding the Desktop Publishing Process

beginning work. In many cases the reproduction charges will materially limit or alter the project's format. Some format choices, such as number of colors or oversized paper, may be expensive to print. It's important to find this out before you design the piece. If other services such as imagesetter film, photography, outside writing, or illustrations are required for the project, these must also be included in the budget.

3. *Schedule*: Most publishing revolves around a schedule (usually tight). In the newsletter example, you would work with your writer to develop a schedule so that the two of you work in harmony on the project and it gets completed on time.
4. *Assemble*: Create the publication on the desktop and incorporate the copy, pictures, and other components of the job. We provide more details on this process within PageMaker later in this chapter and throughout the book.
5. *Check*: Carefully check the work for errors and proof the copy—including all captions and headlines. Have more than one person check the document. It's very difficult to proof your own typing and document assembly.

TIP

Don't proof your job on-screen! Take it from us, typos and mistakes often get missed on-screen no matter how many times you go over the document for errors. These errors then show up at the print shop—and then it costs money to repair. Save yourself the eyestrain and catch more mistakes by proofing your job on printed output from your computer printer. (A laser printer is highly recommended if you use PageMaker.) You can also catch other errors, such as misplaced design elements, better from "hard copy" than you can on-screen.

6. *Reproduce*: Have the job printed at a print shop, on your laser printer, or at the copy center depending on the needs of the project. If you will be creating a high-quality document, you will have an intermediate stop at a service bureau (see Chapter 11 for information on service bureaus) to run film of the job on an imagesetter before plates can be made at the print shop.

7. *Learn*: Study the completed job and evaluate the process of creating it. The best way to learn from your mistakes and triumphs is to carefully review the process to understand what went right and what went wrong. This knowledge will make things go faster and smoother on your next publishing project.

TIP

If your projects will finish at the print shop, and you are new to desktop publishing and PageMaker, initially take on simple black and white (or one-color) projects and gradually build your skills by taking your projects into print. After one-color projects, try projects in two colors, and after you master those, try a four-color project. Full-color publications are by far the most difficult and fraught with potential problems. Never try a full-color project as your first publication in PageMaker or in any new product for that matter.

Desktop Design and Assembly with PageMaker

Within the framework of the desktop publishing steps just described, you most likely will follow a specific series of steps when creating documents with PageMaker. For documents containing large amounts of text, you will usually create the text in a PageMaker-compatible word processor. Text can of course be added directly to a PageMaker layout, but for voluminous text, you will probably find a word processor more convenient to work with.

Next, a layout is created within PageMaker. Copy is added and design elements arranged and manipulated on the desktop. Images and graphics are often scanned or designed after the initial layout is "roughed out." By waiting to see how much space is available for each graphic component, you can design illustrations or scan photos to fit your layout precisely. This saves time and disk space.

Once all of the elements are in place, the document is fine-tuned and proofed for errors in copy and in design. Then the approved document is printed on a printer or sent to an imagesetter for high-resolution output and subsequent printing at a commercial print shop.

Understanding the Desktop Publishing Process

CHECK YOURSELF

What are the seven steps of the desktop publishing process?

▲ Plan, Budget, Schedule, Assemble, Check, Reproduce, and Learn.

QUICK COMMAND SUMMARY

Shortcut Keys	***Commands***	***Procedures***
N/A	Mouse click	Selects an icon or inserts cursor in a word
N/A	Two clicks	Launches an application from its icon or selects a word of text
(File menu)		
Ctrl+N	New. . .	Opens a new PageMaker document
	Ctrl+Q	Exits PageMaker
Alt S→S	Save. . .	Saves the open document after prompting for a name for the document if it hasn't been saved previously
Alt S→A	Save As. . .	Allows an existing document to be saved under a new name
(Help menu)		
Alt H→C (or F1)	Contents	Opens PageMaker's Help index
Alt H→S	Search	Opens Search window in Help
Alt H→K	Shortcuts	Help for shortcuts
Alt H→U	Using Help	How to use PageMaker's help facility

Shortcut Keys	***Commands***	***Procedures***
(Window menu)		
Alt W→T	Tile	Fits all open PageMaker documents on-screen at once
Alt W→C	Cascade	Stacks the windows of open PageMaker documents on top of each other

PRACTICE WHAT YOU'VE LEARNED

What You Do	***What You'll See***
For readers new to the mouse:	**For readers new to the mouse:**
1. Use the mouse to open the Windows **Control Panel** by double-clicking on it.	1. A new window appears with several Control Panel icons displayed.
2. Use the mouse to open the Windows **Color Control Panel** by double-clicking on it.	2. The Color Control Panel is displayed.
3. Click on the button to the right of the **Color Schemes** box to display the color schemes.	3. A list of color schemes pops up.
4. Click on several color schemes to see what they look like.	4. As each scheme is selected, the color changes to the Windows desktop are displayed in the Control Panel.
5. Select one you like and close the Control Panel using the mouse.	5. If a color scheme is selected different than the one used before this exercise, the new colors are used for the Windows desktop.

What You Do	*What You'll See*
For all readers:	**For all readers:**
6. Double-click on the PageMaker icon to launch PageMaker.	6. PageMaker begins its loading sequence and finally displays the menu bar.
7. Select **New...** from the **File** menu.	7. The New dialog box appears on-screen.
8. Create an 8" by 8" document and set the margins so that they are 1" from all edges of the page. Click **OK**.	8. PageMaker produces a blank page on the monitor that measures 8" by 8" with 1" margin guides on all sides.
9. Drag the **Styles** palette to a new place on the screen.	9. The Styles palette follows the mouse until it is released.
10. Close the **Toolbox** by double-clicking on its **Control-menu** box.	10. The Toolbox palette disappears from the screen.
11. Bring up PageMaker's **Help** window by hitting the **F1** key	11. PageMaker's Help window appears on the screen.
12. Use **Search** to get help on the following topics: Control Palette, Rotating Tool, Autoflow.	12. The correct help topics appear on the screen inside the Help window.
13. Open a second letter-sized PageMaker document, and tile the windows using the **Tile** command under the **Window** menu.	13. A new PageMaker document opens. Choosing Tile reduces the size of the documents and displays them side by side on the monitor.

What You Do	*What You'll See*
14. Exit PageMaker without saving changes.	14. PageMaker asks whether you want to save changes. Click **No** to discard this chapter's session with PageMaker. You are returned to the Windows desktop.

WHAT IF IT DOESN'T WORK?

6. If you can't get PageMaker to launch and present you with the **New** dialog box, make sure that your system has enough memory available for it by closing other open applications.
9. If the **Styles** palette isn't present on-screen when you start PageMaker, click on the **Styles** palette from the **Window** menu to open the palette on-screen.

In this chapter you have learned the basic mechanics of using a mouse and opening a PageMaker document. You have also taken the nickel tour of PageMaker's desktop and have been introduced to the desktop publishing process. In the next chapter you will learn how to perform basic operations inside of PageMaker and navigate around the PageMaker desktop.

2

Getting Started

PageMaker for Windows provides a number of powerful features for setting up documents. In this chapter you'll learn how to work with the basic document assembly features such as adding pages. You will also learn to navigate within a PageMaker document after it has been defined. In addition you will complete your tour of the PageMaker desktop and see some of PageMaker's floating palettes in action. In this chapter, you will learn how to:

- **Set up a multipage document**
- **Use the Facing pages option**
- **Add and delete pages**
- **Move around in documents**
- **Use PageMaker's floating palettes**

Setting Up Multipage Documents in PageMaker

Although page layout programs are frequently used for one-page documents such as ads and one-page datasheets, the majority of page layouts consist of more than one page or *spread*. (A spread is two pages that open together to form one double-sized area, as you get when you open a brochure to the middle.) PageMaker is capable of handling long documents, like books, that contain several hundred pages. The practical limit to the number of pages is constrained by the amount of empty storage available on your hard disk. Unless you exclusively design one-page documents such as ads and posters, the option to have multiple pages and facing pages is key to speedy assembly of documents.

Facing pages are like the ones found in this book. There is a left-hand page and a right-hand page. The **Facing pages** option in PageMaker is particularly important because it allows you to run design elements across two pages. For example, in a publication you might want to add a decorative line that starts near the left edge of the left page of a spread and crosses over the right page of the spread, stopping near the right page's right edge.

Facing Pages

When you open a new document in PageMaker, the **New** dialog box has a check box called **Facing pages**. If you have defined a multipage document and checked the **Double-sided** option, **Facing pages** becomes available. Checking this option tells PageMaker to place pages next to each other on the desktop. Using the **Facing pages** option allows you to design documents with elements that cross from the left page to the right page as shown in Figure 2.1.

PageMaker's first page in a multipage document has no facing page. That is because the first page of most documents is the cover page, just like the cover of this book.

▼ *Figure 2.1. Facing Pages*

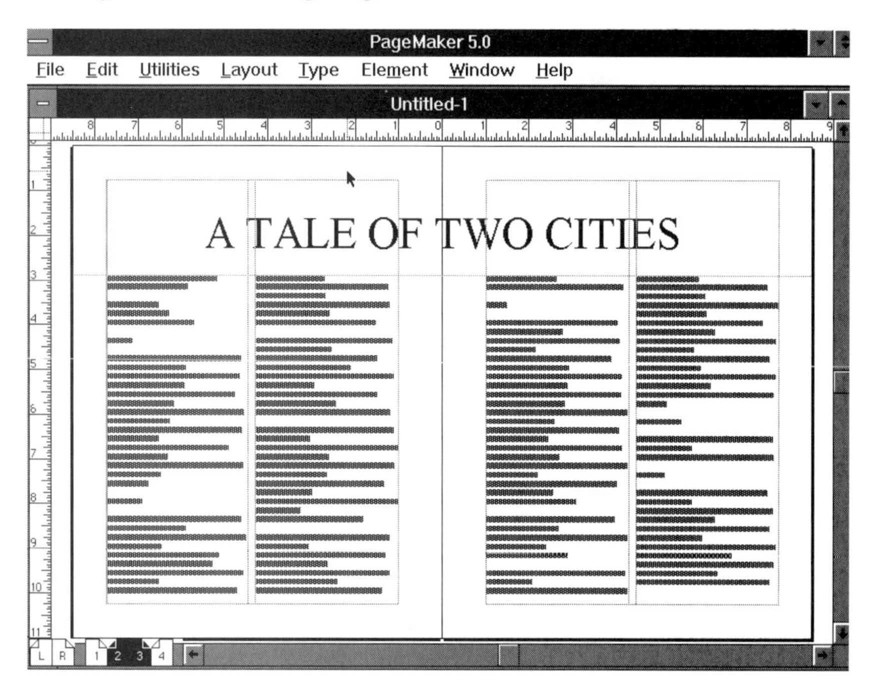

Setting Up Multipage Documents in PageMaker

Inserting and Deleting Pages in PageMaker

Pages can be added to or deleted from PageMaker documents using menu items found under the **Layout** menu shown in Figure 2.2. However, you can't delete text that jumps from page to page with the commands in this menu. If pages are deleted that contain part of the text, the text is not deleted but stays connected to the PageMaker document, ready to be placed on a new page that you insert later.

To add pages in PageMaker:

1. Open the **Layout** menu and select **Insert pages....**
2. Enter the number of pages you want to insert.
3. Choose where you would like the new page or pages inserted in your document and then click **OK**.

To delete pages and their contents (except text) from a PageMaker document:

1. Open the **Layout** menu and select **Remove pages....**

▼ *Figure 2.2. PageMaker's Layout Menu*

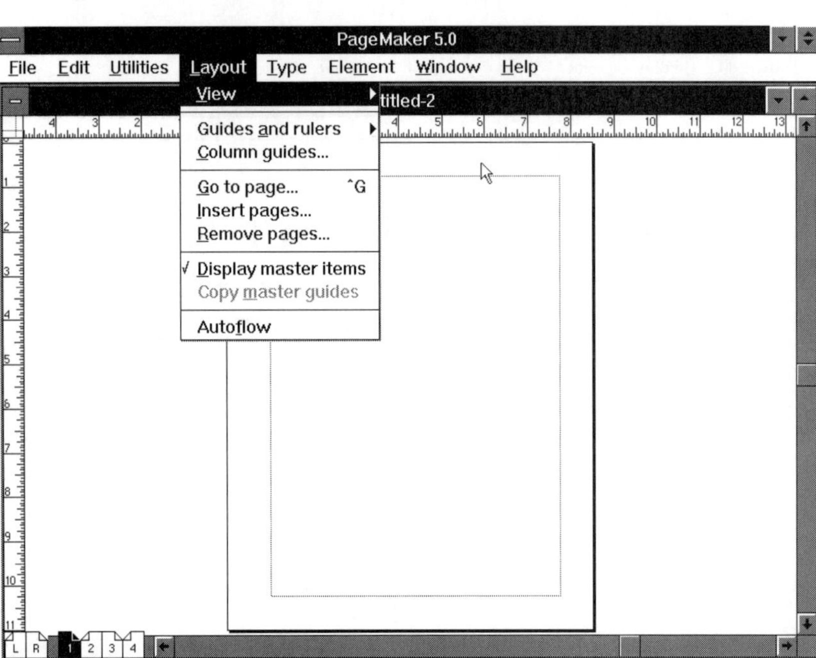

2. Enter the page number or a range of page numbers to be deleted in the boxes and click **OK**.

Setting Up a Multipage Document

When setting up a document within PageMaker, you can add pages in two ways—add all the pages when you start or add pages as you need them. The method you choose depends on your personal style of working and whether you already have a predefined number of pages for the document. PageMaker lends itself readily to either method of setup and allows you to create a longer document than necessary while you complete your design and modify elements such as copy and *headlines* to actually fit the required number of pages. (A headline is the large piece of text at the top of the ad, intended to catch the eye and deliver the ad's main message.)

The first method requires planning your document in advance based on your needs, budget, and working style. For example, if you are assembling a brochure, you may have a set page count based on the budget. Adding one extra page to an eight-page brochure makes it into a twelve-page document in print because one entire sheet of paper must be added—and that brings along an extra three pages you don't need. This will most likely blow your budget even if you had enough copy and pictures to fill the new pages.

Setting Up Multipage Documents in PageMaker

To set up your document using the first approach, you choose the page size and turn on the **Facing pages** option if required when starting your design. Then, once PageMaker is open, you use the **Insert pages...** command to add exactly the number of pages you plan to work with. You then add the design elements and copy a page at a time until the document is complete. If you have more copy than will fit in the budgeted number of pages, you will know that you must make changes to the design or the copy, or to both.

The second method of working is much less formal, and in the case of a document where the final page count is neither critical nor predictable, it is the method of choice. To put this method to work, you again set up your document and turn on the **Facing pages** option if required. But, instead of immediately adding all of the pages you might require, you add them one or two at a time as you assemble the publication. By working this way, the design or copy dictates the final page count. This second option is used for longer documents such as books, where an exact page count may initially be impossible to judge without time-consuming counting of words and precise specifications for illustrations.

For documents that contain a large number of pages, such as a book, PageMaker can also be set up to add pages automatically as text is typed or when a large word processing file is imported that contains the bulk of the book's text. (We show you how to do this in Chapter 5 when we discuss importing text.)

CHECK YOURSELF

1. Start PageMaker and set up a new document with the **Facing pages** option turned on. Adjust the **View** to 25%. Then add four pages to the end of the document. What do you see on-screen?
   ▲ You should be able to see all five page icons on the lower left of your screen. Pages two through five should display

side by side. Note how upper left or right edges of the icons are folded to indicate left or right in facing pages.

2. Delete pages four and five in your PageMaker document using the **Remove pages...** command. What do you see on-screen?
   ▲ You should see that only three page icons remain of the original five.

Going Places in PageMaker

PageMaker provides several ways to move around in a publication. The easiest way is to click on the page icon of the page you want to move into. The associated icon is then highlighted. If you are working with the Facing Pages option on, each page will be displayed with its respective mate and both page icons will be highlighted.

In addition to clicking on the page icons, PageMaker provides three other methods for traversing your document: the **Go to page...** command, the scroll bars, and the two navigation keys. The **Go to page...** command is found under the **Layout** menu. This command allows you to enter a page number and then go directly to the specified page after clicking the **OK** button.

If you are not already familiar with scroll bars, they are the bars displayed at the right edge and bottom of a PageMaker document's window. The bottom scroll bar allows you to move horizontally in a PageMaker document to see facing pages or more of PageMaker's pasteboard. The vertical scroll bars allow you to scroll vertically in a document to see the top or bottom of a page, or in the case of a multipage document like the one you created in the last Check Yourself, the scroll bars allow you to move vertically through the multiple pages. The scroll bars can accomplish the following three types of movement, depending on how you use them, as shown in Figure 2.3:

▲ Holding down and dragging the vertical scroll box allows you to move vertically through the entire document in one motion. Holding down and dragging the horizontal scroll bar scrolls

▼ *Figure 2.3. A Scroll Bar and Where to Click*

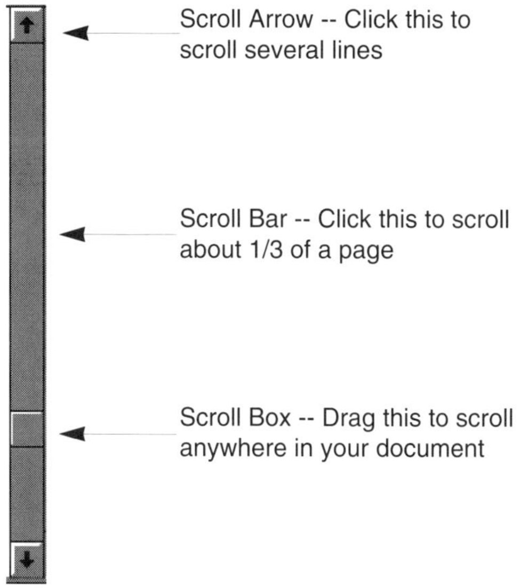

Scroll Arrow -- Click this to scroll several lines

Scroll Bar -- Click this to scroll about 1/3 of a page

Scroll Box -- Drag this to scroll anywhere in your document

Going Places in PageMaker

left to right through a document with large page sizes or with facing pages.

- ▲ Clicking on either of the arrows displayed at the end of the scroll bars scrolls the displayed document approximately a line at a time at 100% magnification.
- ▲ Clicking on the scroll bar's gray area between the two arrows scrolls the screen a larger amount than clicking on the arrows. In an 8 1/2" by 11" document, for example, clicking on the gray area moves the screen about one-third of a standard page for each click.

The two navigation keys are the **F11** and **F12** keys. **F11** moves backward one page and the **F12** moves forward a page.

To see more of a PageMaker document, the **Maximize** button can be used to enlarge the window to its maximum size on your monitor if it's not already as large as will fit, as shown in Figure 2.4. Using the maximized view shows a larger percentage of your document, but if you have floating palettes open, you will need to move them when you want to work on the parts of your document underneath the palettes.

▼ ***Figure 2.4. PageMaker Document before and after Maximize***

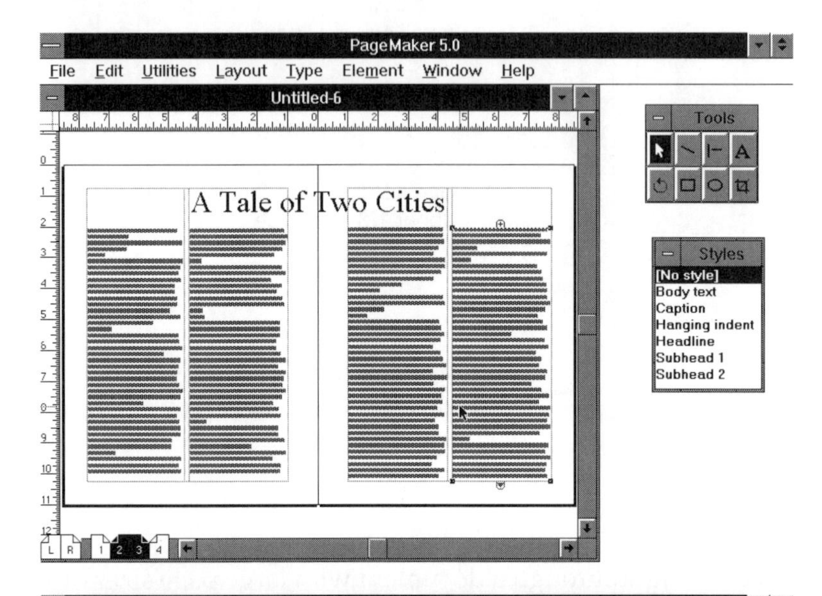

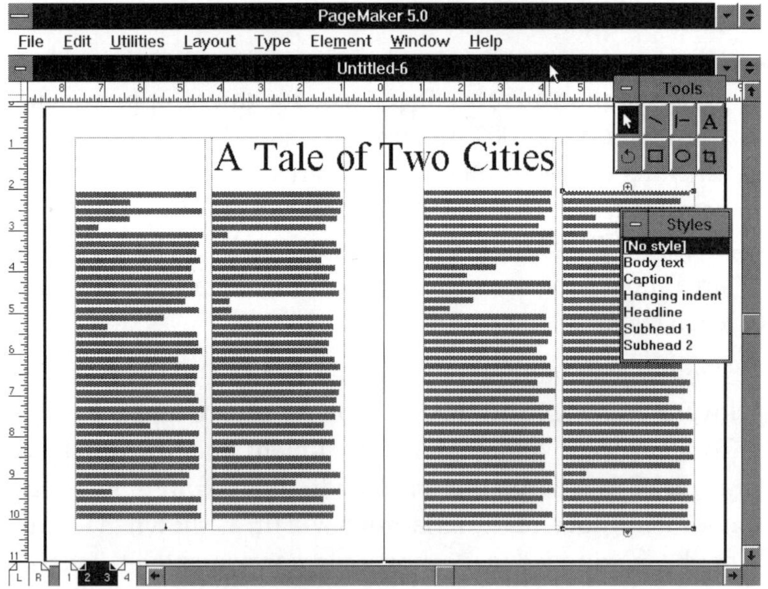

CHECK YOURSELF

1. Start PageMaker and set up a new document with the **Facing pages** option turned off. Add six pages to the document. What do you see?

Going Places in PageMaker

- ▲ You should see seven page icons in the lower left. The page 2 icon should be highlighted, indicating that it is currently displayed on your monitor.

2. Click on the page 6 icon. What happens?
   - ▲ The page 6 icon becomes highlighted and page 6 appears in the window.
3. Open the **File** menu and go to the **Page setup** menu. Click on **Facing pages** to turn it on. What happens?
   - ▲ Pages 6 and 7 are shown in the window and the two page icons are highlighted
4. Use the **Go to page...** dialog to move to page 1. What happens?
   - ▲ You are back where you started.

Meet More of PageMaker's Floating Palettes

We introduced the concept of floating palettes in Chapter 1. PageMaker has five powerful floating palettes that provide a wide range of commands able to be carried out without using PageMaker's drop-down menus. These palettes can save considerable time when assembling and fine-tuning documents, because you can make a variety of adjustments and changes in a matter of seconds by simply pointing and clicking with the mouse.

The five palettes are:

- ▲ The **Toolbox**—This palette contains drawing tools, text tools, and selection tools. You'll learn more about the Toolbox palette in Chapter 3.
- ▲ The **Control** palette—This powerful palette allows you to make a number of changes to type, graphic elements, and lines. You'll learn more about this palette in Chapter 4.
- ▲ The **Styles** palette—This palette allows you to directly apply predefined text styles to the copy used in your page layout. Styles and the Styles palette are covered in Chapter 8.

- ▲ The **Colors** palette—The Colors palette allows you to apply color to objects and text in your page layout. You'll learn how to apply color to PageMaker elements and publications in Chapter 10.
- ▲ The **Library** palette—The Library palette gives you access to groups of text or graphics objects that are often used. The palette lets you create, organize, and search for individual items within one or more libraries. We'll examine the Library palette in Chapter 9.

Using PageMaker's Floating Palettes

As mentioned in Chapter 1, PageMaker's floating palettes can be displayed or put away when not in use to free up screen space on a crowded monitor. If you are fortunate enough to be working on a large monitor, you may have enough room to display a document full-size, as well as room for two or three floating palettes. Palettes can be moved around on the screen and the Colors and Styles palettes can also be resized, as in Figure 2.5, to better fit the desktop and the current project requirements. Remember that you enlarge or reduce a palette the same way you enlarge or reduce a window, by dragging on the corner or edges of the palette.

▼ ***Figure 2.5. PageMaker's Styles Palette Normal and Resized***

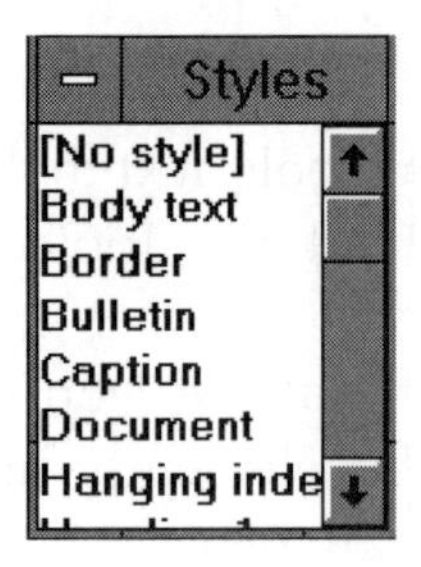

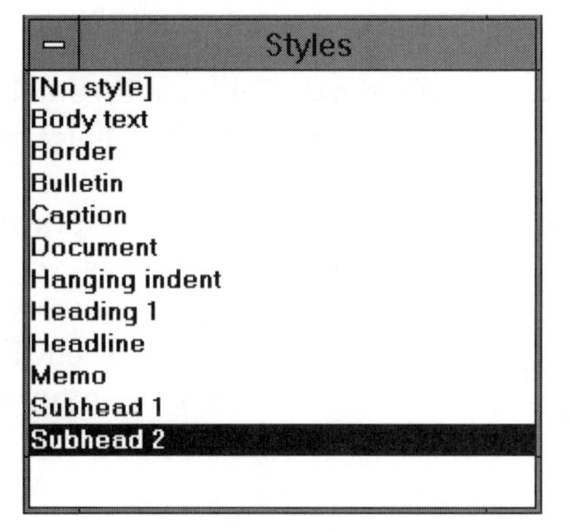

Meet More of PageMaker's Floating Palettes

When PageMaker starts up, only the Toolbox and the Styles palette are visible. To show the other palettes, click on the **Window** menu. Notice that there is a check mark to the left of the Toolbox and the Styles palette. Clicking on the Colors palette puts a check mark to the left of it, closes the menu, and displays the Colors palette. Similarly, opening the **Window** menu and clicking on a checked item removes the check mark and removes the palette from the screen. Between work sessions PageMaker remembers which palettes were open the last time you used PageMaker and reopens them in the same place you left them the next time you start the program.

ALTERNATE METHOD

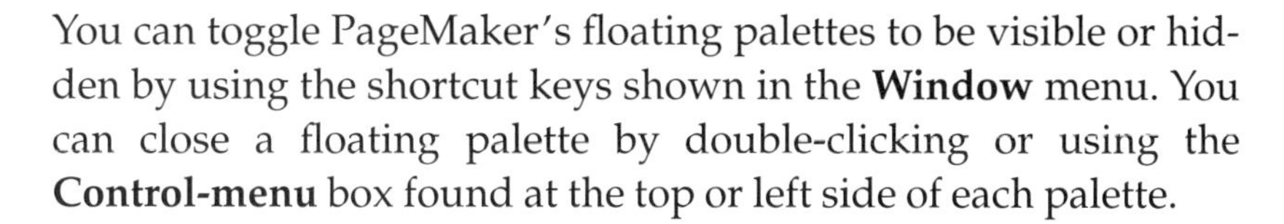

You can toggle PageMaker's floating palettes to be visible or hidden by using the shortcut keys shown in the **Window** menu. You can close a floating palette by double-clicking or using the **Control-menu** box found at the top or left side of each palette.

CHECK YOURSELF

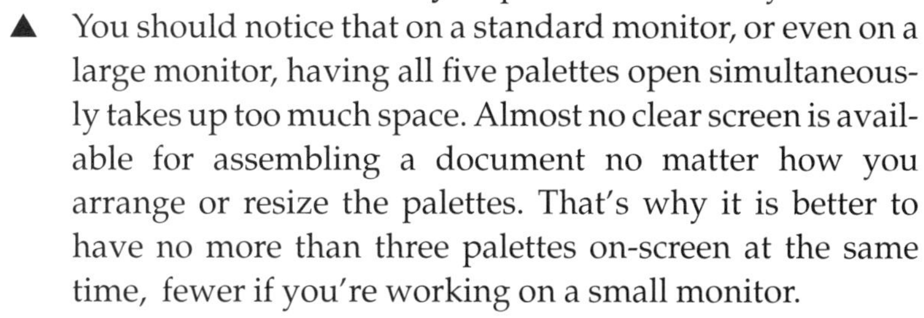

Open a new letter-sized PageMaker document. Next, open each of the floating palettes and leave them on your screen. Study each of the palette's, names and functions. Note where PageMaker automatically places each one when you display it for the first time. Use the drag boxes in the lower right corners of the palettes to adjust the size of the **Colors** and **Styles** palettes. What do you see?

- ▲ You should notice that on a standard monitor, or even on a large monitor, having all five palettes open simultaneously takes up too much space. Almost no clear screen is available for assembling a document no matter how you arrange or resize the palettes. That's why it is better to have no more than three palettes on-screen at the same time, fewer if you're working on a small monitor.

QUICK COMMAND SUMMARY

Shortcut Keys	*Commands*	*Procedures*
(Layout menu)		
Alt L→I	Insert. . .	Adds a page or pages to a document
Alt L→D	Delete. . .	Deletes a page or pages from a document
Alt L→G	Go to. . .	Jumps to the selected page
(Keyboard)		
F11	Back	Moves back one page
F12	Forward	Moves forward one page
(Window menu)		
Ctrl 6	Toolbox	Toggles the Toolbox palette on/off
Ctrl Y	Styles palette	Toggles the Styles palette on/off
Ctrl K	Colors palette	Toggles the Colors palette on/off
Ctrl '	Control palette	Toggles the Control palette on/off

PRACTICE WHAT YOU'VE LEARNED

What You Do	*What You'll See*
1. Launch PageMaker and select **New. . .** from the **File** menu.	1. PageMaker launches and the New dialog box opens.
2. Create a new letter-size publication with the **Facing pages** option checked. Click **OK**.	2. A new letter-sized PageMaker document is displayed on the desktop.
3. Select **25%** view using the **View** submenu from the **Layout** menu.	3. The page layout appears at 25% of its actual size.

What You Do	*What You'll See*
4. Insert eight pages into the document with the **Insert pages. . .** command.	4. Eight new pages are added to the layout. Notice that PageMaker defaults to the Facing pages option.
5. Double-click on the **Control-menu** boxes of the **Styles** palette and the **Toolbox** palette.	5. The palettes are removed from the screen.
6. Select **75%** from the **View** submenu.	6. The dark line down the middle of the page is the intersection of the left and right pages. The blue lines are the respective margins.
7. Drag the vertical scroll box about one fourth of the way from the top.	7. You should see the top margin of the two pages.
8. Drag the horizontal scroll box about one fourth of the way from the right.	8. The top right corner of the page should appear.
9. Click on the page icon for page 9.	9. Pages 8 and 9 are both shown. The view has changed to **Fit in window**.
10. Click on the icon for page 3.	10. Pages 2 and 3 return, still in the 75% view.
11. Exit PageMaker and do not save your work.	11. You are returned to the Windows desktop.

WHAT IF IT DOESN'T WORK?

7. If the top margin is not visible, try dragging the vertical scroll box up and down a few times to bring the margin into view. If finer adjustments to your position are needed, click on the two arrows at either end of the vertical scroll bar.

This chapter has shown you how to create multiple-page PageMaker documents with empty pages, ready for you to add text and graphic elements. It has also demonstrated how to move around in PageMaker and has introduced PageMaker's five floating palettes. In the next chapter, we'll put PageMaker to work by exploring the capabilities of the powerful Toolbox palette.

3

The PageMaker Toolbox

Designers use a wide variety of pens, pencils, burnishers, knives, and brushes to create conventional graphic designs and page layouts. PageMaker's **Toolbox** palette (also called simply the **Toolbox**) contains an assortment of tools that duplicate (and enhance) the functions of these conventional tools. In this chapter, you will be introduced to each tool in the Toolbox and will learn how to:

- ▲ **Draw lines, squares, rectangles, circles, and ellipses**
- ▲ **Add text to PageMaker page layouts**
- ▲ **Select fonts and font sizes**
- ▲ **Use PageMaker's ruler guides features**

Toolbox Overview

You were introduced to the Toolbox in the last chapter. Like all of PageMaker's floating palettes, the Toolbox can be repositioned on the desktop by moving the cursor into its drag zone (the title bar) and dragging the palette to a new location. When you start PageMaker, the Toolbox is in the middle of the screen. It is helpful to drag it to the upper right corner. Most palettes are left on the desktop only when they are in use, but the Toolbox is usually left on the desktop during all PageMaker sessions because it must be frequently accessed. To select a tool in the Toolbox palette, you simply click once on the desired icon in the palette. This activates that tool. If you do remove the Toolbox from the desktop, individual tools can also be activated by shortcut keys.

There are eight tools in the Toolbox as shown in Figure 3.1. The tools are:

- ▲ **Pointer**—used to select objects
- ▲ **Line** tool—draws with any orientation
- ▲ **Constrained-line** tool—draws lines at 0, 45, and 90 degrees
- ▲ **Text** tool—for inserting text
- ▲ **Rotation** tool—rotates desktop objects
- ▲ **Rectangle** tool—draws boxes
- ▲ **Ellipse** tool—draws circles and ellipses
- ▲ **Cropping** tool—crops graphics

▼ ***Figure 3.1. The Toolbox***

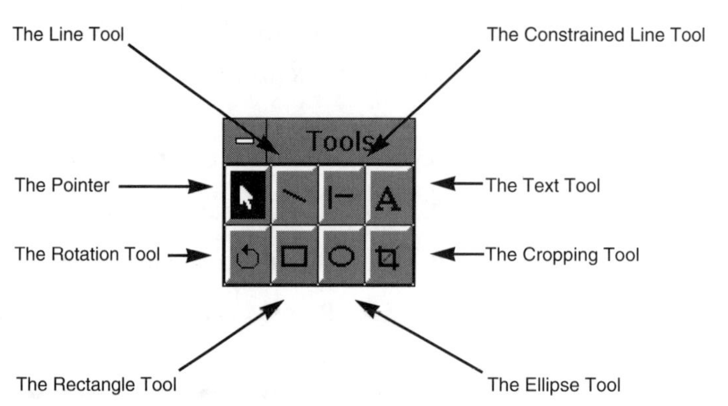

The **Line** tool, **Constrained-line** tool, **Rectangle** tool, and **Ellipse** tool are collectively known as the *shape tools*.

Tool Basics

Tool Basics

All page layout operations in PageMaker are based on the manipulation of objects. Objects are defined by PageMaker to be anything that is on the desktop layout that will print. Thus lines, text, and graphic elements are all objects. Other elements of the desktop, including margin guidelines and the user-definable guides, are not considered objects because they do not print, but they appear on the desktop while you are working to assist you in accurately laying out pages.

The advantage of an object-oriented orientation is that all items on the desktop, be they lines, text, shapes, or images, can be positioned and or have their characteristics changed instantaneously using the tools in the Toolbox. You can fine-tune your layout as much as you like and even save multiple versions so that you can come back later and choose the one you like best from the various versions.

Objects

To make it easier to describe operations in PageMaker, throughout the book we will refer to the elements in a PageMaker page layout generically as *objects*. You will also see this phrase used in PageMaker's manuals to describe items on the desktop. Remember, anything you add to a layout that prints—shapes, text blocks, and lines—is an *object*.

Selecting and Deselecting Objects

Similar to the way you must select text in your word processor before making changes to its font, type size, or style, in PageMaker you must select objects before making changes to them. Using the

Pointer tool, you *select* an object by clicking on it. When an object becomes selected, small rectangles, called *handles*, appear on the objects border. Clicking elsewhere in a publication *deselects* the object and the handles disappear. Only when an object is selected can you make changes to it. Selecting is also called *highlighting* when you are selecting text. (Text can be selected by dragging over the text with the mouse button down. You'll get more practice doing that later in this chapter.) Deleting objects is accomplished by first selecting the object, then hitting either the **Backspace** or **Delete** keys.

The reason that objects must be selected individually is that a page layout may contain 50 or more individual objects. Before you can make changes to just one or two objects without affecting the other 50, PageMaker must know which ones you want to change or adjust and which ones to leave alone.

When an object is selected, PageMaker looks to see what kind of object it is and then modifies some of the items on the floating palettes, pull-down menus, and dialog boxes to make them "compatible" with the range of manipulations possible for the kind of object selected. For example, if the selected object is text, the Control palette is modified to add controls for modifying the text's font, style, and size. If the object selected is a line, the Control palette is modified to display controls for line styles and widths.

As you work through this book, you will see this modification process in action. It is in part PageMaker's ability to change its palettes, menus, and dialogs interactively that gives the product great power and flexibility. PageMaker always provides exactly the right command set at the right time for the job at hand.

Selecting Multiple Objects

We mentioned selecting multiple objects in the Introduction, but it is probably a good idea to remind you of the procedure now that you know more about objects. To select more than one object at a time, just click on the first object you want to select. Then hold down the **Shift** key and click the next object. Continue to hold down the **Shift** key and click on each object or portion of object you want to select. When you are done selecting, you can execute

Tool Basics

a command and that command will be applied to all the selected objects. This **Shift-click** method is useful, for example, if you want to make the same size change to a number of objects or if you want to delete a number of objects at the same time. We'll give you a chance to practice selecting and deselecting multiple objects later in the chapter.

The Pointer Tool

The **Pointer** tool is an important general purpose tool for moving and selecting objects. Though you don't have anything to move or select yet, we want to introduce this tool to you now, because it is the most commonly used tool and will affect how the objects created with the other tools can be manipulated. PageMaker's Pointer tool, which looks like an arrow in the palette, is shown in Figure 3.2. It is used to select, move, and resize objects on PageMaker's desktop. After you select an object with this tool, clicking on the object causes the Pointer to change shape and function. For example, if you select a rectangle, then move the Pointer to a handle on the side and click, the Pointer changes into a two-headed arrow used to change the width of the box. If you click on the border of that rectangle (but not on a handle), the Pointer becomes a four-headed cross. This enables you to reposition the box. We'll show you how to move and resize objects with the Pointer tool after you have drawn some shapes later in this chapter.

The Pointer tool can also be used to select multiple objects. There are two ways of doing this.

To select multiple objects:

1. Use the **Shift-Click** procedure described earlier.
   or

▼ ***Figure 3.2. PageMaker's Pointer Tool***

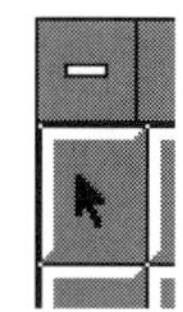

2. With the **Pointer** tool active, *lasso* the objects by clicking outside the objects and holding down the mouse button while dragging. As you drag, a rectangular "lasso" with a dashed border will grow. Drag until it surrounds, but doesn't touch, all of the objects you want to select. When you release the mouse button, all of the included objects will be selected. You should see the handles of all the objects you have selected. Remember, you can use the **Shift-Click** method to deselect any objects you don't want selected after they have been selected with the lasso method.

The Shape Tools

Recall that PageMaker has four shape tools that are used for adding elements and graphics to PageMaker documents. The tools are the **Rectangle**, **Ellipse**, **Line,** and **Constrained-line**. The shape tools work in basically the same ways. You may wonder how useful squares, rectangles, circles, and ellipses are going to be in designing page layouts on the desktop. Obviously a square can be used to put a decorative box around a block of text, but what else can it be used for? Well, these tools have other functions, which include the following:

▲ *Holding Pictures:* All of these shapes can be used to hold a picture or graphic created with another program or scanned into the computer with a scanner. (The process of importing graphics is explained in Chapter 8.)

▲ *Creating Charts:* Combining shapes with words is an easy way to create a variety of charts and graphics.

▲ *Modifying Graphics:* If you import a black-and-white image of a pair of woman's eyes where white is transparent, you can place two blue ellipses behind the pupils to make her eyes appear blue. There are many similar modifications that can be made to graphics with the shape tools.

Drawing, Dragging, and Resizing a Rectangle

Drawing, Dragging, and Resizing a Rectangle

Now you are ready to draw a rectangle with the **Rectangle** tool. The **Rectangle** and **Ellipse** tools work in similar ways. The following exercise will teach you the basics of using all these tools inside PageMaker.

Start by opening the **File** menu and selecting the **New...** command.

To create a rectangle:

1. Click on the **Rectangle** tool in the Toolbox to select it. The Rectangle tool is simply the shape of a rectangle.
2. Place your cursor in the middle of the desktop. Hold down on the mouse button and drag until a rectangle appears. Drag until the rectangle is about two inches wide. Then release the mouse button. Congratulations! You have drawn your first rectangle.

Notice that the rectangle you have created has eight tiny boxes with one in each corner and one in the middle of each side. These are the handles and are shown in Figure 3.3. Once you release the mouse, PageMaker allows you to use the **Pointer** tool to resize the box you've drawn. To resize the box, hold down and drag any one of the handles. The handles in the corners resize two sides at one time. Dragging a handle in the middle of a side resizes the box either horizontally or vertically, depending on the side selected.

If you select the **Pointer** tool, you will also be able to move the rectangle around the layout. Try it! To move your box, place the tool anywhere on the outline of the rectangle except on a handle. Now hold down and drag. The box will move as you move your mouse (until you release the mouse button).

You may also add rounded corners to a rectangle or square. Under the **Element** menu is a submenu, **Rounded corners,** with six corners of varying radii or "roundness." To round the corners of a rectangle, select it with the **Pointer** tool, then open the **Element** menu and click on the **Rounded corners** submenu. Click on the

▼ ***Figure 3.3. Drag Handles on a Rectangle***

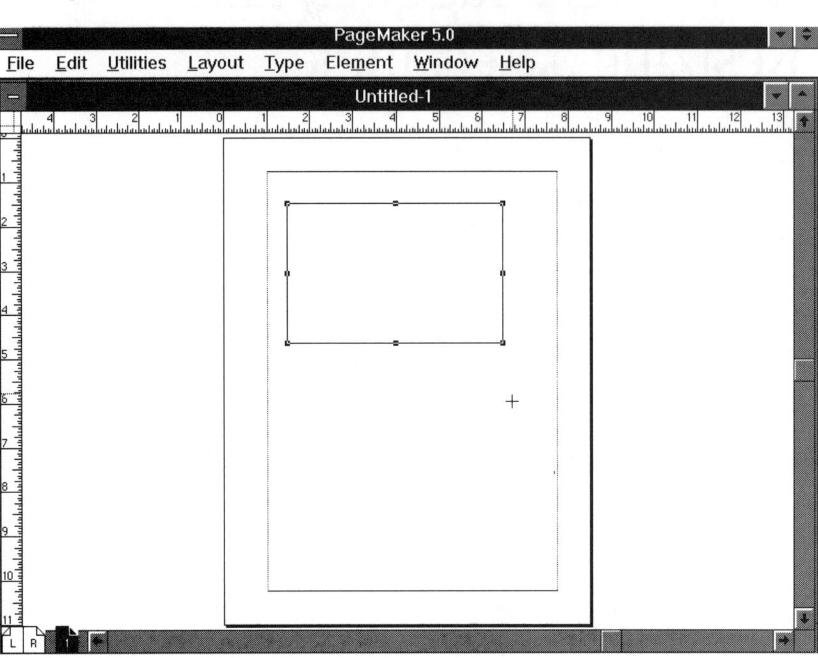

style corner you want and hit the **OK** button. The rectangle's corners are now changed.

Another Way to Position Objects

In addition to using the Pointer tool, objects can also be moved using the arrow keys (sometimes called "cursor keys"). Instead of moving the object quickly around the layout as the mouse can, the arrow keys nudge it one pixel at a time on your monitor, making precise movement much easier than working with the mouse. This is particularly useful for moving tiny objects that you can't grab with the mouse and avoids the problem of accidentally grabbing a handle and resizing the object by mistake.

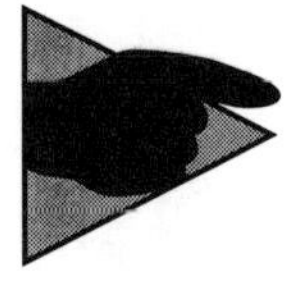

ALTERNATE METHOD

Objects can also be repositioned and resized with great precision using the **Control** palette explained in the next chapter.

The Ellipse Tool

Drawing, Dragging, and Resizing a Rectangle

In addition to the Rectangle tool, PageMaker also allows you to draw circles and ellipses and add them to your layout. To draw a circle or ellipse, follow the same steps that you used to create a rectangle, but select the **Ellipse** tool instead of the Rectangle tool. Both ellipses and circles can be created with the same **Ellipse** tool—it just takes practice dragging the shapes.

Try drawing some of these shapes and moving them around on the page. Just follow the steps given earlier for creating and moving a rectangle.

The Constrain Key

As you've been drawing, you may have noticed that it is difficult to create a perfect circle or square shape. Actually, it's easy if you know the trick. To create a perfect square, circle, or a square with rounded corners instead of a rectangle shape or slightly lopsided circle, hold down the **Shift** key as you draw with the shape tools. This "constrains" the shape being drawn into a perfect square or circle automatically and certainly beats "eyeballing" to achieve the perfect shape.

Shift can also be used to control the movement of objects vertically and horizontally. If you hold **Shift** down while dragging an object such as a rectangle, it will only move horizontally or vertically. The choice of direction is made when you begin moving the object. So, if you move it slightly horizontally with the constrain key (**Shift**) held down, vertical movement will become impossible until you release the key, or until you move the object back to its original position on the layout.

ALTERNATE METHOD

You can also create "perfect" shapes by drawing the kind of shape you want and then changing its size using the **Control** palette discussed in the next chapter. This palette allows you to modify a shape's size after you draw it by directly specifying its dimensions.

The Rotation Tool

To rotate objects quickly to new angles, use PageMaker's **Rotation** tool, which looks like a curved arrow pointing counterclockwise on the Toolbox. The Rotation tool is a fast way of rotating objects to the angles used for other objects. For example, if you create a slanted line and want to align a rectangle to the same angle as the line, the Rotation tool can quickly position the rectangle. The Rotation tool allows shapes to be freely rotated to any angle.

To use the Rotation tool:

1. Select the object to be rotated.
2. Click on the **Rotation** tool.
3. Click inside or outside the object with the tool and a "star burst" symbol will be displayed. This acts as the point of rotation for the object. Without letting go of the mouse button, hold down and drag away from the target to create a line as in Figure 3.4. At one end of the line is a cross that marks the point of rotation; at the other is the star burst.
4. Move this line in any direction to rotate the object. For more precision drag the line further away from the target.

TIP

To limit the rotation of objects to multiples of 45 degrees, hold down the Shift **key while using the Rotation tool.**

When you have the rotation you desire, release the mouse and the object will remain rotated in its new location. PageMaker offers several other ways of rotating objects that you'll learn in later chapters. While the other methods offer precision down to $^{1}/_{100}$ of a degree, only the Rotation tool allows you to align objects visually.

▼ *Figure 3.4. The Rotation Tool in Action*

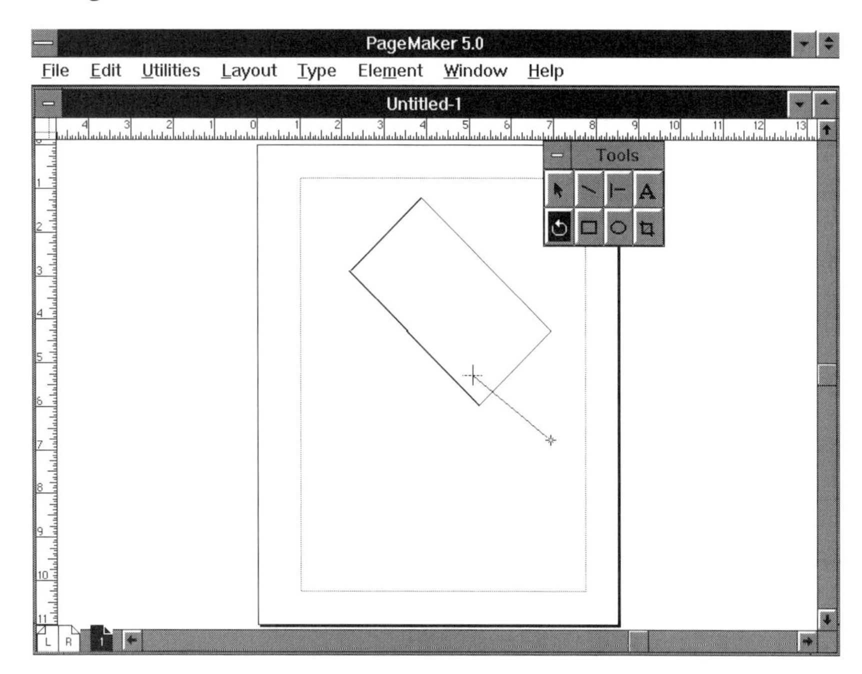

Drawing, Dragging, and Resizing a Rectangle

CHECK YOURSELF

1. Open up a new letter-sized PageMaker publication. Click on the right mouse button to change the view to **Actual size**. Draw a rectangle anywhere on the screen, then select the **Pointer** tool from the **Toolbox** and click on the rectangle to make its handles visible. Now hold down the **Shift** key, and click on any one of the rectangle's handles. What happens?
   ▲ The rectangle instantly becomes a square.
2. Click elsewhere on your layout to deselect the square. What happens?
   ▲ The handles disappear.
3. Click on the square to reselect it using the **Pointer** tool.
   ▲ The handles reappear.
4. Select the **Rotation** tool and rotate your rectangle. Notice that once you release the mouse after rotation, the rectangle stays selected. You may choose another point of rotation for the object and rerotate it.
   ▲ The square rotates as much as you specify.

5. Draw two more shapes of your choice on the desktop close to the rectangle. Now select the two of them by holding down on the **Shift** key while you select them one at a time. Use the **Rotation** tool to rotate the group of objects.
   ▲ Both objects are rotated.
6. Delete the selected objects with the **Backspace** key.
   ▲ Two of the objects are deleted, but the other object remains on the desktop.

Using the Line Tools

Lines can be added to PageMaker documents with either of two tools: the **Line** tool and the **Constrained-line** tool. Lines created with either tool can be used to divide text, added as a decorative touch, or drawn as rules to become part of a chart or illustration. PageMaker provides a number of different styles of lines, plus you can instantly change the thickness of a line to make it appear heavier or lighter as called for in your design.

The **Line** tool can be used to draw lines at any angle. The **Constrained-line** tool draws lines only vertically, horizontally, and at a 45-degree angle. The latter tool is a convenient way of adding decorative lines to a publication without the risk that they will be crooked when printed.

To draw a line:

1. Select one of the line tools from the **Toolbox**.
2. Click and hold down the mouse button where you want the line to begin.
3. Drag until a line of the correct length has been created. If you are using the **Line** tool, this step can also be used to assign an angle to the line. Just drag in the direction that creates the desired angle. To create a horizontal or vertical line with the **Constrained-line** tool, drag vertically or horizontally as required.

Once you finish drawing your line, PageMaker leaves the line selected and returns you to the Pointer. You can immediately use the tool to change the position, angle, or length of the line. Exception: If you create a line with the Constrained-line tool, you can only change its angle in 45-degree increments. PageMaker will not allow you to assign another angle to it. If you need a line that has a nonconstrained angle, delete the line and re-create it using the **Line** tool.

Using the Line Tools

TIP

If you read books on design, discuss your work with a print shop, or talk with designers, you may hear the word *rule* used to refer to lines. Don't worry, the word *rule* and the word *line* mean exactly the same thing. Another word you'll hear is a reference to *line weight*. Line weight simply refers to the thickness of the line. A line is said to be "heavier in weight" when it's thicker. This refers to the "visual weight" of the line. A thicker line is more noticeable and is therefore said to be heavier than a thinner line.

Line Styles and Width

Once a line is created, you can make changes to its width or style. The *width* is specified in points (approximately 72 points equal one inch); the *style* assigns the look of the body of the line (i.e., solid, dashed, doubled, dotted, etc.). These characteristics can be changed using the **Line** submenu of the **Element** menu shown in Figure 3.5. Notice that there is a selection of common line styles and widths and also a button for **Custom**. You can either select from the menu of common line types, or click **Custom** to bring up the dialog box shown in Figure 3.6. Here you enter the width of the line in points and select the line style from the drop-down menu.

ALTERNATE METHOD

You can exercise fine control over the appearance of lines using the **Control** palette, discussed in the next chapter.

▼ ***Figure 3.5. The Line Submenu***

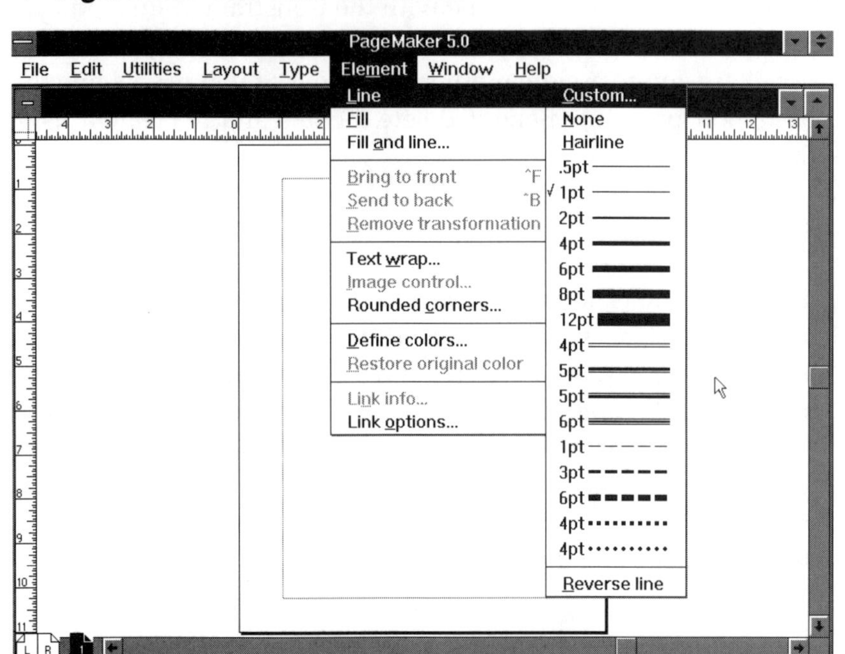

CHECK YOURSELF

1. In an open PageMaker document, draw a line using the **Constrained-line** tool. Its length does not matter. Now, use the **Line** menu to change its width to 18 points. What do you see?
   ▲ The line becomes much thicker.
2. Use the **Line** menu to change it into a dashed line. What do you see?
   ▲ The line becomes dashed.

▼ ***Figure 3.6. Custom Line Dialog Box***

Custom line

Line style:

Line weight: 1 points

Line background:

Transparent Opaque

OK

Cancel

Using the Text Tool

Using the Text Tool

We will look at entering text in detail in Chapter 5, but to finish our discussion of shape objects, we take a brief look at the **Text** tool. Like the other tools you have been experimenting with, the Text tool creates an object that can be resized and rotated and manipulated. The Text tool appears as a capital "A" in the Toolbox. Once you select this tool you will see a flashing vertical bar at the left margin. This vertical bar is called the *insertion point* and marks where your text will appear. As you type, text flows across the page until hitting the right margin, where it wraps around to the next line. The lines of text are known as a *text block*. After entering text, use the **Pointer** tool and click anywhere within the text to select the text block as you would any other object. Figure 3.7 shows a few lines of text that have been typed and selected. There is a border, called a *windowshade,* above the text and below the text, but no side borders. The two handles in the middle of the top and bottom borders are called the *windowshade handles*. Dragging the top window-

▼ ***Figure 3.7. Selected Text Block***

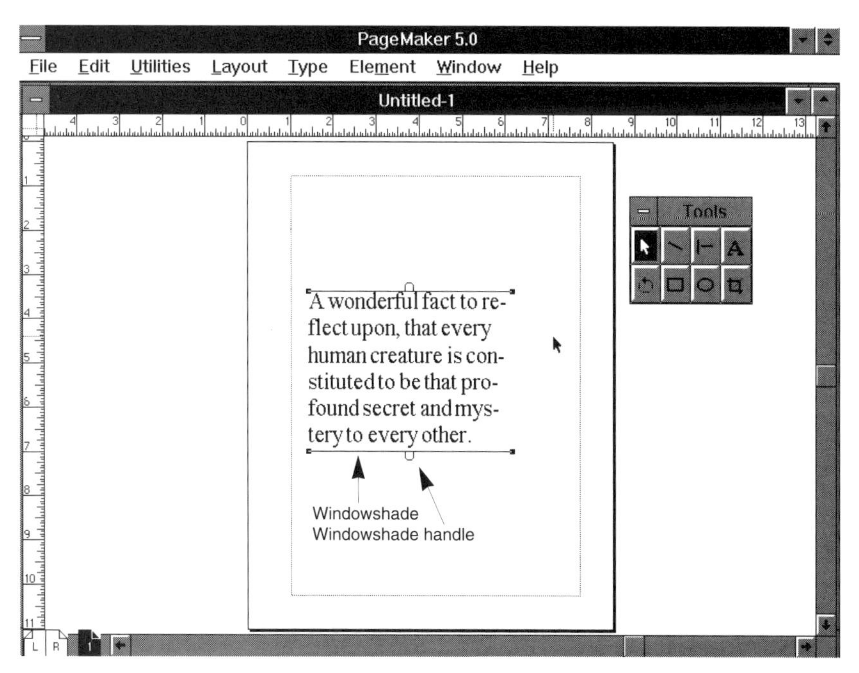

shade upward moves the entire text block perpendicular to the top windowshade. The bottom handle is used to control the flow of text, as we will see in Chapter 5.

The text object behaves slightly differently than other objects. When you hold down the pointer anywhere in the text, the four-headed arrow appears and you can move the text block. Like the other objects, holding down the **Shift** key first constrains the movement to one direction. Holding down at a corner produces the double-headed arrow for resizing the block, but the height of the block is limited by the amount of text available. If there are only four lines of text, then the block can only be four lines high, no matter how much you pull on the handle. As the width of the box is changed, the text is reformatted to fit in the wider or narrower space.

The **Rotation** tool can be used to rotate text blocks exactly the same as other objects. Once a text block is rotated, the windowshades still work the same; that is, the top shade will move the block only perpendicular to its orientation.

CHECK YOURSELF

1. Bring up a new PageMaker document and set the view for "Actual size." Close the **Styles** palette and move the **Toolbox** to the left side of the screen so that the page edge and left margin (blue line) are completely visible. Click on the **Text** tool to select it, then click anywhere in the document to the right of the margin guide. What do you see?

   ▲ A flashing vertical bar at the left margin.

2. Enter three lines of text. Do not hit the **Enter** key at the end of each line. What happens?

   ▲ As you type, the display moves to follow your typing. When you get to the right margin, the text is wrapped automatically.

3. Select the **Pointer** tool and use it to click anywhere within the text. What happens?

   ▲ The two windowshades appear.

Using the Text Tool

4. Hold down on the top windowshade handle and drag it up a couple of inches. Now pull down the bottom windowshade also.
   ▲ The text block moves up with the top windowshade. The bottom windowshade snaps back to its original position when released.
5. Hold down on the handle at the bottom left of the text block and drag it to narrow the block. What do you see?
   ▲ The text block is reformatted to fit the new dimensions.
6. Select the **Rotation** tool. Click anywhere in the text block and rotate the text. What happens?
   ▲ The text block moves to the new orientation.
7. Select **Remove transformation** from the **Element** menu. What happens?
   ▲ The text block returns to its original position.
8. Leave your work on-screen for the next Check Yourself.

Selecting Fonts and Font Sizes

There are many type designs, or *typefaces*, available for use in your publications. Typefaces are often called *fonts* in the computer world. A font is the complete set of characters for a particular typeface. All fonts have names so that they can be easily specified. The size of a font is described in points, as are the width of lines. The fonts used in books commonly range from 10 to 30 points with larger fonts being used for chapter titles or for emphasis. Fonts, typefaces, and type attributes are extensively covered in Chapter 7. For now we just want to look at a few basic operations.

The most common operations you will perform on text are selecting the font or size. To select a font before entering text, open the **Type** drop-down menu and select **Font**. Click on the font you want. Use the **Size** submenu to select the point size of type. Whatever text you now enter will appear in that font and size until you change the specifications.

Modifying Text Font or Size

Often you will look at text after it has been entered and want to change the font or size. You do this by first selecting the text to change, then specifying the changes you want to make.

To change text font or size:

1. Select the **Text** tool.
2. Position the tool at the beginning of the text you want to modify.
3. Holding down the left mouse button, move the **Text** tool to the end of the text you want to change. The text you have selected will be highlighted.
4. Use the **Font** and **Size** submenus of the **Type** menu to make the desired changes.
5. Notice that the text stays highlighted. If you not like the changes you have just made, go back to **Font** or **Size** and try again.
6. When you are satisfied with your changes, click anywhere outside of the selected text. The highlighting will vanish and the changes will be set.

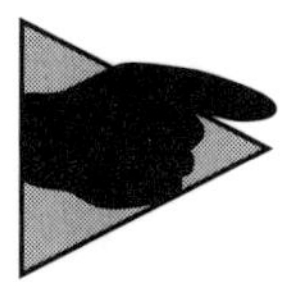

ALTERNATE METHOD

The Control palette also allows you to make fine adjustments to text appearance. We will look at its use in Chapters 4, 7, and 10.

CHECK YOURSELF

1. Continue with the publication from the last Check Yourself and open the **Type** menu and select **Font**. Click on **Arial.** Open the **Size** submenu and click on **24**. Now click on the **Text** tool and move it somewhere below the text block you typed in the last Check Yourself. Click to position the insertion point and type two lines of text. What do you see?
   - ▲ The text style is different and the size is larger than the last text you entered.

Using the Text Tool

2. Position the **Text** tool at the start of the text you typed during the last Check Yourself. Hold the left mouse button down and move the tool to the end of the text. Release the button. What do you see?
   ▲ The text is highlighted.
3. Open up the **Size** submenu under the **Type** menu. Click on **24**. What do you see?
   ▲ The type changes to the same size as the text you just entered.
4. Use the **Font** submenu and select **Arial**. What happens?
   ▲ The text looks the same as the text you just entered.
5. Click anywhere outside of the text blocks. What do you see?
   ▲ The highlighting disappears.

Deleting Text Blocks and Objects

To delete text blocks or object—including any shapes created with the shape tool—simply select them with a single-click of the mouse using the **Pointer** tool and press the Backspace key on your keyboard. This will delete the text in a text block as well as the box.

If you make a mistake, you can undo the deletion immediately after you press the Backspace key by choosing the **Undo** command from the **Edit** pull-down menu. However, you cannot undo the deletion of objects after you have entered other commands—so be careful that you really want to delete the object or text forever.

ALTERNATE METHOD

The **Cut** command under the **Edit** pull-down menu can also be used to delete objects. We will cover this method and other text and object manipulation options under the Edit menu in Chapter 4.

Using Ruler Guides to Place Objects

When you start PageMaker, the margin guides are visible as blue lines at the left, right, top, and bottom. These guides are useful for aligning text and objects. You can also create your own guides, called *ruler guides,* to help you place text and graphics in the publication. Say you want to draw three boxes on a page, one at the top, one in the middle, and one at the bottom of the page, but you want them to all line up vertically. You can drop a guide along the vertical line and then easily position the rectangles so that they border on the guide.

Creating Ruler Guides

Ruler guides are simple to create. To create a horizontal guide, move the cursor into the horizontal ruler and hold down the mouse button. The cursor will change into a two-headed arrow. With the button still held down, move the cursor back onto the desktop. A horizontal cyan line appears across the screen. In the vertical ruler, a solid line tracks the guide. When the guide is positioned where you need it, release the mouse button and the black line turns to cyan. You can now use the guide.

To make it even easier to line up objects, the guides can be specified as *snap-to guides.* A snap-to guide exerts a magnetic attraction on objects close to it, pulling them into alignment. The snap-to attribute can be toggled on and off from the **Guides and rulers** submenu of the **Layout** menu; a check mark to the left of **Snap to guides** indicates the guides are magenta.

In addition to **Snap to guides**, there is also **Snap to rulers** on the same menu. The horizontal and vertical ruler tick marks form an invisible grid behind the desktop. In the case of the default ruler, this places a tick mark every 1/32". By toggling on **Snap to rulers**, objects are drawn to these intersections when they are placed on the desktop. **Snap to rulers** is actually most useful when placing ruler guides. By turning on **Snap to rulers**, the guides are more easily aligned along the ruler. After placing the guides, **Snap to rulers** may be toggled off.

Using Ruler Guides to Place Objects

Once ruler guides have been placed, they can be relocated. Move the cursor so that it just touches one of the guides and hold down the mouse button. The cursor will turn into a double-headed arrow, and the guide will become a black line again. Continue to hold down the mouse button as you drag the guide to its new location. Release the button and the guide is set.

CHECK YOURSELF

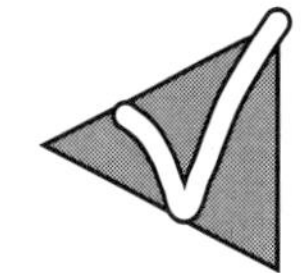

1. Bring up a new PageMaker document and set the view to 400%. Close the **Styles** palette and move the **Toolbox** to the left side of the screen so the page edge and left margin (blue line) are completely visible. Click on **Snap to rulers** in the **Guides and rulers** submenu of **Layout**. Move the cursor into the horizontal ruler and hold down the mouse button. Move the cursor into the desktop and move it around. Look at the tracking line in the vertical ruler. What do you see?
   ▲ The ruler guide jumps from tick mark to tick mark in the vertical ruler.

2. Let go of the mouse button. What happens?
   ▲ The ruler guide sticks in place.

3. Toggle off **Snap to rulers**. Position the cursor so that it just touches the ruler guide you created. Click and hold down the mouse button. What happens?
   ▲ The ruler guide turns black and the cursor becomes a two-headed arrow.

4. Move the guide up and down. What do you see?
   ▲ The guide travels smoothly over the vertical ruler and does not jump from tick mark to tick mark.

5. Let go of the mouse button to set the guide. Use the **Rectangle** tool to draw a rectangle above the ruler guide. Use the **Pointer** tool to select the rectangle and move it over the guide line several times. What happens?
   ▲ As the rectangle passes over the ruler guide, it "sticks" at the guide before passing over it.

QUICK COMMAND SUMMARY.

Shortcut Keys	*Commands*	*Procedures*
(Toolbox)		
Shift F9	Pointer tool	Creates, moves, and resizes objects.
Shift F4	Text tool	Used to create boxes that will hold text
Shift F5	Rectangle tool	Used to create rectangles
Shift F7	Ellipse tool	Used to create circles and ellipses
Shift F3	Constrained-line tool	Used to create vertical or horizontal lines
Shift F2	Line tool	Used to create lines with non-constrained angles
Shift F6	Rotation tool	Allows free rotation of objects
Shift F8	Cropping tool	Adjusts the size of imported graphics
F9		Toggles between the last selected tool and the pointer

PRACTICE WHAT YOU'VE LEARNED

What You Do	*What You'll See*
1. Create a new PageMaker 8 1/2" by 11" letter-sized layout.	1. A new document is opened, ready for a new page layout to be created.
2. Using the **Rectangle** tool, draw a rectangle in your PageMaker layout. Now using the **Pointer** tool, resize the rectangle by dragging the object's handles.	2. A rectangle is created on screen with handles showing, indicating that it is selected. Using the Pointer tool, the rectangle is resized.

What You Do	*What You'll See*
3. Use the **Ellipse** tool to draw an ellipse of any size. Now, using the **Pointer** tool, click elsewhere on your layout to deselect it. Then reselect and delete the shape.	3. An ellipse is created. By clicking elsewhere, the handles disappear. Clicking on the ellipse with the **Pointer** tool and then entering a backspace deletes the ellipse.
4. Use the **Shift** key to constrain the tool and, with the **Ellipse** tool, draw a circle.	4. No matter how you move the mouse, instead of creating an ellipse, a circle is created.
5. Use the Rotation tool to rotate your rectangle in any direction.	5. The Rotation tool creates the "star burst." As you move the mouse away from the star burst, a line from the target to the pointer (of your mouse) appears and becomes longer. Then, as you move the line in a circular motion around the target, the object rotates.
6. Draw a vertical line using the **Constrained-line** tool. Now, with the **Pointer** tool selected, change the length of the line.	6. A vertical line appears. As you move the mouse, the line lengthens.
7. Using the **Line** menu, change your line's width to four points and make it into a dotted line.	7. The line becomes thicker and then becomes a dotted line.
8. Use the **Text** tool to enter several sentences explaining what you plan to use PageMaker for (or a topic of your choice).	8. Text flows between the two margins. When selected, windowshades and handles delineate the text block.

What You Do	*What You'll See*
9. Lasso the text block and any other shape together. Use the **Rotation** tool to turn them.	9. Handles appear on both the text block and the second selected object. They are turned as one unit.
10. Use the **Shift** key and the **Pointer** to select everything except the text block. Delete the selected objects.	10. Everything except the text block is removed from the desktop.
11. Drop a vertical ruler guide 1" from the left-hand margin. Rotate the text box so it is vertical and align it with your ruler guide.	11. A cyan ruler guide appears on screen. The text box aligns to the ruler guide.
12. Use the **Text** tool to select the text you typed.	12. The text is highlighted.
13. Select the **Font** submenu and click on **Courier New**.	13. The text changes to new font.
14. Select the **Size** submenu and click on **36**.	14. The text appears much larger.
15. Use the **Pointer** tool and click anywhere in the text block.	15. The text block is selected. Windowshades and handles appear at the borders.
16. Use the **Backspace** key to erase the selected text block.	16. The text block is removed from your desktop.
17. Select **Undo** from the **Edit** menu.	17. The text block reappears.
18. Exit PageMaker without saving changes.	18. PageMaker returns you to the Windows desktop.

WHAT IF IT DOESN'T WORK?

9. To lasso the objects, use the **Pointer** tool and click somewhere outside of the objects you want to select. Hold the left mouse button down and move the mouse. A rectangle with a dotted border will appear. Size the rectangle so that it surrounds the objects you want to select. Release the mouse button.

In this chapter, you've learned how to put PageMaker's Toolbox to work defining objects, moving and resizing them, and have learned the basics of text entry and guide lines. In the next chapter we'll explore the Control palette, which will enhance your ability to manipulate objects.

PageMaker's Control Palette

In Chapter 3 we looked at the creation of various types of PageMaker objects—rectangles, ellipses, lines, and text blocks. Each of these objects has certain characteristics or attributes such as height, width, location, and angle of rotation. Some attributes, such as the Font of a text block, are unique to that particular type of object. Others, like height and location, are common to all objects. PageMaker's Toolbox provides the tools necessary for creation and editing of various objects. In this chapter we discuss the **Control** palette, which allows you to precisely manipulate the attributes of objects on the desktop. You will learn how to:

- **Use controls in the Control palette**
- **Use the Proxy**
- **Resize and move objects**
- **Accurately rotate objects**
- **Use the Control palette to change text font and size**

Control Palette Overview

The **Control** palette is normally hidden when you start PageMaker. To toggle it visible, go to the **Window** menu and click on **Control palette**. The palette appears on-screen as in Figure 4.1. Notice that there is no title bar on the top edge. Instead, the area immediately below the Control-menu box functions as a *drag zone.* To reposition the palette, move the cursor into the drag zone, hold down the mouse button and drag the palette. Releasing the mouse button sets the palette in place. The Control-menu box functions somewhat differently than in the other palettes: There is no menu and a single-click on it closes the palette.

The only information initially displayed on the Control palette is the type of tool selected, represented by the black arrow, and the current location as shown in the X and Y fields. The location is specified with reference to the zero point of the rulers. By default, the zero point is at the top inside edge of the page (the top left edge if your publication is a single page).

▼ *Figure 4.1. The Control Palette*

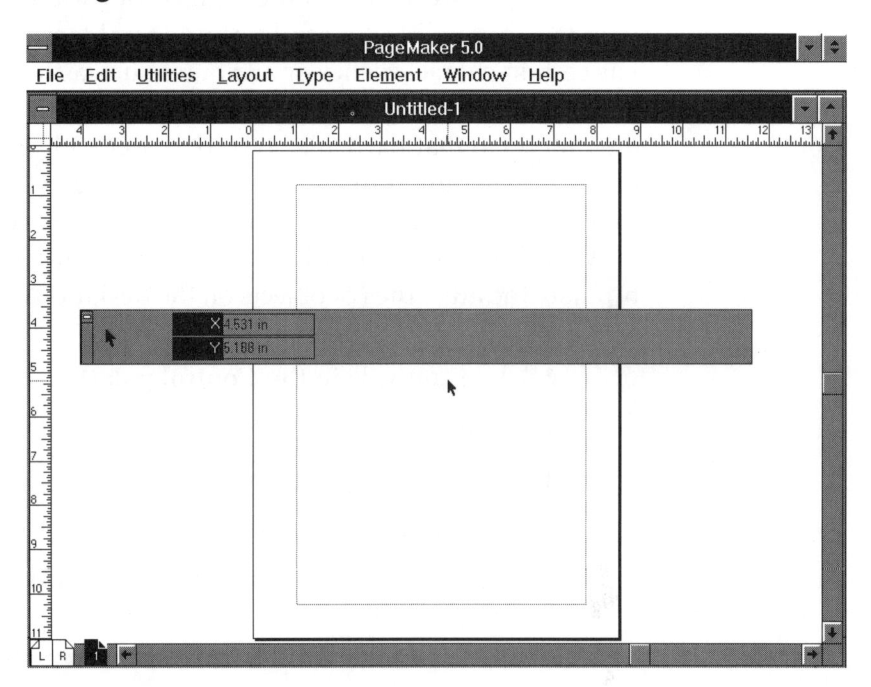

Control Palette Overview

Because the Control palette is so useful, it is convenient to keep it on the desktop at all times. But it is so large that it is difficult to find anywhere to place it without obscuring something else. A good compromise is to shrink the desktop slightly and position the Control palette below the horizontal scroll bar.

To position the Control palette:

1. Move your cursor to anywhere along the lower border of the desktop (the outside border of the horizontal scroll bar). The cursor should change to a double-headed arrow.
2. Click and hold down the left mouse button. The outside border of the desktop will become dotted.
3. Still pressing the mouse button, move the mouse up and the lower border of the desktop will follow. Allow approximately enough space for the height of the **Control** palette.
4. Release the mouse button and move the cursor into the **Control** palette's drag zone. Click and hold the left mouse button.
5. Drag the palette down to the bottom of the screen and release the mouse button.
6. Adjust the lower border of the desktop to fit snugly on top of the **Control** palette. Your screen should look similar to Figure 4.2.

A Tour of the Control Palette

Once a tool is selected, the layout of the Control palette changes to help place and size the object. Figure 4.3 shows the palette while sizing and placing an ellipse. The **X** and **Y** fields give the horizontal and vertical location of the cross hairs with respect to the zero point. The **W** and **H** fields change to reflect the width and height of the ellipse. Once the object is positioned, the Control palette changes, as in Figure 4.4, to show what attributes may be manipulated.

A close-up of the palette is shown in Figure 4.5. At the far left is the **Apply** button, which changes to reflect the type of object selected. If no object has been selected, it indicates the current tool. Next to it is the **Proxy,** a miniature of the object. At the Proxy's perimeter are six boxes that correspond to the object's handles as well as one box in the center. Any time an object is selected, one

▼ *Figure 4.2. After Positioning the Control Palette*

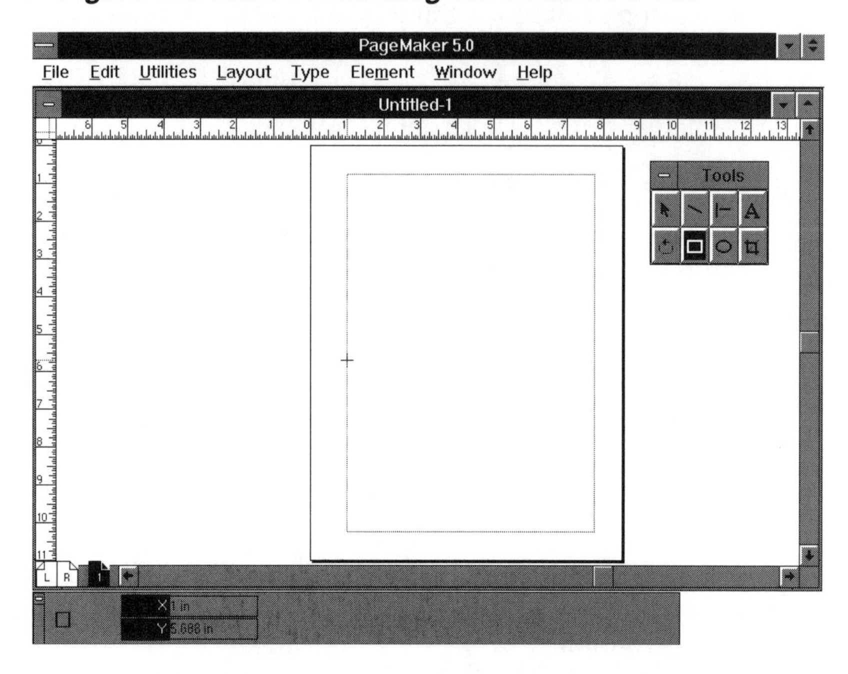

▼ *Figure 4.3. Using the Control Palette to Help Place an Object*

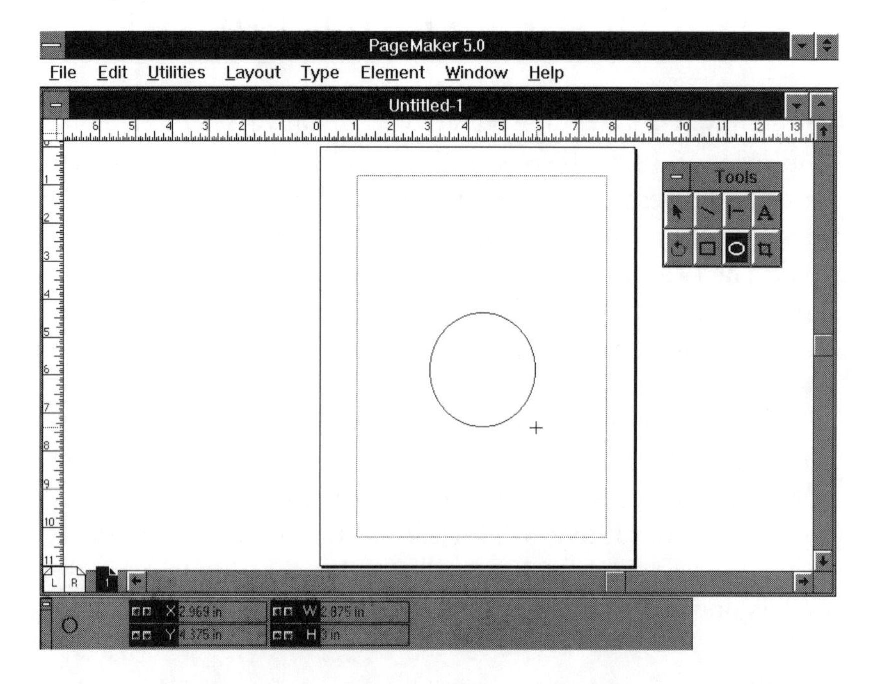

▼ Figure 4.4. The Control Palette after Placing an Object

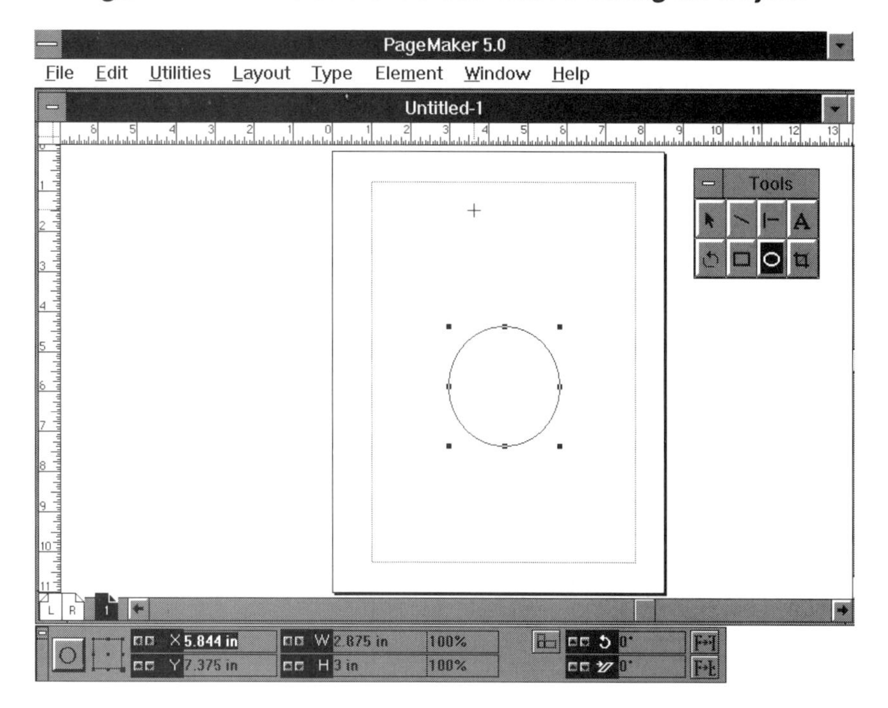

A Tour of the Control Palette

▼ Figure 4.5. Close-up of the Control Palette

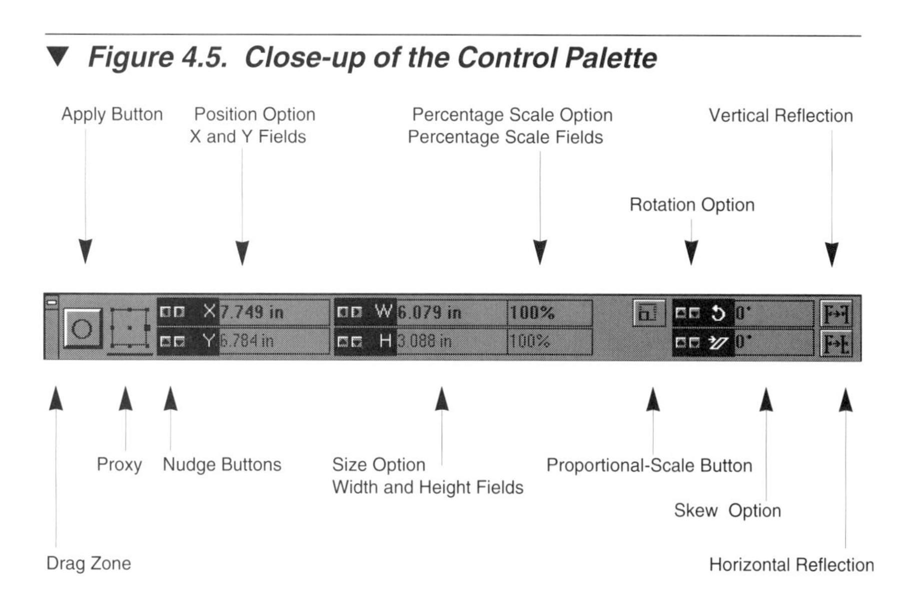

box is larger than the rest to indicate the reference point for the object. X and Y coordinates, angle of rotation, and skew are all measured with respect to this reference point. To change the reference point for an object, click on another box in the Proxy or on any of the actual object's handles.

Moving Objects

The **X** and **Y** fields of the **Position** option may be used to control an object's location. The **Proxy's** reference point controls which dimensions are available to be modified. If the reference point is at any of the four corners or in the center, both dimensions may be changed. However, if the reference point is located on one of the two vertical sides, you will notice that the **X** field appears bold with respect to the **Y** field and only the horizontal dimension can be adjusted. Similarly, if the reference point is on one of horizontal sides, only the Y dimension is available.

Double-clicking in the **X** or **Y** field highlights the field and allows you to enter a new coordinate for the object. Remember, this coordinate is with respect to the reference point shown on the Proxy and the zero point on the rulers. For example, in Figure 4.6, the upper left box on the Proxy is enlarged so the X and Y coordinates represent the distance from the upper left handle of the ellipse to the horizontal and vertical rulers' zero point.

You may also click once at the end of the **X** or **Y** field to position an insertion point. Here you can enter an arithmetic expression to change the current value. To add, subtract, multiply, or divide, use the characters +, −, *, or /, respectively. Hit the **Enter** key, or click the **Apply** button, and the change will be implemented.

The **nudge** buttons to the left of the **Position** option provide extremely fine control. The direction of the arrow on each nudge

▼ ***Figure 4.6. The Proxy Showing Point of Reference***

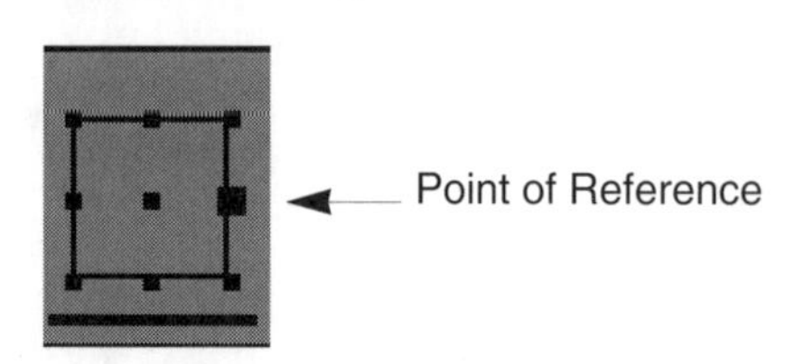

button indicates the direction the object will move. Each click on the button moves the object .01". This "nudge value" can be changed by altering **Preferences** as discussed in Chapter 6.

Sizing Objects

Sizing is similar to moving. Observe that the change in size is accomplished by moving the side opposite the side where your reference point is located. If the reference point is positioned in the middle, both sides move toward, or away from, the center. As in positioning objects, you can directly enter the new values, express them as an arithmetic expression, or use the nudge buttons for fine control.

PageMaker also enables you to adjust size as a percentage of the original size by using the **Percent-scale** fields. By double-clicking on the **Percent-scale** field, you can directly enter a value. You may single-click at the end of the field and enter an arithmetic expression.

To maintain an object's original *aspect ratio* (the ratio of height to width) scale, click on the **Proportional-scale** button located to the right of the **Percent-scale** option. The icon changes from two rectangles to the double square as shown in Figure 4.7. Now when you enter a new value for the width or height, PageMaker will adjust the other dimension to maintain the object's scale. This is extremely useful when you want to retain the original shape of an object while adjusting its scale, as in enlarging circles or squares.

▼ ***Figure 4.7. The Proportional-Scale Button***

Unconstrained

Constrained

CHECK YOURSELF

1. Open up a new PageMaker document and accept the default settings. Close the **Styles** palette. Go to the **Window** menu and click on the **Control** palette. Click and drag on the palette's drag zone to position it near the bottom of the page. Move the cursor around the desktop. What do you see?
   ▲ The Control palette appears on-screen. A black arrow on the left of the palette shows the Pointer tool is in use. The X and Y fields track the cursor's coordinates.
2. Select the **Rectangle** tool and draw a rectangle approximately 2.5" wide by 3" high anywhere on the desktop. What happens?
   ▲ The Control palette first changes to show the Rectangle tool is in use. Once the rectangle is drawn, the palette changes again to display the object attributes.
3. Click on the top left handle of the rectangle. Double-click on the **X** field of the **Control** palette and change its value to 1". Do the same for the **Y** field. Click on the **Apply** button. What happens?
   ▲ The rectangle jumps to the upper left of the page.
4. Use the nudge buttons to make the rectangle into a 2" by 2" square. Click on the upper left handle. Click on the **Proportional-width scale** button. Click at the end of the **Percent-scale** field for the width and type in ***2.** Then, either click the **Apply** button, or hit the **Enter** key. What happens?
   ▲ The square doubles in size. Because Proportional-scale is selected, the Y dimension is changed in response to the change in the X dimension.
5. Leave the square on-screen for the next Check Yourself.

Object Transformations

Rotating, skewing, and reflecting are examples of object *transformations*. They affect the shape of an object, not its dimensions. In Chapter 3 we experimented with the rotation tool available on the Toolbox. The **Control** palette's **Rotation** option offers finer control

Object Transformations

but does not allow the arbitrary points of rotation as the Rotation tool does. As with the other controls, rotation from the palette is done with respect to the reference point on the Proxy. To rotate an object, first set the reference point and then use the nudge buttons to adjust the desired angle. The upward button rotates the object counterclockwise and the downward button rotates clockwise.

As shown in Figure 4.8, a rectangle is *skewed* when two of its sides are no longer at right angles to each other. In the case of a circle or an ellipse, the two axes are no longer perpendicular to each other. To achieve this effect, choose your reference point and use either the **Skewing** option's nudge buttons or directly enter a skew angle.

Reflecting is the process of creating a mirror image of an object. Two buttons are associated with the **Reflection** option: The top button is for horizontal reflection, the bottom for vertical. Again, the direction of reflection is determined by the reference point. The reflection will always take place around an axis that passes through the reference point. An object can also be rotated first, so that the object is not purely vertical or horizontal. The skewed rec-

▼ *Figure 4.8. A Skewed Rectangle*

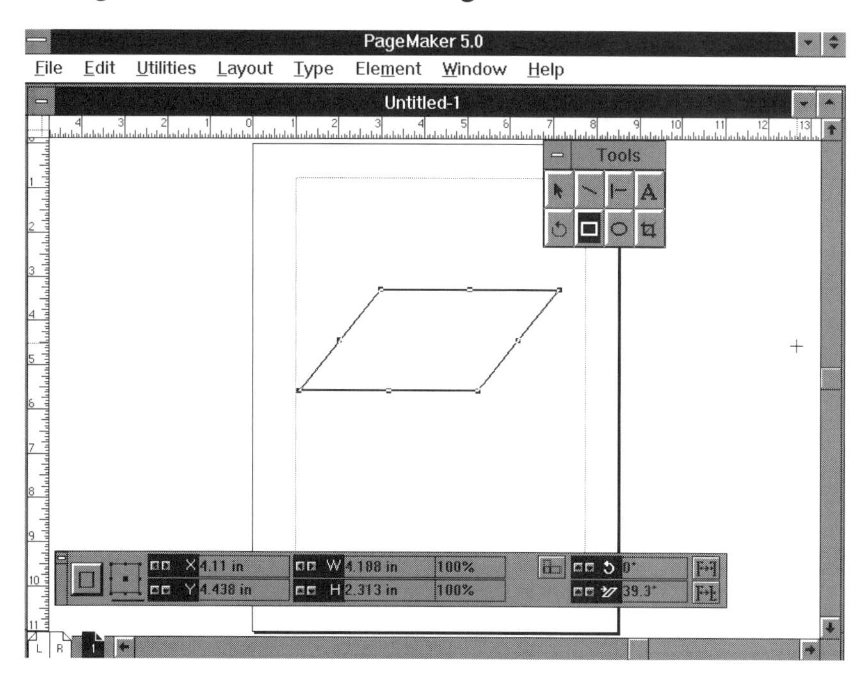

tangle from Figure 4.8 is shown reflected about the horizontal axis in Figure 4.9. You can also group objects together and then reflect the whole group. Text blocks can be reflected to create backward or upside-down text, as shown in Figure 4.10, where the text has been reflected about the vertical axis.

If you make complex transformations on an object only to decide that you liked it better way back at the beginning, don't despair; PageMaker obligingly remembers how your objects began life. Go to the **Element** menu and click on **Remove transformation.** Like magic, your object will be returned to its undistorted shape.

CHECK YOURSELF

1. Use the rectangle from the last Check Yourself. Drag it into the middle of the page. Use the **Line** tool to draw a slanted line anywhere in the rectangle. Look at the angle of rotation. Now click on either of the other boxes on the **Proxy** and look at the angle of rotation. What do you see?
   ▲ The Control palette changes to display attributes for the line. No matter what reference point is chosen, the angle

▼ ***Figure 4.9. The Skewed Rectangle Reflected Horizontally***

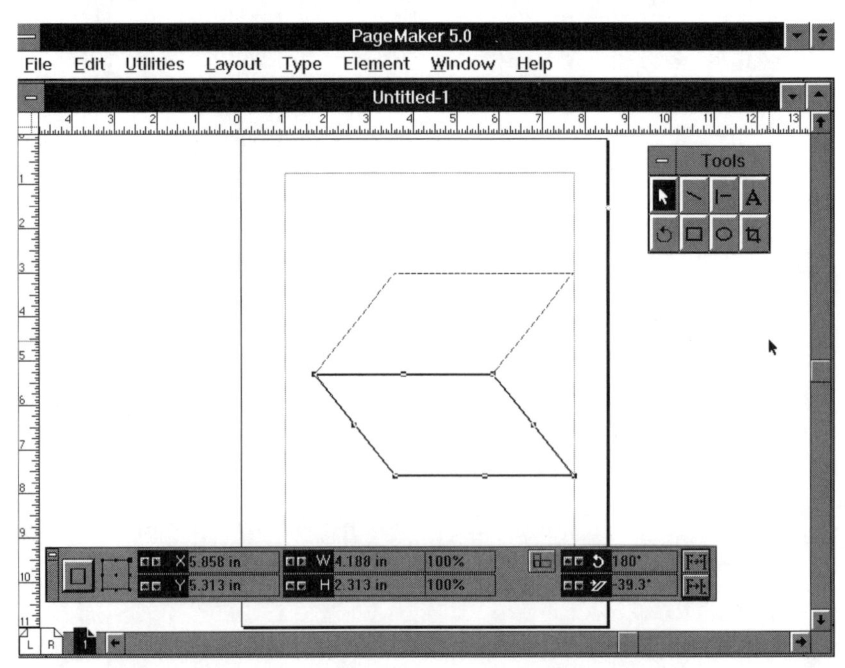

Object Transformations

▼ ***Figure 4.10. A Reflected Text Block***

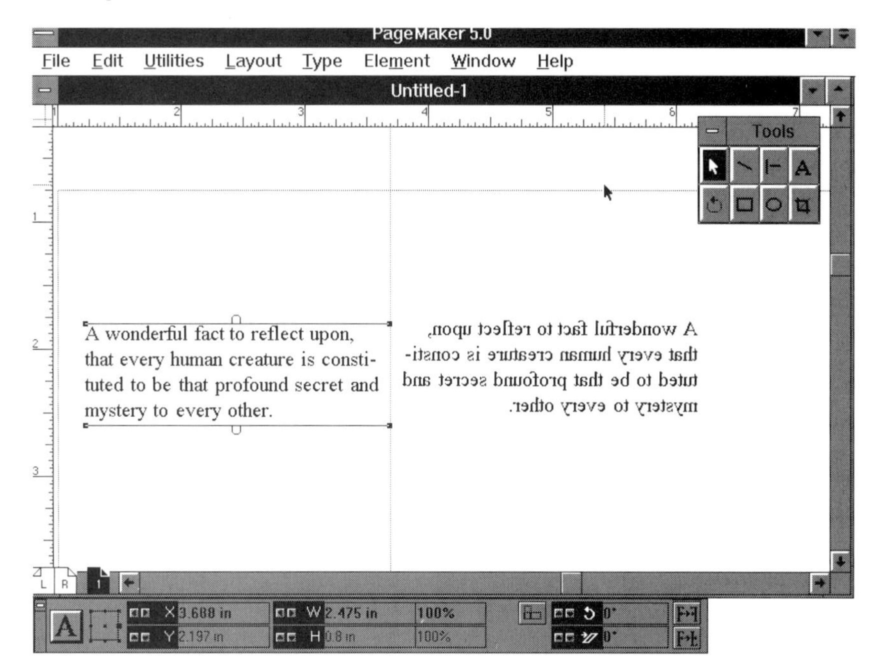

of rotation for a line is always measured with respect to its left endpoint.

2. Lasso the line and the rectangle together. Choose a point on the rectangle and click on it. Click on the **Vertical Reflection** option. What do you see?
   ▲ The rectangle and the line are both reflected.

Selecting Fonts and Font Size

So far we have used the Control palette to manipulate objects. It is also useful for adjusting text attributes. When the **Text** tool is selected, the face of the **Control** palette changes as shown in Figure 4.11. All of the typographic controls available from drop-down menus are now found immediately at hand. The advanced functions will be discussed in Chapters 7 and 8. Here we will look at font selection and sizing.

▼ ***Figure 4.11. The Control Palette in Text Mode***

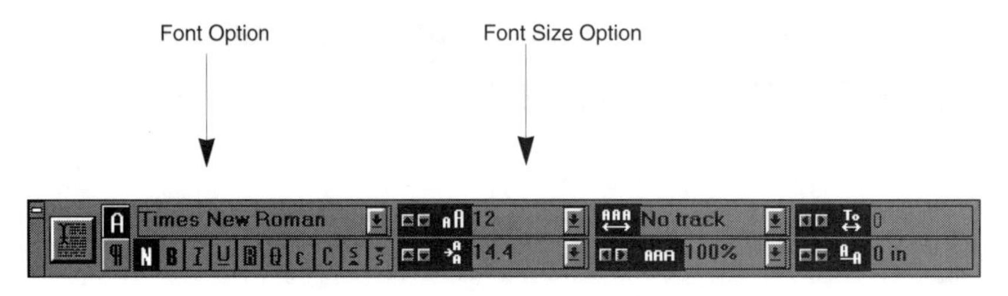

To select a font for entering text, first position the insertion point. Then use the **Control** palette's **Font** button to display the font selection menu. The **Control** palette menus act somewhat differently than the drop-down menus. After you position the cursor on the **Font** button, hold down the left mouse button to display the associated menu. Continue to hold the button down while you slide the mouse to move the highlight to your selection. Releasing the button closes the menu. However, the selection does not take effect until you hit the **Apply** button. The same procedure applies to selecting a font size.

To modify text, first use the **Text** tool to highlight the text you want changed. Open the **Font** menu and select a new font. The selected text will appear in a new font. It is surrounded by a solid rectangle to indicate that your changes are not final. You can go back and select another font to see how that looks or try out various sizes until the text appears exactly as you wish. As you can see, this ability to quickly change and review text attributes is extremely powerful.

QUICK COMMAND SUMMARY

Shortcut Keys	***Commands***	***Procedures***
Ctrl '		Toggles Control palette on/off
(Control palette)		
	Apply	Implements changes
	Proxy	Assigns point of reference
	X field	Changes horizontal position
	Y field	Changes vertical position
	W field	Changes object width
	H field	Changes height of an object
	Proportional-Scaling	Allows change in only one direction

Shortcut Keys	*Commands*	*Procedures*
	Rotation tool	Used to rotate object
	Skewing	Used to change the angles of an object's sides or axes.
	Reflection	Creates mirror images of objects.

PRACTICE WHAT YOU'VE LEARNED

What You Do	*What You'll See*
1. Open a new PageMaker publication and accept the defaults. Remove the **Styles** palette. Move the **Toolbox** to the upper right of the desktop. Position the **Control** palette below the horizontal scroll bar.	1. The screen appears as in Figure 4.2
2. Choose **View** from the **Layout** menu and select **Actual size**. Use the horizontal scroll bar to move the publication so the left margin is lying close to the vertical ruler.	2. The blue line of the left margin is visible close to the left side of the desktop.
3. Use the **Ellipse** tool to draw an ellipse approximately 3" wide by 2" high with the left point at 6" on the vertical ruler and 1.5" on the horizontal ruler.	3. An egg-shaped ellipse is drawn.
4. Select the ellipse with the **Pointer** tool. Click on the center point of the **Proxy**. Double-click on the **X** field and enter 3.00. Double-click on the **Y** field and enter 6.00. Click on the **Apply** button.	4. The ellipse moves so that its center point is exactly at 3 horizontal and 6 vertical.

What You Do	*What You'll See*
5. Use the nudge buttons on the **W** and **H** fields to adjust the size of the ellipse to 3" wide by 2" high.	5. The size of the ellipse is modified.
6. Click outside of the ellipse to deselect it, then click on it again to select it. This resets the **Control** palette. Click on the **Proportional-scale** button. Set the height to 2.5".	6. The width of the ellipse is automatically changed to 3.75".
7. Select the **Text** tool and position the insertion point at the left margin, an inch or so above the ellipse. Type in **The yolks on you.**	7. The text appears at the left margin.
8. Use the **Pointer** to select the text block. Double-click on the **W** field and set the width to 2". Click on the **Apply** button.	8. The text block shrinks.
9. Click on the center point of the **Proxy**. Set the **X** field to 3.0 and the **Y** field to 6.0. Click on the **Apply** button.	9. The text block is moved inside of the ellipse.
10. Get the **Text** tool and select the text you typed. Use the **Control** palette to set the font to **Arial** and the size to **18 point.**	10. The text changes style and gets larger.

What You Do	*What You'll See*
11. Use the **Pointer** tool to lasso the text block and ellipse together. Click on the middle left box of the **Proxy**. Double-click on the **Rotation** option and enter **45**. Click on the **Apply** button.	11. The ellipse and the text rotate to a 45-degree angle.
12. Exit PageMaker without saving your publication.	12. You are returned to the Windows program manager.

WHAT IF IT DOESN'T WORK?

2. If you do not see the left margin, look at the horizontal ruler. Use the horizontal scroll bar to position the 1" mark just to the right of the vertical ruler. The left margin guide should now be visible.
4. If the ellipse does not move where you expect it to, make sure that you have clicked on the center point of the **Proxy**. This sets the reference point for the X and Y position at the ellipse's center.
11. If both the ellipse and text are not rotated, select **Remove transformation** from the **Element** menu to start over. Make sure that when you lasso you capture both the text and the ellipse. The rectangular lasso you draw must surround, but not touch, the ellipse. When you release the mouse button, you should see the handles on both the ellipse and the text box.

In this chapter you have learned how to use PageMaker's powerful Control palette to manipulate the attributes of objects. As we investigate advanced text and graphics operations in later chapters, we will revisit the Control palette and learn additional functions. In the next chapter, we'll look at entering text in PageMaker.

Text Processing with PageMaker

The ability to manipulate text on a page is one of the most fundamental features of a desktop publishing program, and PageMaker 5.0 for Windows offers a wide range of text editing and manipulation capabilities. The functions covered in this chapter are the basics, similar to the type-handling functions found in most word processors. Some of the editing functions covered in this chapter, such as copy and delete, can also be used to move and manipulate objects drawn with the shape tools. Text editing and object manipulation within a PageMaker document are fast, easy, and flexible. In this chapter, you will learn how to:

- **Select type for editing and use the Undo command**
- **Format text with the Control palette**
- **Use guides for placing text and objects**
- **Copy and move text and objects**
- **Use PageMaker's text import function**
- **Use the story editor and the spelling checker**
- **Use columns**

Selecting, Editing, and Deleting Text

In Chapter 3, you learned how to create text blocks and add text to them. If you do not enter text exactly right the first time, PageMaker allows you to make changes as you would in a word processor. To add or delete words, change spellings, or make other small changes, select the text tool and click to locate the insertion point where you want to start.

To make large-scale modifications, such as changing font or size, you must first select the text to work on. Choose the **Text** tool and then hold down the left mouse button while moving the mouse. The text is highlighted as the mouse moves over it. Releasing the mouse button will leave the selected text highlighted, as in Figure 5.1. Selected text can be deleted by pressing either the **Backspace** or **Delete** key, replaced by typing new text, or it can be manipulated in other ways that you'll learn in this chapter.

▼ ***Figure 5.1. Selecting Text***

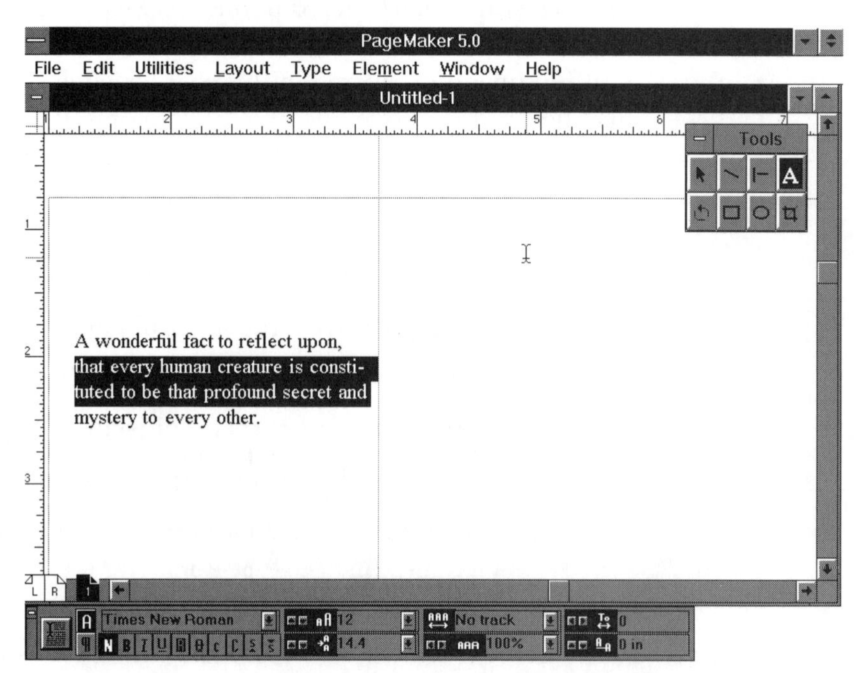

Selecting, Editing, and Deleting Text

Text can also be selected by using the cursor keys to move the cursor to the beginning or end of the text you want to select. As you'll recall from Chapter 3, holding down the **Shift** key while clicking on objects allows you to select multiple objects. Holding the **Shift** key down while moving the cursor through text with the **cursor** keys selects the text the cursor travels over. *Note:* Remember that selected text is called "highlighted text" in other programs. You might be more familiar with that term.

Cutting, Copying, and Pasting

Because objects and blocks of text often need to be rearranged in a document or moved from one document to another, PageMaker supports copying and pasting of objects and text. *Copying* an object or text leaves the original where it is and stores a copy of it in the Window's **Paste** buffer. The **Paste** buffer is a place in memory where text or objects can be temporarily stored before being moved to another place in the layout. When you *paste* from the buffer, a copy of the information in the buffer is placed where you specifically tell it to go. *Cutting* the text or object deletes it from the layout but makes a copy of the cut material in the **Paste** buffer.

To copy or cut text, select the portion to copy or cut with the **Text** tool, open the **Edit** menu, and select **Copy** or **Cut**. To copy or cut an object, select it with the tool and do the same.

To paste text into another location, place the cursor at the new location, then open the **Edit** menu, and select **Paste.** To paste an object, select the **Pointer** tool, then select **Paste** from the **Edit** menu. Then move the newly pasted object to the desired location by dragging it with the **Pointer** tool.

WARNING

The Paste buffer is a temporary holding place for text or objects that will be placed into another part of the layout. *Temporary* is the key word here. The same information can be pasted multiple times from the Paste buffer—but as soon as you Cut or Copy something else into the Paste buffer, the previous contents are lost. If you exit PageMaker, the buffer contents are permanently erased. If you used

the Copy command, you can go back and grab the original again if it hasn't been deleted since the Copy operation. Otherwise, it's gone for good.

Because text blocks are objects, as are rectangles, squares, ovals, and other shapes, you can move entire text blocks the same way objects are moved using the commands within the Edit menu.

TIP

You can select all the objects on the visible page of your page layout by choosing Select all **in the** Edit **menu with the** Pointer **tool. If you are working within a text block, the same command will select all of the text in the current block, plus all text threaded with it throughout the layout.**

Fix Mistakes Instantly with Undo/Redo

One of the most convenient features of PageMaker that is now being added to more and more software in the DOS/Windows world is **Undo**. Undo is a single command that allows you to undo your last action should it be made in error or if you don't like the results of a change you've just made. Found under the Edit menu, this single command can be used to fix a wide variety of errors; typing mistakes, changes to graphic elements, and incorrect insertion or deletion of elements and text can all be corrected with Undo.

PageMaker even allows you to Undo an undo! If you use the Undo command and don't like the results of the change, the Undo command turns into **Redo** as shown in Figure 5.2 and lets you keep the changes you made as if you had never used the Undo command.

▼ ***Figure 5.2. Edit Menu with Redo Command Showing***

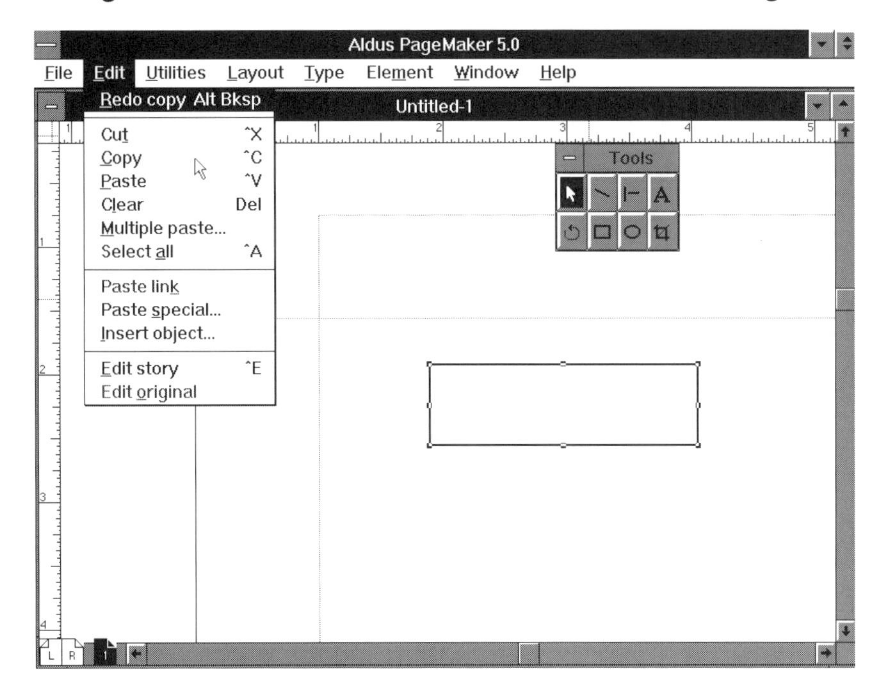

Fix Mistakes Instantly with Undo/Redo

CHECK YOURSELF

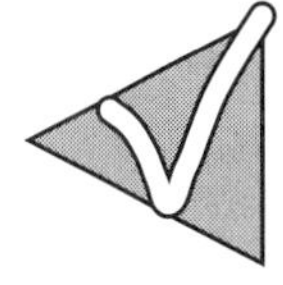

1. Create and save a passage of text for use in this and later exercises in the book. You can use the text suggested here as excerpted from Charles Dickens's *A Tale of Two Cities*. When you are done typing, save the file as DICKENS.PM5 using PageMaker's **Save. . .** or **Save As. . .** command. (PageMaker will automatically add the .PM5 to the filename. PM5 is the PageMaker file extension.)

   It was the best of times, it was the worst of times. It was the age of wisdom, it was the age of foolishness. It was the epoch of belief, it was the epoch of incredulity, it was the season of Light, it was the season of Darkness, it was the spring of hope, it was the winter of despair, we had everything before us, we had nothing before us, we were all going direct to Heaven, we were all going direct the other way-

```
in short the period was so far like the present
period, that some of the noisiest authorities
insisted on its being received, for good or for
evil, in the superlative degree of comparison
only.

There were a king with a large jaw and a queen
with a plain face, on the throne of England;
there were a king with a large jaw and a queen
with a fair face, on the throne of France. In
both countries it was clearer than crystal to
the lords of the State preserves of loaves and
fishes, that things were settled forever.
```

▲ You have now created a page layout containing a text block that is saved on disk for future use in this book.

2. Use the **Text** tool to select the entire second paragraph. Open the **Edit** menu and use the **Cut** command to delete the paragraph. Move the **Text** tool a few lines below the first paragraph and click to position a new insertion point. Select **Paste** from the **Edit** menu to paste the second paragraph into a new text block. Use the **Pointer** tool and click anywhere in the second paragraph. What do you see.
   ▲ The second paragraph is now in a text block of its own.
3. Use the pointer tool to resize the new text block to 1/2 its width. What happens?
   ▲ The text is reformatted to fit the narrower block. An inverted arrow on the bottom windowshade handle indicates that there is more text than is being shown.
4. Use the **Undo** command. What happens?
   ▲ The text returns to full width.
5. Use the **Undo** command again. What do you see?
   ▲ The text goes back to reduced width.
6. Pull down the bottom windowshade handle. What happens?
   ▲ The remainder of the text is revealed.
7. Exit Pagemaker without saving changes.

Working with Text Import/Export

Working with Text Import/Export

Because many page layouts incorporate text that is originally created with a word processor, the ability to import text from other products into a page layout is a useful function. It saves time because you don't need to retype anything. In some situations, you may want to export text from a PageMaker document into another page layout program or word processor. Typically, last-minute changes to documents imported from word processors are made after the text has been placed into PageMaker and readied for output. Typos may need to be fixed, copy cut to fit, or new ideas incorporated. For this reason, the text may need to be sent back to the word processing format so others can work with the modified document inside their familiar word processors instead of within PageMaker.

To practice importing and exporting text within PageMaker, we are going to use the *Tale of Two Cities* excerpt you created in the last exercise. First, we will show you how to export the text into a word processing format. Then, we will reimport the text. That way, if you don't have any text files handy, you can still practice moving the text in both directions.

Exporting PageMaker Text to Word Processors

Text contained in individual text blocks can be exported in one of several word processor-compatible formats or as a standard text-only format called ASCII. For example, you can save text in a format directly readable by popular word processors such as Word for Windows or WordPerfect. If you select one of these formats when exporting, not only is the text saved, but most of the formatting is saved as well. So, if you subsequently open the file in Word for Windows, formatting such as paragraph indents, font sizes, and other information will appear as you specified them in PageMaker.

The ASCII format is used to save text in a format compatible with almost any other program and even with other kinds of incompatible computer platforms. Unlike saving text in a word processor-compatible format, which, in addition to saving the text, also saves invisible control codes that contain formatting information, ASCII consists of only the characters with almost no formatting information, other than line and paragraph breaks. Normally, you export PageMaker text to a compatible word processor for convenience—but if you are exporting to other applications or computer platforms, you may need to export in ASCII.

PageMaker can export an entire story (defined as all the text in related text blocks) or only the text you have highlighted manually within a text block.

To export text from a PageMaker document:

1. To export selected text, highlight it with the **Text** tool, or to export an entire story, click anywhere in the story with the **Text** tool.
2. Open the **File** menu and select **Export....** A dialog box will appear asking you where you want the text saved. In this dialog, there is a menu for you to select the format to save it in and two check boxes that allow you to tell PageMaker to save the entire story or just what is highlighted. (If you have not manually selected a passage of text, the latter option remains grayed out.)
3. Make your choices and click **OK**. The text in the PageMaker document will remain unchanged, but a new file will appear on disk that contains the exported text.

Importing Text into PageMaker Documents

PageMaker can import text documents from a variety of word processors. In addition to importing the text contained in a word processor document, PageMaker also will import any style sheets that may have been defined in the document and convert straight quotes to "curly quotes" (also called "Smart Quotes") automatically. An example of straight quotes and curly quotes is shown in Figure 5.3. Curly quotes are superior to straight quotes because they are less noticeable to the reader and look better with the rest of the text.

▼ *Figure 5.3. Straight Quotes Versus Curly Quotes.*

"Straight Quotes"

“Curly Quotes”

Exporting PageMaker Text to Word Processors

To import a word processing document and place it in PageMaker:

1. Open the **File** menu and select **Place. . .** .When the dialog box appears, choose the **Convert quotes** option if desired, and select the file you want to import. Click **OK** to complete the operation.
2. PageMaker will look at the requested file and attempt to recognize the source application. If PageMaker is unsure of the source, a dialog box will pop up requesting you to identify the source of the file. In either case, PageMaker then chooses the appropriate import filter.
3. The text appears as a loaded text icon as shown in Figure 5.4. Use the mouse to drag the text icon wherever in the publication you want your text to begin. Click, and the text will automatically flow between the page margins to the end of the page or to the end of the text, whichever comes first.
4. If there is more text than fits on the current page, the bottom windowshade handle will display an inverted arrow as in Figure 5.5 and the text icon will change to a pointer. Place the pointer on this arrow, then click and the loaded text icon again appears, representing the rest of the text. Place the text icon at the next spot you want text to start and click. Repeat this until all the imported text has been placed.

TIP

If you do not want to immediately place imported text, move the loaded text icon onto the pasteboard area. Click and the loaded icon will change into a text block. You can leave this block on the pasteboard until it is needed.

▼ *Figure 5.4. The Loaded Text Icon*

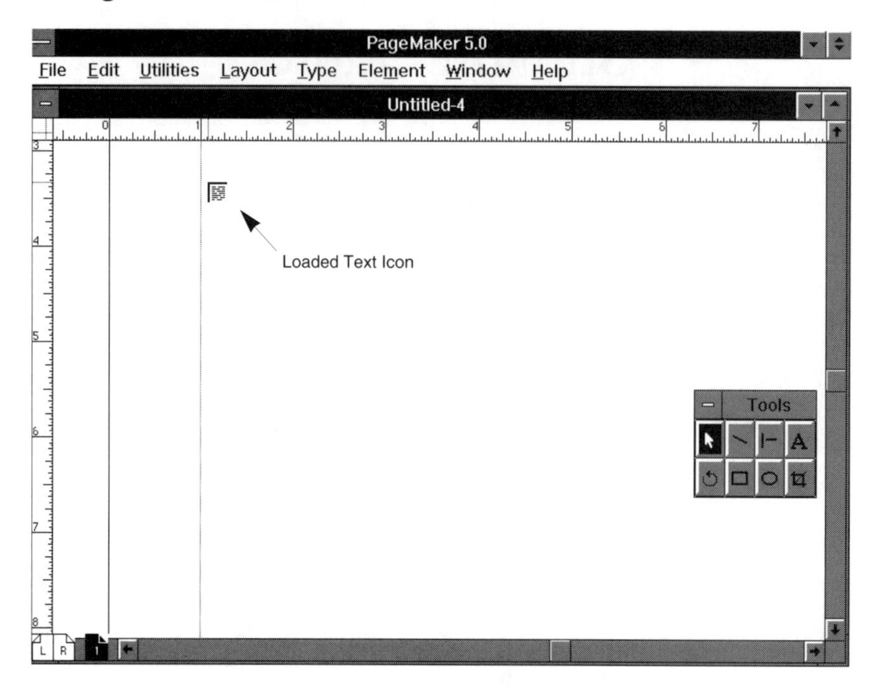

▼ *Figure 5.5. Text Block with Inverted Arrow*

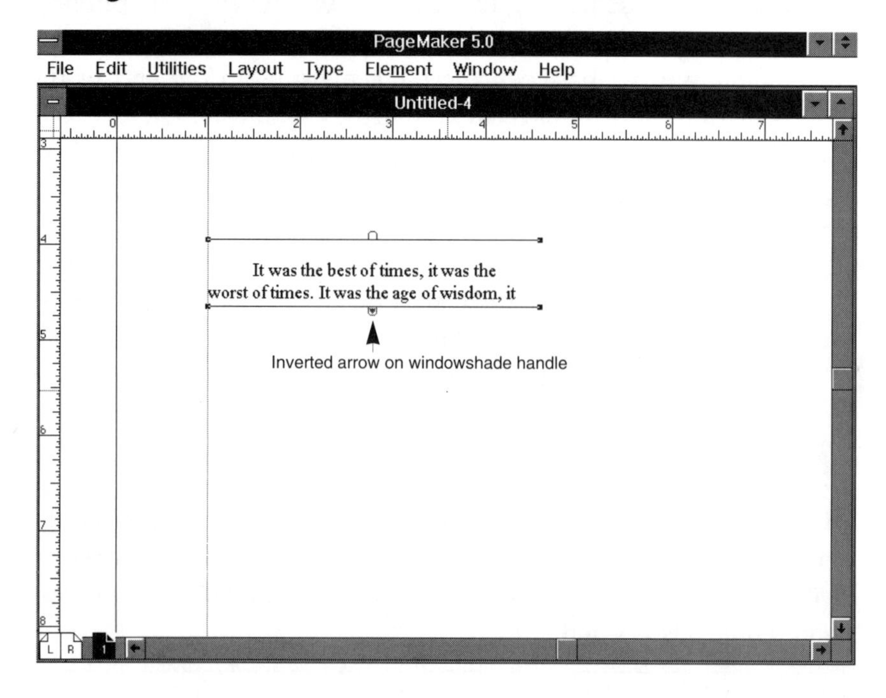

Automatic Text Flow

Exporting PageMaker Text to Word Processors

Placing text manually, as in the example above, offers the maximum control in placement. In cases where you do not need or desire as much control, you can allow PageMaker to flow all of the text by selecting **Autoflow** from the **Layout** menu. With **Autoflow** selected, the text icon appears as in Figure 5.6. Once you place the text icon initially, PageMaker will flow the text through the remainder document. If you did not specify enough pages for all of the text, PageMaker will create new pages as needed.

A variation on this theme is semiautomatic text flow. This pauses text flow at the end of each page but leaves the text icon loaded. To use semiautomatic flow, select **Autoflow** and import your text. The icon will appear as in Autoflow. Place the icon where you want your text to start, but instead of clicking, hold down the mouse button. Text will flow till the end of the page and the icon will be loaded, ready to be placed again. Repeat this until the text is exhausted.

▼ ***Figure 5.6. The Autoflow Text Icon***

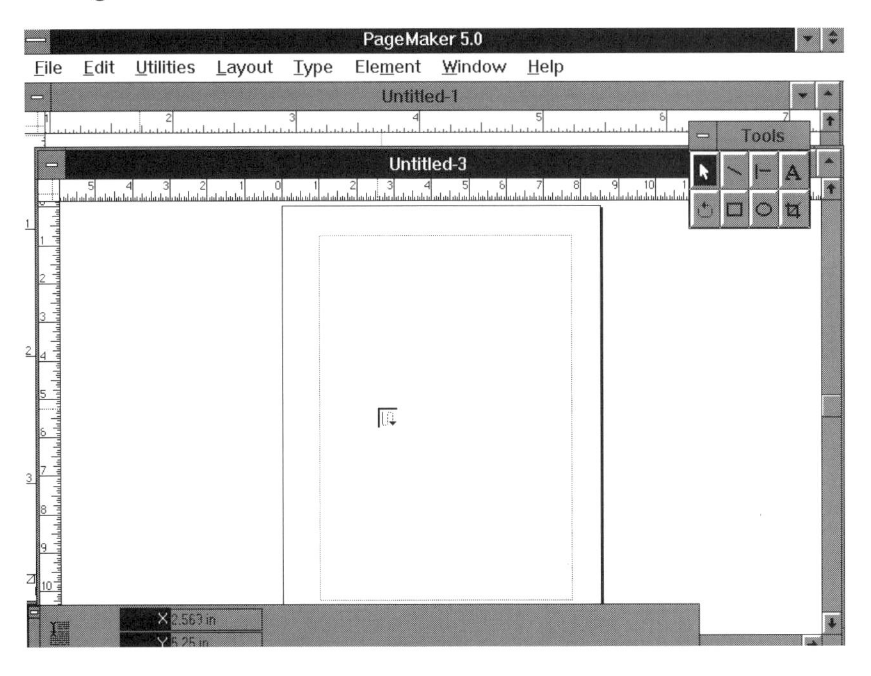

When text runs over several pages, each page is an individual text block. The collection of individual text blocks is known as a *story*. The story is said to be *threaded* through the related text blocks. When a change is made to one page (or text block) the change ripples through the threaded blocks. For example, if text is added to page 2, all of the subsequent text is moved, and new pages created, if needed, to accommodate the change.

CHECK YOURSELF

1. Open the Document DICKENS.PM5. Place the **Text** tool in either paragraph and click. Use Pagemaker's **Export. . .** command and save it as a WordPerfect (not ASCII) document. Call the file DICKENS2. PageMaker will automatically give the filename an extension of "WP5." Close the PageMaker document without saving changes. Use the Windows File Manager to view the contents of the PageMaker directory. What do you see?
   - ▲ The WordPerfect formatted file is saved in the PageMaker directory.
2. Open a new document and accept the defaults (letter-sized). Use PageMaker's **Place. . .** command to import the file DICKENS2.WP5. Accept the default font assignments. What happens?
   - ▲ The file is imported and appears as a loaded text icon.
3. Move the loaded text icon onto the new publication and click. what do you see?
   - ▲ The text flows into your PageMaker publication.
4. Quit PageMaker without saving.

Working with Columns

Often it is desirable to present text in columns rather than in full pages. Basically there are two types of columns: *book columns* and *newspaper columns.* In book columns, the text flows to the end of one column and continues from the top of the next column.

Working with Columns

Newspaper columns are used where the text is to flow down one column and then continue in a column on another page.

To set up columns:

1. Click on the master pages if you want columns throughout the publication, or move to the page where you want columns.
2. Open the **Layout** menu and select **Column guides**. This brings up the dialog box shown in Figure 5.7.
3. If you want different numbers of columns on the left and right pages, click on **Set left and right pages separately.** Fill in the number of columns per page and the amount of space between columns.
4. Click on **OK**.

Blue *column guides* show the column boundaries in your publication. These column guides can be relocated on the master pages or for individual pages. To change the width of a column, use the **Pointer** tool and move the tip to one of the column guides. Click and hold the mouse button. The Pointer turns into a two-headed arrow. Move the mouse and the column guide will move with you. Release the mouse button to set the guide.

▼ *Figure 5.7. The Columns Dialog Box*

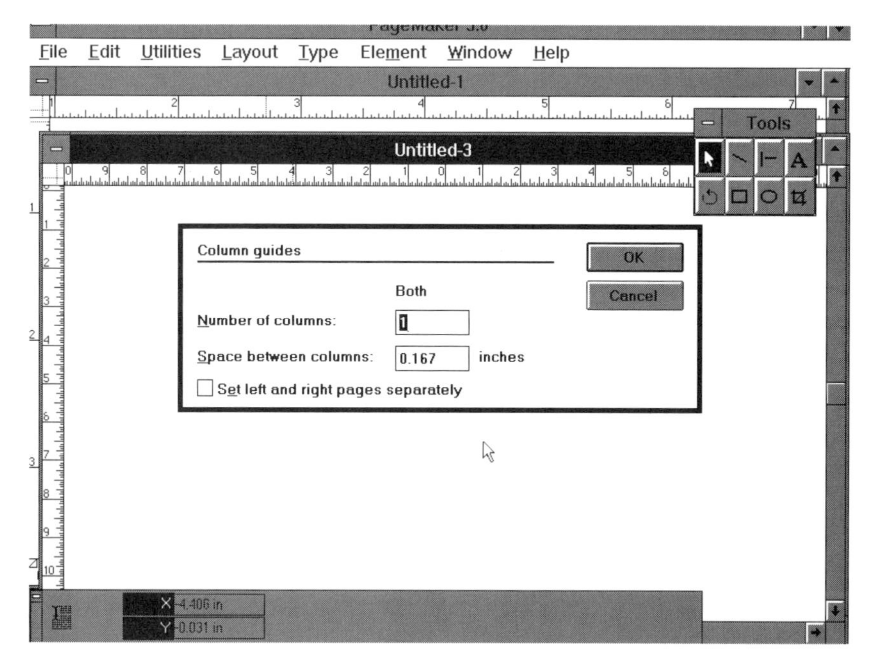

TIP

If you want to be precise when resizing columns, first make the Control **palette visible, then move your guides. The Control palette will display the coordinate of the column edge as you move.**

If you want the text to flow through your columns as in a book, Autoflow will still work. The text will flow through the columns on each page until it is done. Newspaper style columns, however, require manual or semiautomatic text flow. You must fill the desired columns on each page one page at a time.

The Story Editor

You can edit stories in PageMaker's layout view but may find it easier to make major revisions with the *story editor.* The story editor allows you to concentrate on the content of a story while largely ignoring the visual style. To invoke the story editor, use the **Pointer** tool to click anywhere in the current story, then open the **Edit** menu and select **Edit story**. A window similar to Figure 5.8 will appear (if there is no column running along the left side, go into the **Story** menu and click on **Display style names**).

Along the left-hand side of the window is a column that lists the style (discussed in Chapter 8) of each paragraph. Small dots mark the beginning of each new paragraph. The rest of the window is given over to the text itself with most formatting removed. All of the text commands reviewed earlier are available both in layout view or in story editor view. In addition, there are three new text functions accessible only from the story editor: **Find,** to search for words, phrases, or styles; **Change,** to search and replace selected text; and the **Speller**.

Finding and Changing Text

If you have worked with a word processor you are probably familiar with "search and replace" functions for finding words or phrases. The PageMaker **Find** and **Change** commands go beyond simple

▼ ***Figure 5.8. The Story Window***

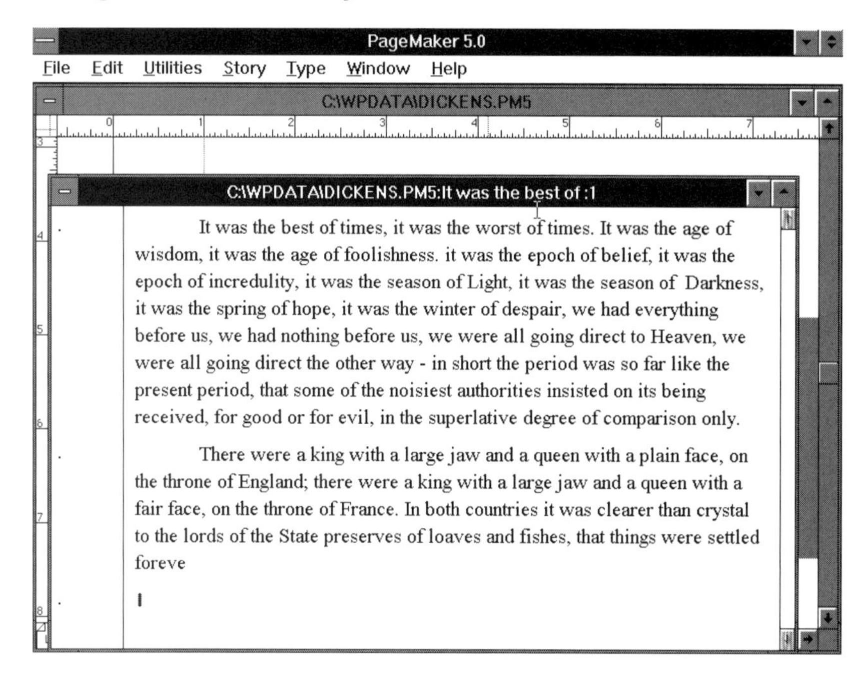

The Story Editor

search and replace, because they not only work on words and phrases but also on text attributes and styles. In addition they can be set to search only the current story, all stories within a publication, or an entire book. In Chapter 12 we will look in-depth at the search and replace function. For now, we'll run through the basics.

To perform a change:

1. Click on the current story.
2. Open the **Edit** menu and select **Edit story**.
3. Open the **Utilities** menu and select **Change** The dialog box in Figure 5.9 appears. Fill in what you want to find and what you want it changed to. Note that you can search through just highlighted text, the current story, or all stories in the publication.
4. If you want to change styles or text attributes, click on the **Attributes** button. The dialog box shown in Figure 5.10 pops up. Here you can find and replace text attributes or styles. By leaving the **Find** and **Change** fields blank in the first dialog box, you have the ability to convert only styles or attributes throughout a publication. This is useful for changing one type font to another or substituting italics for bold.

▼ *Figure 5.9. The Change Dialog Box*

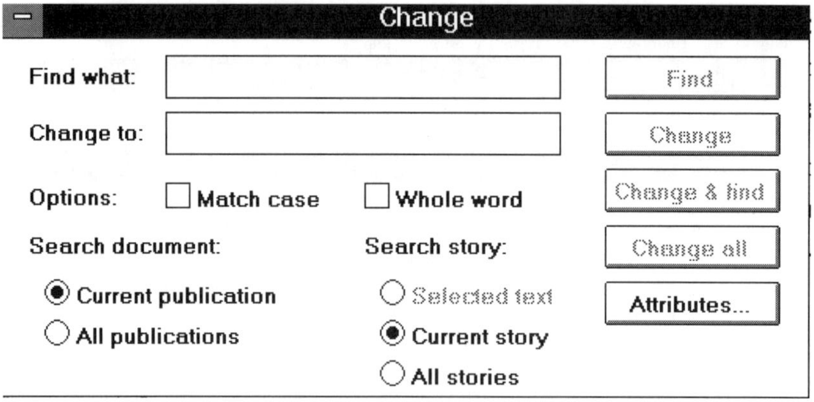

5. When you are done, click **OK** to close the Change attributes dialog boxes and double-click on the **Control-menu** box of the Change dialog box.

The **Find** dialog includes all of the options of **Change,** only without the ability to change items.

Using the Speller

PageMaker has a spelling program that allows you to check the spelling of the text you enter in PageMaker or the text of documents imported from word processors. Because final edit changes

▼ *Figure 5.10. The Change Attributes Dialog Box*

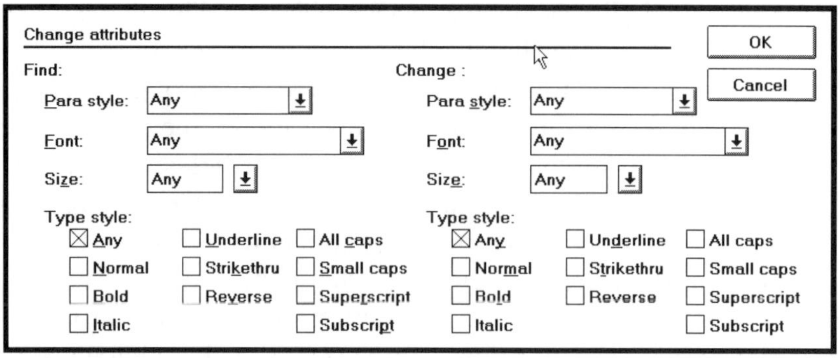

The Story Editor

often are made after a word processing file has been imported, having a speller inside PageMaker helps catch typos added after the file has been imported and placed in the page layout.

Although you may want to use the more powerful spellers contained in a word processor before importing your document, PageMaker's speller is fully capable of checking individual words, selected text blocks and linked stories, or the complete document. PageMaker also allows you to save unique words such as technical phrases in a user-defined auxiliary dictionary.

To use the speller, you must be in the story editor. When you open the **Utilities** menu and select **Spelling. . .**, the dialog in Figure 5.11 appears. You may select to spell-check the current publication or all publications. Within a publication, you can choose to spell-check only the highlighted text, the entire story, or all stories within the publication.

When you have selected the appropriate options, click on the **Start** button. When the speller encounters a word that it doesn't know, it will highlight the word in your text, bring it up in the **Change to:** window in the speller, and suggest possible alternatives in a window below **Change to:**. If one of the alternatives is the correct word, you double-click on it to replace the highlighted word in the text and hit **Start** to have the speller continue. You may

▼ ***Figure 5.11. PageMaker's Spelling Window***

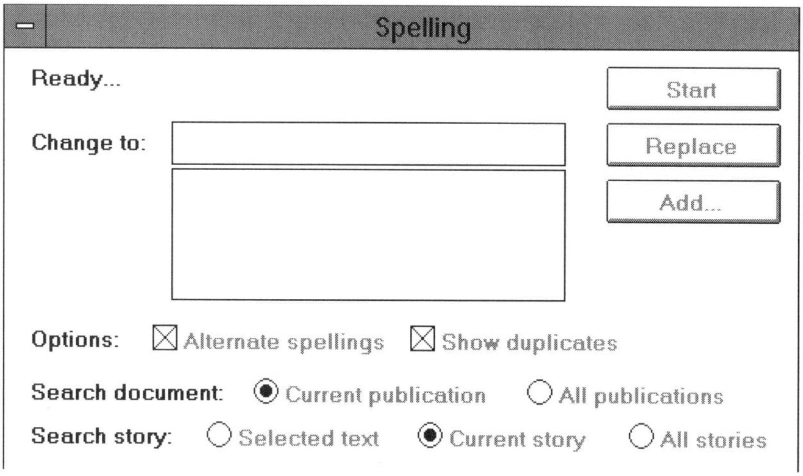

Spelling

Ready...

Start

Change to:

Replace

Add...

Options: ☒ Alternate spellings ☒ Show duplicates

Search document: ◉ Current publication ○ All publications

Search story: ○ Selected text ◉ Current story ○ All stories

also click on **Add**, if you want to add the highlighted word to PageMaker's dictionary. If you would rather edit the misspelled word, then move the pointer to the word and click on it. The speller will be removed from the screen and an insertion point appears next to the word. After changing the word, resume spell checking from the **Utilities** menu.

QUICK COMMAND SUMMARY

Shortcut Keys	Commands	Procedures
(Edit menu)		
Ctrl+C	Copy	Copies the selected text or object into the Paste buffer
Ctrl+X	Cut	Cuts the selected object or text from the layout into the Paste buffer
Ctrl+V	Paste	Pastes the content of the page buffer in a page layout
Alt+Bksp	Undo	Reverses the last change made to text or graphic objects
Alt+Bksp	Redo	"Undoes" the Undo command
(Utilities menu)		
Ctrl+8	Find	Finds text or styles
Ctrl+9	Change	Changes text or styles
Ctrl +L	Spelling	Spell-checks stories
(File menu)		
Ctrl+D	Place. . .	Imports text from a word processing document into a page layout
Alt F→E	Export. . .	Saves text from a PageMaker layout into word processing or ASCII format

PRACTICE WHAT YOU'VE LEARNED

What You Do	*What You'll See*
1. Open a new PageMaker document with the default settings. Adjust the view to 75% and position the left margin close to the left side of the window. Use the **Place...** dialog to import DICKENS2.WP5. Start the text at the top of the page.	1. A new document is opened and the text saved earlier in this chapter is flowed into a text block.
2. Cut the second paragraph and paste it on top of the first paragraph	2. Cutting the second paragraph removes it from the screen. Pasting it at the top places it before the other paragraph.
3. Select the paragraph you just pasted on top and delete it using the **Backspace** key. Immediately use **Undo** to undo the deletion.	3. The paragraph is erased and then reappears when the Undo is used.
4. Select the first paragraph and use the **Control** palette to change it to another typeface (your choice) and make it into 10-point type.	4. The text changes to the new font and becomes smaller once it's resized.
5. Change the second paragraph to 12.57-point type using the **Control** palette.	5. The type changes size.
6. Change the word "wisdom" on the first line of the second paragraph to "wsdom". Use the speller on the entire story. Make corrections as needed.	6. PageMaker stops at "wsdom," highlights it, and offers alternatives. Double-clicking on "wisdom" causes it to appear in place of "wisdom."

What You Do	*What You'll See*
7. Export the text in your publication as a WordPerfect document named TEST2.WP5 using the **Export...** command.	7. The text is saved on disk in a format compatible with Microsoft Word for Windows. Once saved, the text in the PageMaker layout is unchanged. (It doesn't matter if you have Microsoft Word, the text will still be saved in the specified format)
8. Erase the text block from your screen. Place TEST2.WP5 on the bottom half of your screen.	8. The word processing document is imported into PageMaker.
9. Exit PageMaker and do not save changes. You may delete TEST2.WP5; it won't be used again.	9. PageMaker returns you to the Windows desktop.

WHAT IF IT DOESN'T WORK?

1. If you can't select text, make sure that you are using the **Text** tool and not the **Pointer** tool.

In this chapter, we have introduced you to text processing in the PageMaker environment. You have learned how to import and export text, how to create columns, and how to use PageMaker's speller. We build on this text processing foundation in Chapters 7, 8, and 9. In the next chapter, we look at customizing your environment with PageMaker's Preferences options.

6

Setting PageMaker's Preferences

PageMaker allows the user to customize the work environment by selecting the page layout settings that come up when the program is launched. In many programs these settings are collectively known as the *defaults*. Windows programs often refer to them as *preferences*. In this book we use the two terms interchangeably. PageMaker's extensive preference settings are among its most attractive features. The ability to set preferences saves considerable time when assembling large projects. If you are using a new copy of PageMaker for Windows, then the preferences will be those set by the manufacturer. However, you can still set the program up the way you like to work. In this chapter, you will learn how to:

- **Open and use PageMaker's Preferences dialog boxes**
- **Set preferences from PageMaker's menus**

Using PageMaker's Preference Settings

PageMaker has several dialog boxes and drop-down menus with preferences that can be defined and adjusted. These preferences range from the basics, such as margins and orientation, to advanced functions like kerning and linking. The net result is the ability to transform the program environment to fit both your personal taste and the requirements of a particular job.

Preferences are set with no publications open. After starting PageMaker, rather than selecting the **New. . .** dialog, either go to the **Preferences. . .** dialog box or one of the drop-down menus and make the desired changes. If a publication is open while you change settings, then the settings will apply to that publication only; when you next start PageMaker the settings will revert to what they were before you made any changes. This applies to changes made with the **Preferences. . .** dialog as well as the drop-down menus.

This section won't attempt to cover all of PageMaker's preference-setting capabilities, because there are too many options. But it will explain the most important features and how to adjust each set of preferences. You should be able to master the other preference settings as you continue to work with PageMaker.

The Preferences Dialog

The **Preferences** dialog box, shown in Figure 6.1, is accessed from the **File** menu. This dialog box controls a number of useful settings:

▲ **Measurement system**—You may choose to work in inches, inches decimal (ruler increments are in .05 or .001 inch rather than in 1/16" or 1/32"), millimeters, picas, or ciceros.

▲ **Vertical ruler**—The measurement system of the vertical ruler can be set independently of the rest of the publication. This is

▼ *Figure 6.1. PageMaker's Preferences Dialog Box*

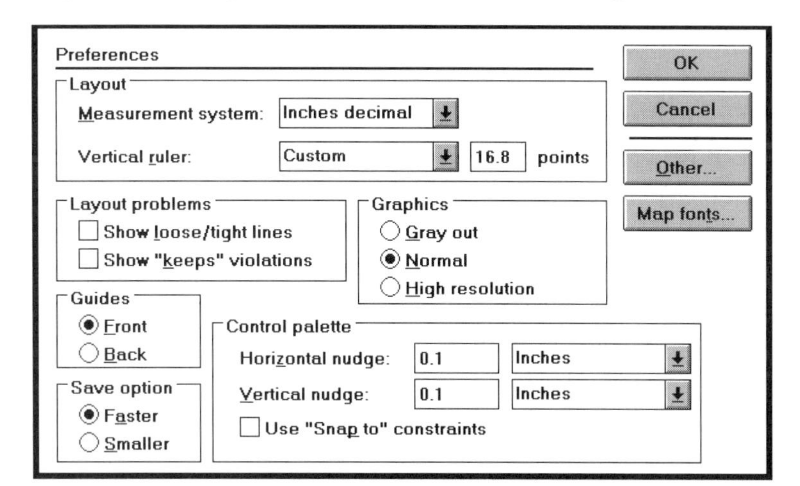

The Preferences Dialog

useful when a project calls for laying down a large amount of text. The vertical ruler is then set to "custom" and the point size of your leading is entered in the **Points** field. *Leading* is the distance from the top of one line to the top of the next line; it will be covered in Chapter 8. The ruler hash marks then fall exactly on the lines of text and it is easy to use **Snap to guides** and accurately align text.

▲ **Layout problems—Show loose/tight lines** has PageMaker highlight lines of text that are identified as having too much letter spacing (loose) or too little spacing (tight). **Show "keeps" violations** highlights any text that does not conform to the text specifications you set in the **Paragraph** dialog of the **Type** menu (covered in the next chapter).

▲ **Graphics**—When using graphics in a publication, screen redraws may be slow. PageMaker offers the option of having graphics **Gray out;** the graphics appear as gray boxes that can be quickly drawn. If you are merely rearranging objects, this will significantly speed up the process. You can then switch back to **Normal** or **High resolution** to see all the detail of your graphics.

▲ **Guides**—Clicking on **Front** causes guide rules to be shown in front of the text in a publication. Clicking on **Back** makes the guides stand in back of the text.

- **Save option**—**Faster** appends to the end of the publication file when you choose **Save** from the **File** menu. **Smaller** rewrites the entire publication when **Save** is chosen. This produces smaller files but takes longer.
- **Control palette**—The value for each click of a **nudge** button can be specified by entering values in the **Horizontal nudge** and **Vertical nudge** fields. **"Snap to" constraints** directs PageMaker to have objects snap to the nearest ruler or guide tick mark when using the nudge buttons. This operates in conjunction with the settings made in the **Guides and rulers** submenu of the **Layout** menu. If **Snap to guides** is turned off and **Snap to rulers** is turned on, then **Control** palette nudges will snap to the ruler tick marks, but not to the guides.

The "Other" Dialog Box

In the **Preferences** dialog box are the **Other** and **Map fonts** dialogs. The **Other** dialog box is shown in Figure 6.2. Some of its useful settings are:

- **Autoflow**—When **Display all pages** is selected, PageMaker displays each page as text is flowed through the publication. If not selected, only the last two pages are shown.
- **Use typographer's quotes**—In Chapter 5 we looked at "curly quotes," which are also called "typographer's quotes." This option replaces straight quotes as you enter text in PageMaker. Note that this only applies to new text entered into PageMaker. Opening previously saved publications will not convert the quotes.
- **Greek text below**—When working with very small type sizes, PageMaker can change the type to lines rather than show the actual text, which would be too small to see at less than 200% view. This speeds up the redraw of screens. Generally, text is greeked at under 8 points.
- **Story editor settings**—The **Font** and **Size** options specify the font used within the story editor. Remember that the story editor is essentially used to enter or edit text; font, size, and other formatting shown in **Layout** mode are not visible in the

The "Other" Dialog Box

▼ ***Figure 6.2. The Other Preferences Dialog Box***

Other preferences
OK
Cancel
Autoflow:
Display all pages
Printer name:
Display PPD name
Size of internal bitmap: 64 kBytes
Auto include images under: 256 kBytes
Text
Use typographer's quotes
Preserve line spacing in TrueType
Preserve character shape in TrueType
Greek text below: 9 pixels
Story editor
Font: Times New Roman
Display style names
Size: 12 points
Display ¶

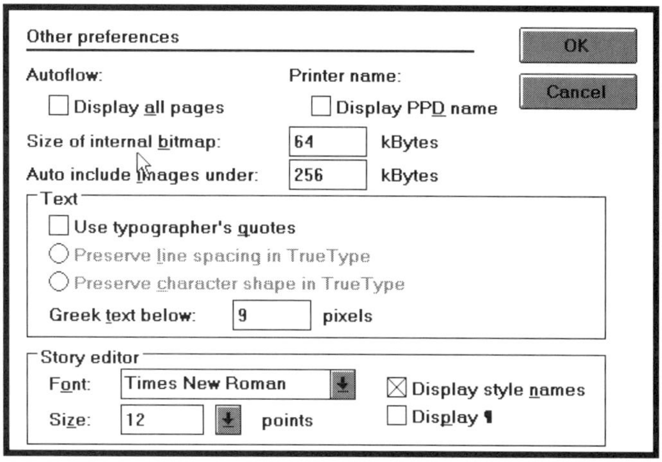

story editor. **Display style names** shows style names in story editor's left-hand column. Styles are discussed in Chapter 8. **Display ¶** enables the display of the end of paragraph symbol (¶) in the story editor.

The Map Fonts Dialog Box

One of PageMaker's strengths is its ability to interchange publications between the MacIntosh and the PC. Occasionally, problems arise when different fonts are available on the MacIntosh than are on the PC, or the same fonts are known by slightly different names. For instance, a font known as Times Roman on the MacIntosh may be called New Times Roman in PC Windows. The **Map fonts** dialog, accessible from **Preferences**, allows you to specify how fonts will be converted or *mapped* when moving PageMaker publications across platforms. We will defer discussion of this facility until the end of Chapter 7, after a discussion of type and fonts.

Setting Defaults from the Menus

Many defaults are set directly from their associated drop-down menus. Remember, like the **Preferences** dialog, you must not have any publications open when you alter a default setting or it will affect only that publication. We will look at some of the settings available from each of the menus. Note that not all options on the menus are available for default setting.

1. The **File** menu

   ▲ In **Page setup** you can change any of the default settings that appear when you open the **New** dialog box. These include the page size, margins, and orientation.

2. The **Layout** menu

   ▲ Use the **Guides and rulers** submenu to select whether or not to default to **Snap to guides** and **Snap to rulers.** Select **Rulers** if you want the rulers to appear on the desktop when PageMaker is started.

   ▲ Open **Column guides** to specify the default number and size of columns for a publication.

   ▲ Set **Autoflow** on to have PageMaker automatically flow text when importing to a publication.

3. The **Type** menu

   ▲ **Type specs. . .** is used to set all of the default type attributes except the default font, which always reverts to the first font on the font list. Note that for most of these defaults, you must type in the value rather than select from a menu. Type attributes are discussed in the next chapter.

   ▲ The individual menus—**Font**, **Size**, **Leading**, **Set width, Type style, and Track**—offer subsets of the selections available in the **Type specs. . .** dialog.

   ▲ **Alignment** sets up the default justification.

   ▲ **Paragraph. . .** and **Indents/tabs. . .** set default paragraph characteristics as explained in the next chapter.

   ▲ **Hyphenation** lets you set rules for how words are broken at the end of lines. We will look at hyphenation in Chapter 8.

   ▲ **Style** selects the default paragraph style for publications. Creating and using styles is also discussed in Chapter 8.

Setting Defaults from the Menus

4. The **Element** menu

   ▲ Choose default line width and style using the **Line, Fill,** or **Line and fill. . .** menus. Remember that the chosen line width is also the default width for the border of rectangles and ellipses.

   ▲ Set how text flows around graphics (discussed in Chapter 9) in the **Text wrap. . .** dialog.

5. The **Windows** menu

   ▲ A check mark next to any of the palettes indicates that it will appear on your desktop when PageMaker is started.

TIP

At some time you may want to discard all of the default settings you have altered and return to the factory defaults. This is most easily accomplished by renaming the file that contains the defaults and allowing PageMaker to build a new one. The file to rename is "PM5.CNF" and resides in the "\aldeo\usenglsh" directory. First close PageMaker. Then rename the file to something such as "PM5.OLD." Now start up PageMaker once more and a new default file will be built with the factory settings.

QUICK COMMAND SUMMARY

Shortcut Keys	*Commands*	*Procedures*
(File menu)		
Alt F→R	Preferences	Changes many of PageMaker's defaults
Alt F→G	Page setup	Changes defaults for the New dialog box.
(Layout menu)		
Alt L→A	Guides	Selects how PagerMaker treats guides and rulers
Alt L→C	Column guides	Default number and size of columns
Alt L→F	Autoflow	Default text flow

Shortcut Keys	***Commands***	***Procedures***
(Type menu)		
Alt T→S	Size	Default font size
Alt T→L	Leading	Default leading
Alt T→W	Set width	Sets default font width
Alt T→R	Track	Default tracking
Alt T→Y	Type style	Sets caps, italics, bold, etc.
Ctrl+T	Type specs	All of the above, in one place
Alt T→A	Alignment	Default justification
Ctrl+M	Paragraph	Default text attributes
Ctrl+I	Indents/tabs	Default tab and indentation
Ctrl+H	Hyphenation	Default hyphenation
Alt T→S	Style	Default text style

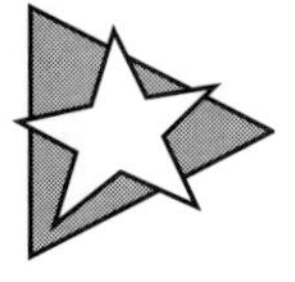

PRACTICE WHAT YOU'VE LEARNED

What You Do	***What You'll See***
1. With PageMaker launched but no document open, open the **Preferences...** dialog from the **File** menu. Set the measurement system to inches decimal, the vertical ruler to 16.8 points, and click **OK**. Open **Page setup...** and set the orientation to **Wide**. Click on **OK** to save and close.	1. The **Preferences** dialog appears, changes are made, and it is put away when **OK** is clicked.
2. Go to **Layout** and open the **Guides and rulers** submenu. Click on **Rulers** and **Snap to rulers** to select them.	2. Check marks appear next to **Rulers** and **Snap to rulers** to indicate that they have been selected.
3. Open **Type specs...** from the **Type** menu and set the size to 14 points and the leading to normal. Click on **OK**.	3. Changes are made to the **Type specs** dialog and are saved.

What You Do	*What You'll See*
4. Go to the **Line** submenu in **Element** and set the default line to a 4-point double line. Click on **OK** to close the dialog box. Exit PageMaker.	4. A check mark is placed next to the 4-point double line.
5. Restart PageMaker and open a new publication. Accept the defaults in the **New** dialog box.	5. A new PageMaker publication appears. The page is in wide (landscape) orientation, as is the default in the page setup. The horizontal ruler is now in decimal inches and the vertical ruler is in points.
6. Set the **View** to **Actual size**. Move your publication around the desktop so that you can see the upper left vertical and horizontal margin. Click on the **Text** tool and position the insertion point along the left margin, near the top.	6. The intersection of the two margins should be visible on the desktop. The blinking insertion point is at the left margin.
7. Drop a horizontal guide to the top of the insertion point. Drop another guide to the bottom of the insertion point.	7. The two guides line up exactly with tick marks on the ruler when placed at the top and bottom of the insertion point. There are exactly three ruler tick marks between the top and bottom. This is because the vertical ruler was set to the same point size as the normal leading for the 14-point font (16.8 points). Leading will be discussed in the next chapter.

What You Do	*What You'll See*
8. Type five or six words of text. Click on the **Text** tool and select the text you just chose.	8. When the text is selected, the highlight fits exactly between the two guides.
9. Select the **Rectangle** tool and draw a rectangle below the text. Also draw an ellipse.	9. The rectangle and the ellipse both have double lines for a border as we specified in the **Line** submenu.
10. Exit PageMaker without saving changes.	10. You are returned to Windows.

In this chapter you learned how to set PageMaker's basic preferences. These settings will remain constant throughout the rest of this book—unless you change them. In later chapters, you will put some of the other settings to work.

Now that you know about setting your preferences and using the basic features of PageMaker, we are ready to move on to more advanced topics. We'll start by explaining more of PageMaker's typographic functions in Chapters 7 and 8, because typographic control within PageMaker for Windows is one of its most powerful features for creating professional-level publications.

Working with Type and Fonts

The ability to extensively format type is important, because every attractive document that makes it into print, be it a simple newsletter or a complicated brochure, uses type as part of the design aesthetics. PageMaker for Windows is a powerful set of tools for controlling text formatting and type specifications. We'll cover typography within PageMaker in two chapters. Basic typography and type controls are covered in this chapter and more advanced functions are covered in Chapter 8. This chapter introduces you to the Type menu and the type facilities on the Control palette. You will learn how to:

- **Recognize the five major families of type**
- **Change font, size, and style and align type**
- **Set tabs and create indented paragraphs**
- **Imbed lines (rules) in the text**
- **Create superscript and subscript type**
- **Use PageMaker's Map Fonts settings**

The Basic Families of Type

You learned earlier that a font is a complete set of characters with a particular design and purpose. In the computer world, the word font is commonly (and technically speaking, incorrectly) used to mean both typeface and character set. Technically, a font is a rendering of the characters in a typeface for display or reproduction in a certain size or weight. The typeface is the actual look and design of the characters in the font. To be precise, Times Roman is a typeface, Times Roman 14-point Bold is a font, and Times Roman 14-point Italics is another font. In this book, we will continue the practice of using the word font to mean both "set of characters" and "typeface" for simplicity—though we acknowledge that this is technically imprecise.

All fonts used by PageMaker have names so they can be easily specified. There are two major typeface (font) families of which you should be aware: *serif* fonts and *sans serif* fonts. Serif fonts have a short stroke that protrudes from the ends of each character. Sans serif fonts do not have this short stroke (*sans* is French for "without"). Two commonly used fonts are *Times*—a serif font, and *Helvetica*—a sans serif font. Three of the Times serifs are circled in Figure 7.1

You will encounter three other classifications of fonts in desktop publishing—*display* fonts, *script* fonts, and *symbol* fonts.

▼ ***Figure 7.1. Serif and Sans Serif Fonts***

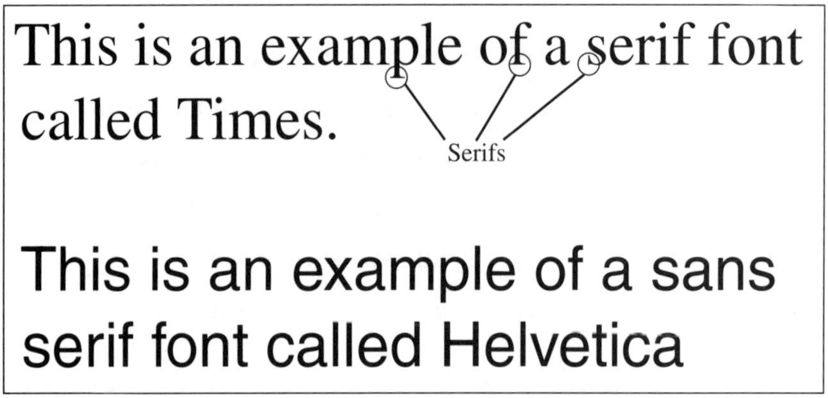

This is an example of a serif font called Times.

Serifs

This is an example of a sans serif font called Helvetica

The Basic Families of Type

Examples of each are shown in Figure 7.2. Display fonts are used to get attention in ads and on signs and billboards. Script fonts are used for wedding invitations and other formal correspondence. There are also special purpose fonts for printing mathematical symbols and decorative characters called *dingbats* (for example, there is a font named Zapf Dingbats—it contains no letters, only symbols and icons.)

Today there are literally thousands of fonts available to desktop publishers, many of them originally designed in the 19th and 20th centuries for newspapers and book printers. Recently the traditional typefaces have been converted into formats suitable for computers to use. The availability of sophisticated computer-based fonts has partially fueled the growth and success of desktop publishing and products like PageMaker.

It is often confusing to see that fonts from three different manufacturers may look alike but have different names. This is because the exact font name is often copyrighted and trademarked. For example, the names "Times" and "Helvetica" are trademarks of Linotype AG. Only licensees of Linotype are entitled to use the names. Several other companies have developed fonts that look very close to Times and Helvetica, but they must use different names. Microsoft uses "Times New Roman" and "Arial" for its fonts that closely resemble Times and Helvetica whereas Bitstream calls its versions "Dutch" and "Swiss." These fonts are so close that differences are often not discernible to the average eye.

▼ ***Figure 7.2. Other Font Families***

This is an example of a display font
called Caslon 540

This is an example of a script font
called Kuenstler Script

ημακφδπω (Symbols) 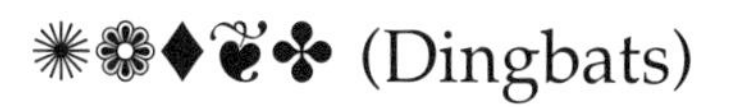 (Dingbats)

Most publishing, both on the computer and using conventional methods, is done using typefaces very similar to Times New Roman and Arial. There are hundreds of variations of these enormously popular typefaces, such as Times, Palatino, Futura, and others. Why? Because they are the easiest typefaces to read. Imagine reading a daily newspaper printed entirely with an elegant script font—it would be quite fatiguing for the eyes!

PageMaker is capable of manipulating a number of fonts. Windows includes basic fonts for you to use. You can buy additional fonts from a number of suppliers and install them in your system for use with PageMaker.

TIP

When assembling documents on the desktop, particularly if a large number of fonts have been installed, resist the temptation to use more than one or two faces in the same document. Too many fonts in a document make it look amateurish and/or difficult to read. Study existing publications such as ads, brochures, and books to learn how to better select and use type in your documents.

CHECK YOURSELF

1. This is Garth Graphic. This is Univers.
   In the examples above, which font is a serif typeface and which one is sans serif?
   - ▲ Garth Graphic has serifs so it is a serif font and Univers does not, so it's sans serif.
2. **Sample Typeface** Is this a display font or a script font?
   - ▲ It is Bodoni Poster and is an example of a display font.

Using PageMaker's Type Menu

You can take advantage of almost all of PageMaker's type handling commands directly from the **Type** drop-down menu, shown

Using PageMaker's Type Menu

in Figure 7.3. The commands in this menu can be used to control everything from selecting fonts and font sizes to setting tabs. To change fonts, you simply select the text you want to modify, open the **Type** menu, and then select the **Font** submenu. A list of available fonts will pop up to the side of the **Font** menu. Move the pointer to your choice and click. A check mark will appear next to your selection and the text will be redrawn on the screen in the new font.

Resizing Type

In addition to changing fonts, PageMaker allows you to change the size of the type through the **Size** submenu. Rather than being measured in inches or centimeters, type sizes are measured in the old print shop standard of points. A point is $^{1}/_{72}$ of an inch and type is measured vertically from the top of an ascender to the bottom of a descender as shown in Figure 7.4. (There are actually 72.27

▼ ***Figure 7.3. The Type Menu Is a Powerful Tool for Designing with Type***

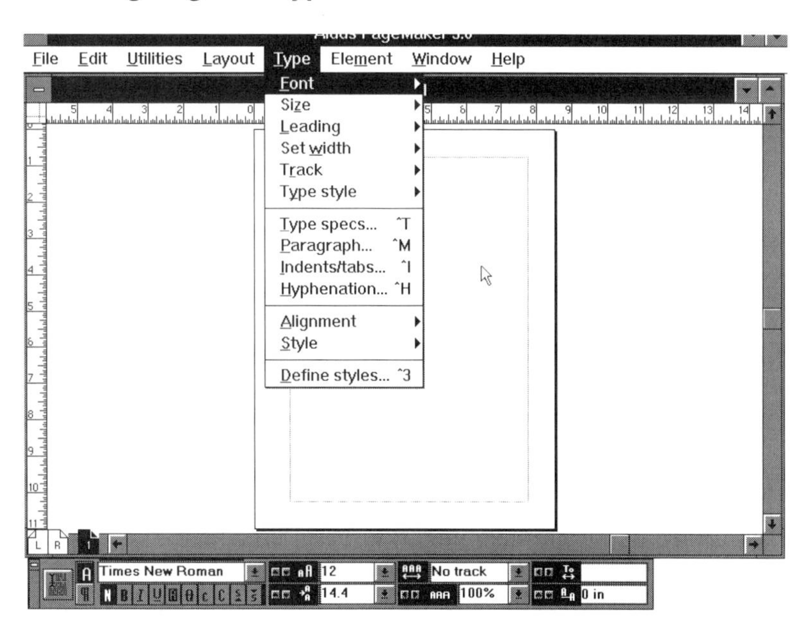

▼ ***Figure 7.4. An Example of 48-Point Type Showing How Point Sizes Are Measured***

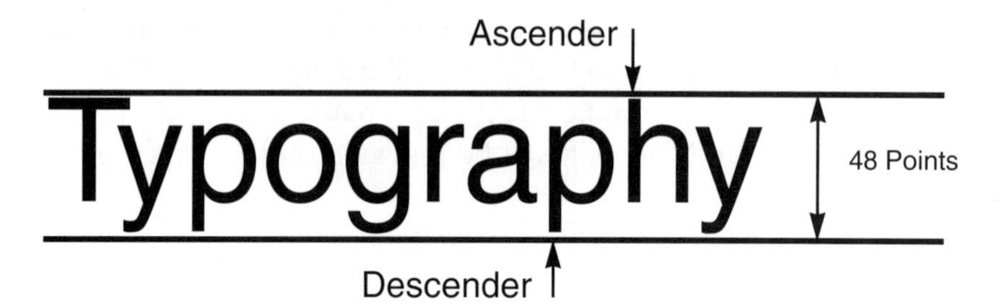

points to an inch, but for all but the most precise documents, this tiny extra fraction can be ignored.)

For most publications, sizes between 10 points and 14 points are the most readable for body copy like the material you are reading right now. PageMaker's **Size** selection provides 14 preselected type sizes based on the most commonly used sizes from 6 points to 72 points. If you want to use a size other than the selections shown in the pull-down menu, select **Other. . .** from the top of the menu. This will produce a dialog box in which you can enter the exact value you want down to 1/10th of a point.

To resize type:

1. Select the type to resize.
2. Open the **Type** drop-down menu and select the desired new size from the **Size** menu item.

TIP

To select all of the text in a single text block, instead of using the mouse and dragging from column to column or page to page, position the insertion point anywhere in the text, then use the command Select all **from the** Edit **menu or its keyboard equivalent** Ctrl+A. **This selects all of the text in a single block or series of blocks.**

The best way to learn about the fonts available on your system is to print out a list of them. For each font, type a line "This is an example of Palatino." Make one line for each typeface and substitute the correct font names as you make up the list. Set each entry in 14 point or larger type so you can easily see the subtle difference in closely related fonts. Print this list and keep it near your computer as a reference. Update it as new fonts are added to your system.

CHECK YOURSELF

1. How do you enter a font size that's not already in the Size selection?
   ▲ Use the **Other**. . . selection under the Size menu item and enter a value for the number of points desired.
2. How many points are in an inch?
   ▲ There are approximately 72 points in an inch.

Changing the Type Style

You can easily change the look of the type by applying any of PageMaker's six different styles. These styles are available through the **Type style** submenu. Simply select the type to modify with the **Text** tool and then choose a style from the list.

To change the style of a section of text, you select it and choose the style from the **Type style** menu's selection. It is important to remember that with PageMaker's Font, Size, and Style selection possibilities, you can make your text look and fit almost any way you can imagine! The six style choices are shown in Figure 7.5.

The most commonly used styles are Normal, Bold, and Italic. The other styles are used for special treatments and decorative effects. Unless you handle projects that require special characters in a hard-to-read type style, such as letters with lines through them (Strike Thru) used in legal documents, most of your work will probably be confined to these three styles.

Using PageMaker's Type Styles in Page Layouts

As a generalization, **Bold** is used for emphasis in a document otherwise composed of plain text. Bold characters are identical (in

▼ *Figure 7.5. Type Style Choices in PageMaker*

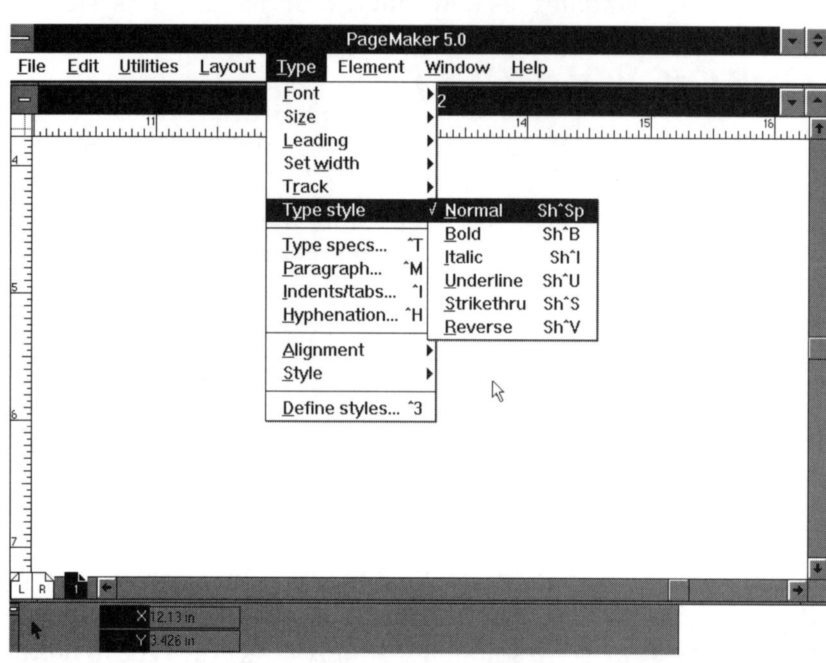

most fonts) to normal characters, but the lines used to draw the character have been thickened to make them look darker. Like bold, *Italic* may be used for emphasis, for the names of books, or as a decorative touch. Italics are different than the plain characters in a font. Though "Ital" may look like a slanted variation on the font's normal letters, a true Italic font is a completely different variation of the font, drawn at an angle using thick and thin lines.

To change type styles in PageMaker:

1. Select the type with the **Text** tool.
2. Select a new style for the text from the **Type style** submenu.

TIP

Bold and Italic should not be overused in a document because Bold loses its emphasis when used too many times and paragraphs set in Italic are difficult to read, particularly in small point sizes.

Using PageMaker's Type Menu

▼ *Figure 7.6. Small Caps Example*

AN EXAMPLE OF SMALL CAPS

One other type style available in PageMaker that is easy to overlook but can be used to create elegant headlines is Small Caps, shown in Figure 7.6. This type style is simply made up of capital letters, but the letters following the first capital in a capitalized word are sized down typically 25 to 35%. Unlike the other type styles, Small Caps is only available from the **Type specs** dialog box. To access Small Caps, open **Type specs**, click on the **Case** drop-down menu, and select **Small Caps**.

In addition to these styles, you can apply multiple styles at one time to type. By choosing all the styles you want applied to the selected type from the **Style** menu, you can create whatever mix you desire. The example in Figure 7.7 is type that has had the Italic, Bold, Strike Thru and Small Caps styles applied to it simultaneously.

Two Other Ways to Control Type

There are two other ways to control type in PageMaker: the **Type Specs...** dialog and the **Control** palette. The most convenient and

▼ *Figure 7.7. Multiple Style Example*

~~AN EXAMPLE OF MULTIPLE STYLES~~

fastest method is using the Control palette, which you explored in Chapter 4. Figure 7.8 shows the Control palette in both character and paragraph view when the Text tool is chosen. The two buttons on the left of the palette control whether you are in Character or Paragraph view. In Character view, all the styles are conveniently

▼ ***Figure 7.8. The Control Palette***

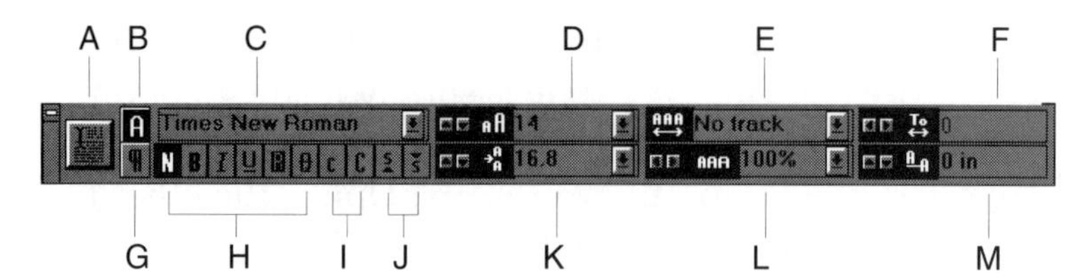

A. Apply button
B. Character view button
C. Font
D. Size
E. Tracking
F. Kerning
G. Paragraph view button
H. Type style buttons:
Normal, Bold, Italic
Underline, Reverse, Strikethru
I. Case buttons:
Small caps, All caps
J. Position buttons:
Subscript, Superscript
K. Leading
L. Set width
M. Baseline shift

CHARACTER VIEW

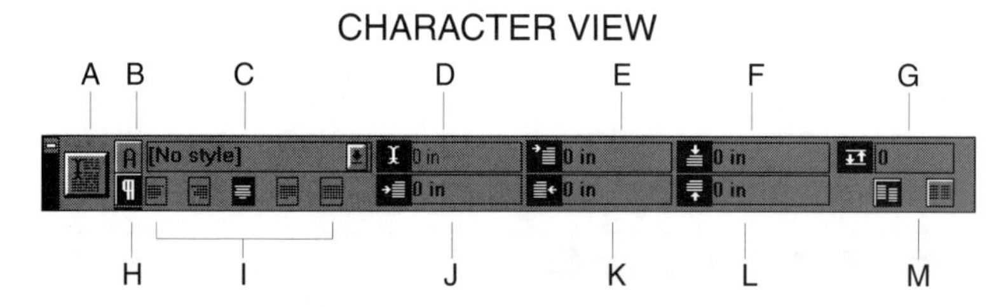

A. Apply button
B. Character view button
C. Paragraph style
D. Cursor position
E. Left indent
F.Space before
G. Grid size
H. Paragraph view button
I. Alignment buttons:
Left, Center, Right
Justify, Force justify
J. First line indent
K. Right indent
L. Space below
M. Align to grid

PARAGRAPH VIEW

available on a button row beneath the font window. By highlighting some text and then clicking on the various style buttons, you can instantly see the effect as you apply single or multiple styles and experiment until you get just the right look for your text.

Two Other Ways to Control Type

Alternatively, you can use the **Type specs** dialog box from the **Type** menu. This dialog, shown in Figure 7.9 contains all of the controls found in the individual submenus that we have already covered.

There are several fields in the Type specs dialog box and the Control palette that we have not yet covered. These will be covered in the next chapter.

Aligning Type

Type alignment is the specification of type lines within the borders of a text block or a column. The five kinds of alignment used by PageMaker are *left justified, right justified, centered, justified,* and *force justified*. Justified means that one or both edges of a column of type is lined up straight vertically with the margins. Left-justified type means that the left edge of the column of type aligns vertically from line to line. Right-justified type is the opposite with the right edge of the text column lined up. You may have seen centered type used to represent poetry or headlines. Each line is centered in the column and neither edge lines up vertically. Justified type is where both edges (right and left) line up vertically. Force-justified

▼ *Figure 7.9. PageMaker's Type Specs Dialog*

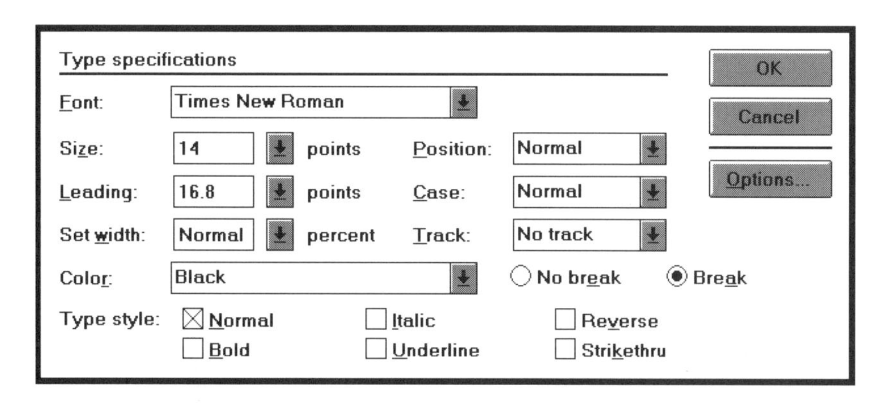

type even justifies lines with only a few characters, such as the last line of a paragraph. This is useful if you have a headline that you want to stretch from left margin to right margin. Because few lines of type have exactly the same number of letters, words, and spaces, justification is accomplished in PageMaker (as it is conventionally) by adding subtle extra amounts of spacing between letters and words to compensate for the variations. Examples of justified text are shown in Figure 7.10.

Aligning Type with the Type Menu and the Control Palette

Aligning type in PageMaker works much the same way that changing type styles is accomplished. The text is selected with the **Pointer** tool and the correct alignment is selected from the **Type** menu.

▼ ***Figure 7.10. Left-Justified Text, Right-Justified Text, Centered Text, Justified Text, Force-Justified Text***

Left justified text means that the left edge of the column of type aligns vertically from line to line.

Right justified type is the opposite of left justified type with the right edge of the text column lined up.

You may have seen **centered type** used to print poetry. Each line is centered in the column and neither edge lines up vertically.

Justified type is where both edges (right and left) line up vertically. Because few lines of type have exactly the same number of letters, words, and spaces, justification is accomplished by adding subtle extra amounts of spacing between letters and words to compensate for the variations.

Force justified type is similar to justified type except that the last line is also justified even if it has only a few characters available for spacing.

To align text:

Two Other Ways to Control Type

1. Select the text with the **Pointer** tool.
2. Open the **Type** menu and choose the desired alignment from the **Alignment** submenu.
   OR
1. Click on the **Control** palette's **Paragraph view** button. The palette should appear as in the bottom of Figure 7.8.
2. Click on one of the **Alignment** buttons. The buttons are self-explanatory because they display an image of type on a page the way it will be aligned.

TIP

In the same way that too many typefaces are hard to read, so are certain kinds of type alignment. Justified and left-justified text are the easiest to read. Centered text and right-justified text should not be used for paragraphs of text because they are difficult to read.

Special Characters

There is more to the keyboard under Windows (and DOS) than meets the eye. There are a host of invisible characters, and you may also own one or more fonts consisting of special purpose symbols. Windows has a simple mechanism for investigating additional characters not visible on the keyboard and symbol fonts that may contain no standard alphabetical characters whatsoever.

To look at your options, within Windows' **Accessories window**, double-click on the **Character Map** icon. This will bring up the **Character Map** window, as shown in Figure 7.11. To use it, select the font you want from the scrollable list.

To bring a special character into a PageMaker Publication from Windows:

1. Open the **Character Map** dialog from within Windows **Accessories**. Choose a font from the menu. Click and hold down on any character to see a magnified view of it.

▼ ***Figure 7.11. Windows Character Map Dialog Box***

2. Double-click on it to add it to the **Characters to Copy** box.
3. Click the **Copy** button and toggle to PageMaker via Windows. (Use the **Alt+Tab** keys to toggle by clicking as many times as necessary to get back to PageMaker.)
4. Use the **Text** tool to place the insertion point where you want the characters in your text. Select the same font as you chose in the **Character Map** dialog. Go to the **Edit** menu and select **Paste** to bring the new characters into your publication.

CHECK YOURSELF

1. Create a new PageMaker document. Accept the defaults and move the **Control** palette to the bottom of the screen. Go to the **Layout** menu and set the **View** to **Actual size**. Move the left margin to the left side of your screen.
2. Click on the **Text** tool and type your name. Now, using the **Control** menu, change the typeface to **36-point Times New Roman** and then add the styles **Bold** and **Small Caps** to it.
   - ▲ It should look something like the following example when you are finished:

YOUR NAME

3. Open the document DICKENS.PM5 that you created in Chapter 5 and set the type as plain **12-point Courier New**. Now select all of the text, and experiment with each of the four alignment options. Read the paragraphs after each change and note how the alignment makes the text easier or more difficult to

read. Exit Pagemaker when you are finished and don't save changes.
4. Open the **Character Map** dialog box from within Windows' **Accessories** group and scroll through your fonts to see what special characters are available.

Two Other Ways to Control Type

Using PageMaker's Map Fonts Facility

Now that we have discussed fonts a bit, we can revisit the **Map fonts** dialog box found in the **Preferences** dialog. As mentioned in Chapter 6, this facility allows the user to transport publications between PageMaker platforms and specify how font inconsistencies will be handled. Sometimes a font on the Macintosh will be known by a different name on the PC or the same exact font will not be available. **Map fonts. . .** tells PageMaker how to substitute fonts when these problems arise.

Figure 7.12 shows the **Map fonts** menu. The **Allow font matching** option tells PageMaker to substitute fonts that are close in style but not exact matches for the original font. If this option is turned off, PageMaker will only make substitutions to correct differences in font name spelling. When this option is turned on, PageMaker will examine the original font and substitute the font closest in

▼ ***Figure 7.12. The Map Fonts Dialog***

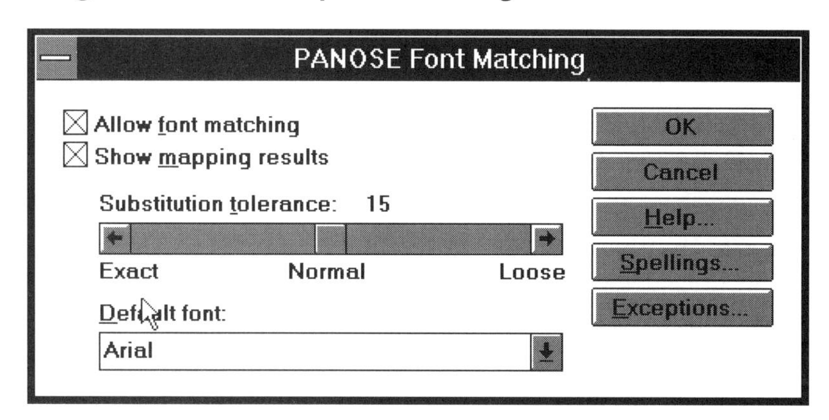

style available on the current system. To see the font substitutions as they are made, check the **Show mapping results** box.

Substitution tolerance controls how close a match you require for substitutions. **Loose** allows a substitution even if the substituted font is not very close to the original; **Exact** makes substitutions only if the new font is very close. **Default font** specifies which font to use if a close match cannot be found at all.

The **Spellings** submenu contains a list of PC fonts and their Macintosh equivalents. You can add to this list as you add fonts to your system. This applies only to fonts from the same manufacturer (e.g., Adobe on the Mac and Adobe on the PC). To substitute fonts from different manufacturers, use the **Exceptions** menu discussed next.

The **Exceptions** submenu allows you to define custom substitutions between platforms even if the two fonts are not even close. This lets the user control how fonts may be substituted. For instance, if you want Arial on the PC to be substituted wherever your Mac document called for New Century Schoolbook, you would enter the substitution in this list.

Indenting Paragraphs and Setting Tabs

PageMaker's **Indents/tabs** dialog box makes setting paragraph indents and tabs easy. Select the text you want to work on, then open the **Type** menu and choose **Indents/tabs....** A dialog box pops up at the top of the selected text, as in Figure 7.13. Notice that the left edge of the ruler (the zero point) is aligned with the left margin.

Adding an Automatic Paragraph Indent

When formatting large columns of text, type is often set so the spacing used between paragraphs is the same as that used between lines of type. When this standard is employed, the first line of a paragraph is indented to indicate a new paragraph. Rather

▼ *Figure 7.13. PageMaker's Indents/Tabs Dialog Box and Ruler*

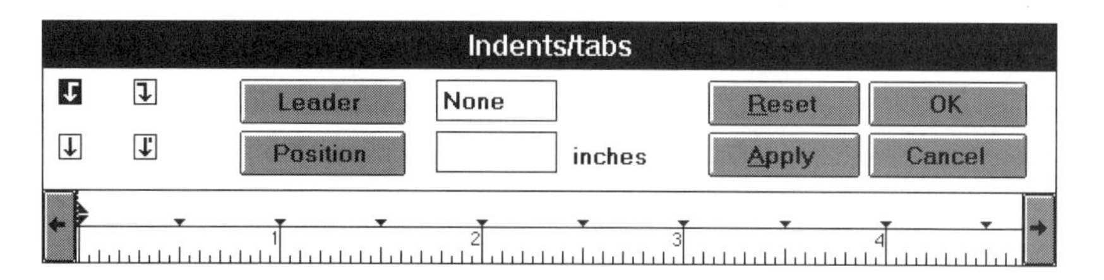

Indenting Paragraphs and Setting Tabs

than using a tab at the beginning of each paragraph, PageMaker can be set up to handle this task automatically in the **Indents/tabs** dialog box.

To indent the first line of each new paragraph:

1. Select the text and pop up the **Indents/tabs** dialog box.
2. Drag the first-line indent icon to the new desired location. Typically the first line is indented about 10 to 20% of its total length. So if a line of type measures 2" in width, the indent might be set to 1/4 of an inch. Click **OK** or **Apply**. Apply will add the indent without closing the dialog box so you can see how it will look. This allows you to experiment with the size of the indent without closing and reopening the dialog box.

To use the Control palette to set indents:

1. Select the paragraph you want to indent by placing the insertion point anywhere in the text.
2. Now click on the **Control** palette's **Paragraph view** button.
3. Double-click on the **First indent:** field and type in a value.
4. Click on the **Apply** button to see the results.

ALTERNATE METHOD

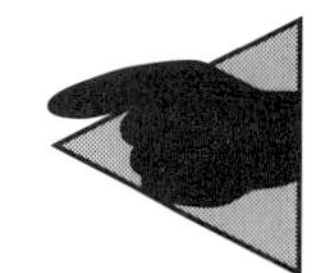

Paragraph indents can also be set using the **Paragraph** dialog box. From the **Type** menu select **Paragraph. . . .** Type the desired indent into the **First indent:** field and click on **OK.** The dialog box will close and the new indents take effect in the selected text.

Setting Tabs in PageMaker

Tabs are useful for formatting tabular information such as simple tables or numerical information. Tabs are also used for aligning lists of bulleted items. PageMaker offers four kinds of tabs, recognizable by the way the symbols appear on the rule (see Figure 7.14) and the results of the tabbing operation itself. Depending on the tab selected, text will appear to the right, left, or center of the tab setting, or some element of the text will align with the table. For example, the **Decimal Tab** lines up the decimal symbol in a dollar amount so the columns of numbers are correctly aligned.

Tabs are set with the **Indents/tabs** dialog box. They can be either set by selecting the kind of tab and clicking on the ruler that appears at the top of the text, or set by position within the dialog box.

To set tabs:

1. Select the text you want to align with tabs and choose **Indents/tabs. . .** from the **Type** menu.
2. Select the kind of tab you want to apply from the dialog box and then click on the open ruler to place the tab. Add as many tabs as you want. Tabs already in the ruler can be moved by dragging them with the mouse or removed by dragging them off the ruler. Tabs can also be added by entering their position within the dialog box. Click **OK**.
3. Move the text into position with the **Tab** key, just as you would with a conventional typewriter.

▼ ***Figure 7.14. PageMaker's Tab Symbols***

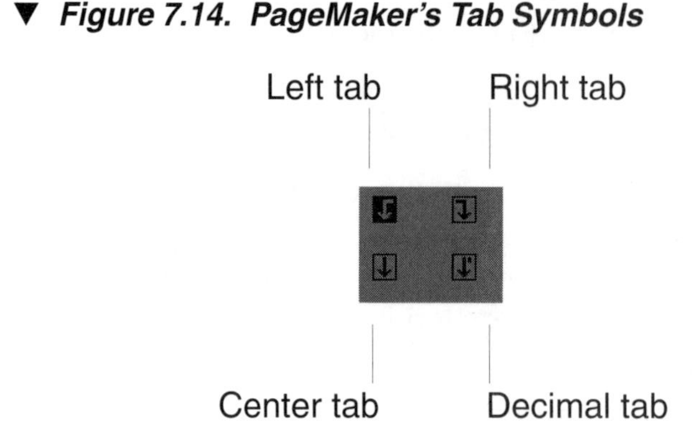

OR

1. Select text.
2. Select the type of tab you want. Enter the tab position in the **Position** field and click on the **Position** button. Select **Add tab** from the drop-down menu. Click on **Apply** or **OK.**
3. Move text into position.

Indenting Paragraphs and Setting Tabs

TIP

All of the menu items contained in the Type menu can be applied to a newly created publication containing no text. Simply set up the format you want. Then, when you add new text, it will be formatted automatically as you type.

CHECK YOURSELF

1. With the DICKENS.PM5 file open, select the text and set its alignment to **Justified**. Then using the **Indents/tabs** dialog box, add a .5-inch indent to the first line of the text. Close the file when you are finished and don't save changes.
   ▲ The paragraph in DICKENS.PM5 should have an indent on the first line only.

2. In a new publication, enter the dollar amounts **$12.60, $200.72,** and **$1.95**. Hit a return after each amount so that they appear on separate lines. Select the three numbers with the **Text** tool and open the **Indents/tabs** dialog box under the **Type** menu. Select the **Decimal Tab** and place it in the ruler at two inches. Click **OK**. Put the insertion point in front of each number and hit the tab key so that the decimal symbols line up with the tab.
   ▲ The three numbers should line up their decimal points with the tab like this:

   $12.60
   $200.72
   $1.95

Adding Lines to Text

Lines are used as design elements to break up sections of text as has been done in this book. The lines can be used to make the organization of a document clearer or just to add interest to the text design. PageMaker has a facility to add lines to blocks of text at the top or bottom. As discussed in Chapter 3, you have the ability to draw rectangles around text, but this has the disadvantage that if the position of the text changes, the lines must be manually moved. PageMaker's **Rules** dialog box resides off of the **Paragraph** dialog. Use the **Rules** dialog box, as shown in Figure 7.15, to create lines—you can tell the lines to flow as the text flows. (Remember: *Rules* are the typographer's name for lines.)

To add lines to text:

1. Place the **Pointer** tool into the place in the text you want a rule added to or select the paragraph or paragraphs with the **Text** tool.

▼ ***Figure 7.15. PageMaker's Rules Dialog***

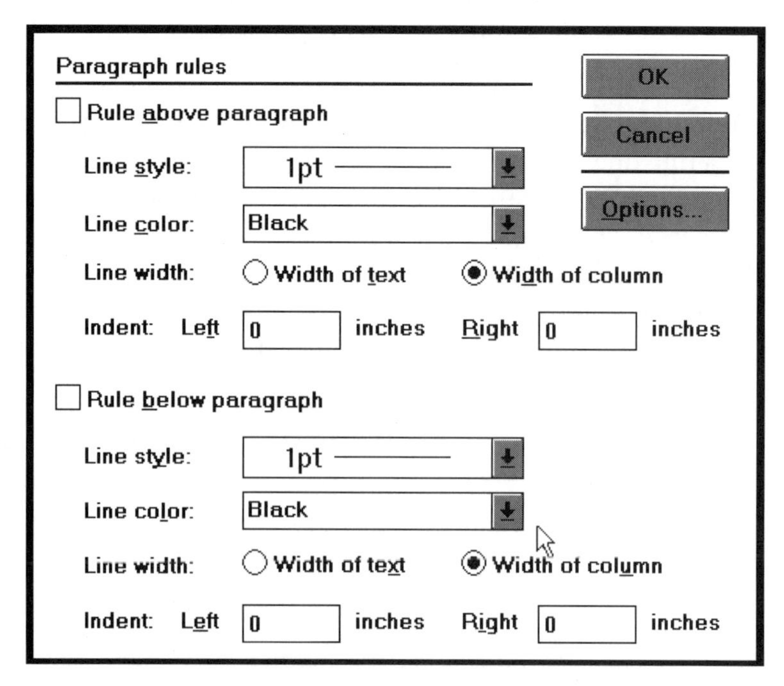

Adding Lines to Text

2. Select **Rules...** from the **Paragraph** dialog box. Click on **Rule above paragraph** to add a rule above selected paragraphs. Click on **Rule below paragraph** to add a rule beneath selected paragraphs.
3. Select the style of line you want and its thickness (in points).
4. Choose whether the rule will span the horizontal width of the text or the width of the column. Select whether it will be indented on the left and right.
5. Click on **Options...** to select the distance between the line and the text by entering the desired value (in points, inches, etc.) in the **inches above baseline** or **inches below baseline** fields. Leaving the default setting will add a line that touches the text. Click **OK** to close the boxes.

CHECK YOURSELF

Open the DICKENS.PM5 file and select and add a rule to the top of the first paragraph and the bottom of the second paragraph. Make the rules .5 inches thick. Click **OK**. Close the file when you are finished and don't save changes.

QUICK COMMAND SUMMARY

Shortcut Keys	*Commands*	*Procedures*
(Type menu)		
Alt T→Z	Size	Changes the size of type
Alt T→Y	Style	Changes the style of type
Ctrl+Shift+L	Left Justified	Aligns type along the left edge
Ctrl+Shift+C	Centered	Centers type
Ctrl+Shift+R	Right Justified	Aligns type along the right edge
Ctrl+Shift+J	Justified	Aligns type along both edges
Ctrl+Shift+F	Force Justified	Aligns type along both edges no matter how small the lines
Ctrl+T	Type specs...	Allows changes to several type attributes at one time
Ctrl+M	Paragraph...	Allows changes to several paragraph attributes at one time
Ctrl+I	Indents/tabs...	Opens the Indents and Tabs dialog

PRACTICE WHAT YOU'VE LEARNED

What You Do	*What You'll See*
1. Open a new letter-sized PageMaker document. Set the view to **Actual size** and move the margin to the left side of your screen. Open the **Control** palette and move it to the bottom of your screen.	1. A new PageMaker publication appears on-screen.
2. Click on the **Text** tool and position the insertion point at the left margin.	2. A blinking cursor is at the left margin.
3. Type **This is an example of type** on one line. Hit the **Enter** key to move the insertion point to the line below.	3. Type appears.
4. Select the text by dragging across it.	4. The text is highlighted.
5. Use the **Copy** command under the **Edit** menu to copy the text.	5. The text is stored in the computer's Copy buffer.
6. Use the **Paste** command to paste the type into the document, then hit the **Enter** key again. Do this four more times to make six new lines of type.	6. Each use of the Paste command adds a line of identical text to the text block.
7. Select the first two lines of type and set it, using the **Control** palette, to **Arial**. Set the next two lines to **Times New Roman**. Set the last two lines in **Courier New**.	7. The type is highlighted and then redrawn in the Arial font. Subsequent lines change to the selected fonts.

What You Do	*What You'll See*
8. Select the first line of each font example and set the first line of each font to 14 points using the **Size** option under the **Type** menu.	8. The first line of each typeface gets bigger, making it easier to compare to other type faces.
9. Set the second line of each font of text to 24 points.	9. The second line of each face is substantially enlarged.
10. Erase all of the text and type in these three dollar amounts, entering one on each line: **$12.00; $234.77; $11,9000.00**. Open the **Indents/tabs. . .** selection in the **Type** menu. Select the **Decimal Tab** option from the dialog box and then place a decimal tab in the middle of the ruler.	10. After the amounts are entered, selecting the Indents/tabs command brings up a dialog box and places a ruler over the text block.
11. Close the **Indents/tabs** dialog box and place the cursor in front of the first value. Press the **Tab** key to tab it over, using the imbedded tabs you created.	11. Inserting the cursor before the first value and hitting the Tab key positions the first number in the middle of the page, its decimal aligned with the tab.
12. Do the same for the other two numbers as well.	12. Tabbing the other two numbers will align their decimal points exactly under the first number's decimal point regardless of the characters in the number.

What You Do	*What You'll See*
13. Erase the numbers and enter a 30-word paragraph on any subject you want.	13. A block of text appears on the screen.
14. Select the paragraph and create a .5" indent on the first line using the **Indents/tabs** dialog box. Click **Apply** to see what happens without closing the dialog box.	14. With the dialog box still open, clicking the **Apply** button will indent the paragraph.
15. Without closing the **Indents/tabs** dialog box, add .4" indents to both its left and right sides and click **OK**.	15. The paragraph will be indented on both the right and left sides and the indent will remain.
16. Select the same paragraph and open the **Rules** dialog selection under the **Paragraph** dialog box. Click on **Rule above paragraph** and **Rule below paragraph** to add a .5-point rule (line) to both the top and bottom of the paragraph. Click **OK**.	16. A horizontal rule (line) will appear above and below the paragraph.
17. Exit PageMaker and do not save changes.	17. PageMaker returns you to the Windows desktop.

This chapter has expanded the basic knowledge of text manipulation you acquired in Chapter 5. You have also added new text formatting capabilities within the PageMaker environment to your skills. In the next chapter, you will learn how to use more of the advanced typographic controls within PageMaker for Windows.

Advanced Type Controls

This chapter will extend your understanding of type and introduce you to features of concern to professional typesetters and type designers. Although type and typography is a vast subject, you can quickly begin assembling professional-looking type designs with what you will learn in this book. In addition to just learning the mechanics of assembling type using PageMaker's commands and specifications, make an effort to study the typography used in ads, brochures, books, and product packaging. This will help you develop an eye for professional type design. In this chapter you will learn how to:

- **Use PageMaker's advanced type controls**
- **Create automatic "drop caps"**
- **Use PageMaker's automatic hyphenation function**
- **Define and use PageMaker's styles**
- **Meet PageMaker's Typographic Preferences dialog**

Advanced Type Controls

If you are new to desktop publishing and working with type, there is an extensive array of tools that can be employed to change how text looks in print and how it fits in your layout. You met several of these tools in the last chapter when you learned how to select fonts, resize them, and apply styles such as boldface and italics to characters. In addition to these basic techniques, there are other type controls that round out the bag of type-manipulation tricks. We'll explain each one and what it is used for in this section. Figure 8.1 shows where some of the functions explained in this section can be controlled through the Control palette.

Adding Leading to Type

Along with changing the size of characters, the space between lines of type can be altered when necessary to make it wider or narrower. This function is called adding *leading*. The term refers to the thin layers of lead strips that were once added between lines of lead type (also called "hot type") to space the lines apart. Today, adjusting leading is simply another task that is easily and elegantly handled by PageMaker. Reducing space between lines of type with leading controls can help you fit text in a tight space on a layout or help you adjust the weight and "feel" of the type on the page. Increasing the space between lines of type with leading controls makes the text easier to read because it increases the amount of white space between lines.

▼ ***Figure 8.1. Control Palette with Call-outs for Tracking, Kerning, and Leading Controls***

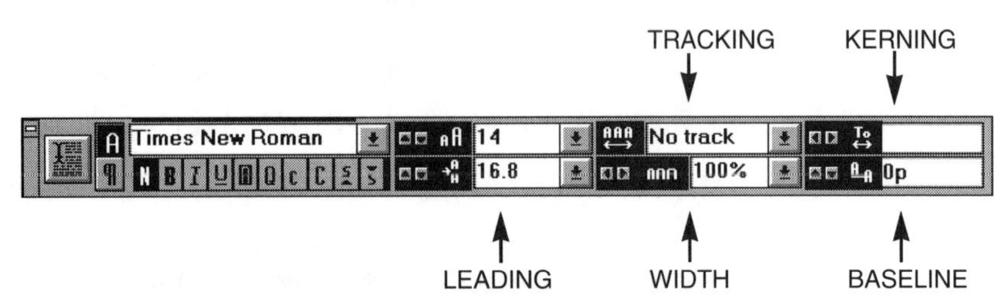

Advanced Type Controls

PageMaker uses automatic leading to space lines of text unless told to do otherwise. It selects the amount of leading to match the size of the font used. This is convenient because you can simply ignore the leading controls unless your copy doesn't fit or if it doesn't look good in a layout. Examine Figure 8.2 to understand the difference leading can make to a body of text.

Like font sizes, leading is measured in points. But there is a twist to it. When specifying type with leading, the leading value is part of the type size equation. So if you have 12-point type with an additional 2 points of leading, it appears as 14 points in the leading field—which indicates the total vertical size of the line of type plus the space between it and the next line. This actually simplifies your work, because instead of treating leading and type point sizes as separate components, this method treats them as a related specification.

To change the leading of text:

1. Select the text you want to adjust. Or, alternately, set the leading before entering any text.
2. Use the leading adjustments found in the **Leading** submenu under the **Type** menu, shown in Figure 8.3, or use the leading controls found on the **Control** palette. The **Leading** submenu allows you to select a preset leading value, or by choosing **Other...** from the menu, directly enter a number (in points) for the leading value. Using the **Control** palette, you enter a value in the **Leading:** field or use the nudge buttons adjacent to the **Leading:** field. Clicking on the up or down nudge buttons adjusts the leading in increments of 1/10th of a point.

▼ ***Figure 8.2. Normal Leading, Too Little Leading***

To be confronted with such pity, and such earnest youth and beauty, was far more trying to the accused than to be confronted with all the crowd. Standing, as it were, apart with her, on the edge of his grave, not all the staring curiosity that looked on, could, for the moment, nerve him to remain quite still.	To be confronted with such pity, and such earnest youth and beauty, was far more trying to the accused than to be confronted with all the crowd. Standing, as it were, apart with her, on the edge of his grave, not all the staring curiosity that looked on, could, for the moment, nerve him to remain quite still.
Normal Leading	Too Little Leading

▼ *Figure 8.3. The Leading Submenu*

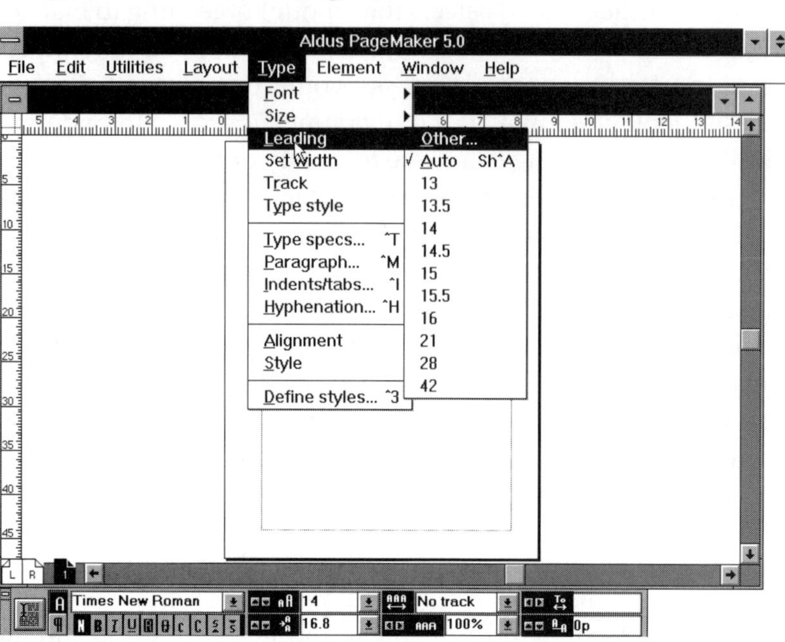

TIP

When setting type that consists of several paragraphs, make it easy on the reader's eyes by using the right leading to type size ratio. Although it's always tempting to use a bigger font size by cutting down on leading, in most designs your project will be easier to read if you use a slightly smaller font size and add more leading. It will be aesthetically pleasing as well if more white space is present.

Changing the Width of Type

When creating headlines for ads, there are often too many words in the headline to use the font size desired in the layout. One simple solution for this problem, which can also be used to create elegant-looking characters, is PageMaker's **Set width** submenu. **Set width** allows you to change the horizontal scale of characters while they maintain their height. Specified as a percentage of normal width (100% is normal), type can be scaled to make characters

Advanced Type Controls

thinner or fatter. A headline that is too long at 100% may fit perfectly if the character's width is changed to 90%. A dull-looking font can be made suddenly elegant by scaling it to 60% and increasing its point size to make it larger and more noticeable, as shown in Figure 8.4.

Type can be scaled to more than 100% of its normal horizontal scale by entering a larger value in the dialog box. This can be used to make a short headline fit the space perfectly or to create special effects. If you are new to type and design, use this function sparingly, because "fat" type often looks unbecoming in print. Width can also be set in the **Type specifications** dialog box.

To see changes as you make them, use the **Set width:** field and nudge buttons on the **Control** palette. Each click on one of the nudge buttons changes the width by 1%.

Width is something you need to play with to understand. Try a range of settings with different fonts in different point sizes to get a feel for the possibilities.

Tracking and Kerning Type

Another way of manipulating type to make it fit better and improve its appearance on the printed page is through two related processes: tracking and kerning.

▼ ***Figure 8.4. Horizontal Scaled Type Examples***

Charles Dickens

Width at 100%

Charles Dickens

Width at 140%

Charles Dickens

Width at 70%

Let's consider tracking first. *Tracking* type is simple to understand—more space is added between individual characters or space is reduced between them. Like the **Set width** command, this is useful for making text fit in tight places. But, also like **Set width**, slightly tightening up type with tracking makes headlines look crisper and reduces the amount of room they take up.

This same command can also be used to add space between characters. Although you rarely want to space paragraphs of text because it makes the copy hard to read, *letterspacing*, as it is called, is an attractive decorative element for certain designs. Letterspacing usually consists of tracking the letters of a single word or two quite far apart to create a decorative effect.

The **Track** submenu of the **Type** menu is used to control tracking. Six tracking settings are seen in Figure 8.5. The default is no tracking. Figure 8.6 shows examples of each tracking setting.

To use PageMaker's tracking controls:

1. Select the text you want to adjust. (You must highlight more than two characters.) Alternately, set the tracking before entering text.

▼ ***Figure 8.5. The Track Menu***

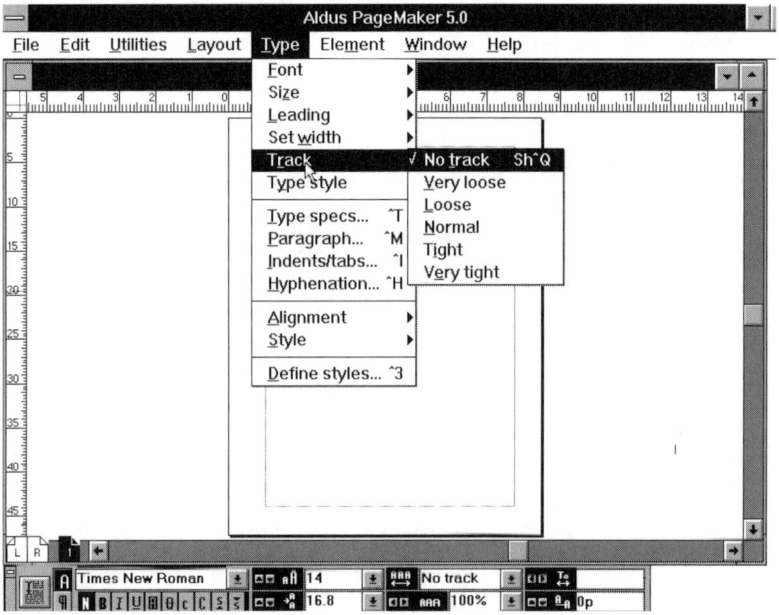

▼ ***Figure 8.6. Examples of the Track Settings***

Charles Dickens

Normal Tracking

Charles Dickens

Very Loose Tracking

Charles Dickens

Very Tight Tracking

2. Select a tracking setting from the **Track** menu. You may also use the **Tracking** menu on the **Control** palette.

Like tracking, *kerning* adjusts the space between characters, but only between individual pairs of characters rather than entire words or sentences. Kerning is often used to manually adjust the space of letters to "tweak" critical headline text. Problem pairs of letters such as "LT," where there may be too much space between the letters, can be fixed using this facility as shown in Figure 8.7.

PageMaker measures kerning by percentages. Each percentage point is equal to 1/100th of an *em*. The em is a printer's measurement unit based on the width of the lowercase letter "m." The kerning percentage can run from −100 to +100. Negative numbers bring letters closer together, positive numbers space them farther apart. This gives you extremely fine control over letter spacing.

To adjust the kerning of two characters:

1. Place the insertion point between the two characters you want to change.
2. Use the nudge buttons adjacent to the kern field on the **Control** palette or enter a percentage value directly in the **Kern:** field.

▼ ***Figure 8.7. Kerning Example Before and After***

LT

No Kerning

LT

Kerning

CHECK YOURSELF

1. Start PageMaker and set up a letter-sized document. Import DICKENS2.WP5 and delete the second paragraph. Set the type to 14 point and then select 2-point leading using the **Leading** submenu command found under the **Type** menu. Study the results. Now, change the leading to Auto and again study the results by reading the text. What do you find?
   ▲ Adding more leading makes the paragraph much easier to read. It also makes it more inviting to the reader's eye.

2. Type your name and resize it to 36 points. After selecting the text with the **Pointer** tool, adjust its tracking first to "very loose" and then to "tight" using the **Track** submenu. How is the type different in appearance?
   ▲ At 140%, the letters look thick and bold, but not very attractive. At 70%, the letters are thin and graceful.

3. Erase your name and enter the uppercase letters "TJ." Then place the cursor in between them and use the kerning field on the **Control** palette. Enter −10. What happens? (Leave this document open for the next Check Yourself.)
   ▲ The letters move closer to overlap in the same space. The result is an artful visual balance of the two letters.

The Baseline Functions

The Baseline Functions

All type has a *baseline*. This is an invisible line that runs through the bottom of a row of characters. When you select text with the **Text** tool, the bottom horizontal of the highlight is aligned with the baseline of the selected text, as shown in Figure 8.8. The baseline is the point at which the type is aligned with other lines of type. This baseline is set for document-wide use, where it is used consistently through pages and the entire document. It allows you to align multiple columns of text to ensure that the text in all columns lines up properly.

Shift Type Vertically Using Baseline Shift

A handy tool for making minor adjustments to the text in a text block containing multiple-sized fonts is the **Baseline Shift** command. This command is found buried in the **Options** dialog box of

▼ ***Figure 8.8. The Baseline***

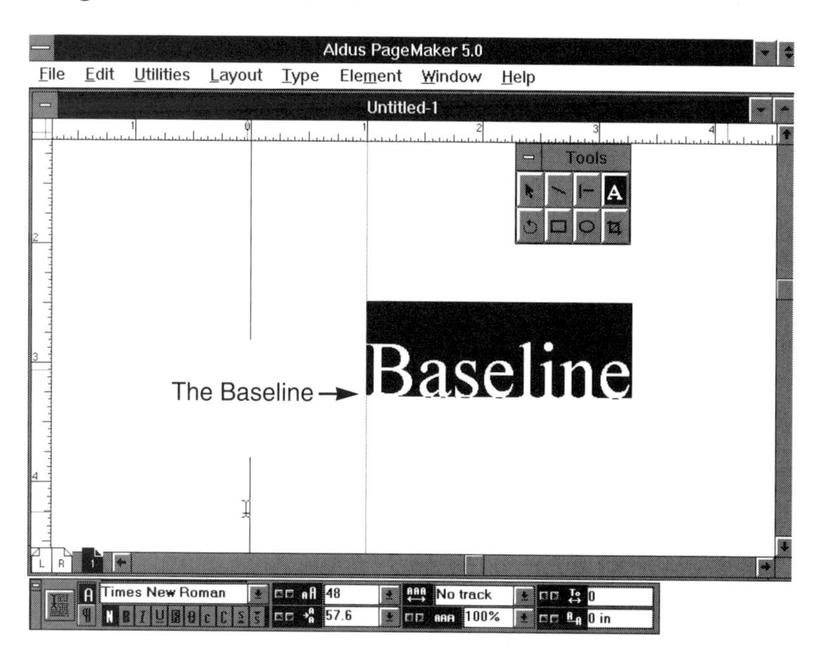

the **Type specs** dialog under the **Type** menu. It enables you to move selected text vertically without disturbing other text or changing its overall baseline. Figure 8.9 shows an example of one line of text with two different baselines.

To shift text baselines:

1. Select only the text you want to shift.
2. Choose **Baseline Shift** from the **Options** dialog box and enter the amount of shift you require in points in the **Baseline shift:** field. Click on **Up** to shift the baseline up or **Down** to shift it down. You can also use the **Control** palette and either enter a value directly into the **Baseline shift:** field or click on one of the associated nudge buttons.

Automatic Drop Caps

Drop caps are a simple but powerful typographic effect used to add interest to pages of text in brochures, magazines, and books. Drop caps are most often used as the first word on a page or to start a new section of a document. To create a drop cap, the first letter in a paragraph is enlarged to four or five times its normal size and then "dropped" into the upper left corner of the paragraph as shown in Figure 8.10.

Some page layout programs require drop caps to be created and added manually to the layout by using text wraparound controls or other clumsy systems. PageMaker makes life much easier by offering an automatic **Drop cap. . .** function inside the **Aldus Additions** submenu of the **Utilities** menu.

To create automatic drop caps:

1. Select the paragraph you want to add drop caps to by clicking on it with the **Pointer** tool.

▼ ***Figure 8.9. Baseline Example and Baseline Shift—Before and After***

The baseline shifts in this line of text.

The Baseline Functions

▼ *Figure 8.10. An Example of a Drop Cap*

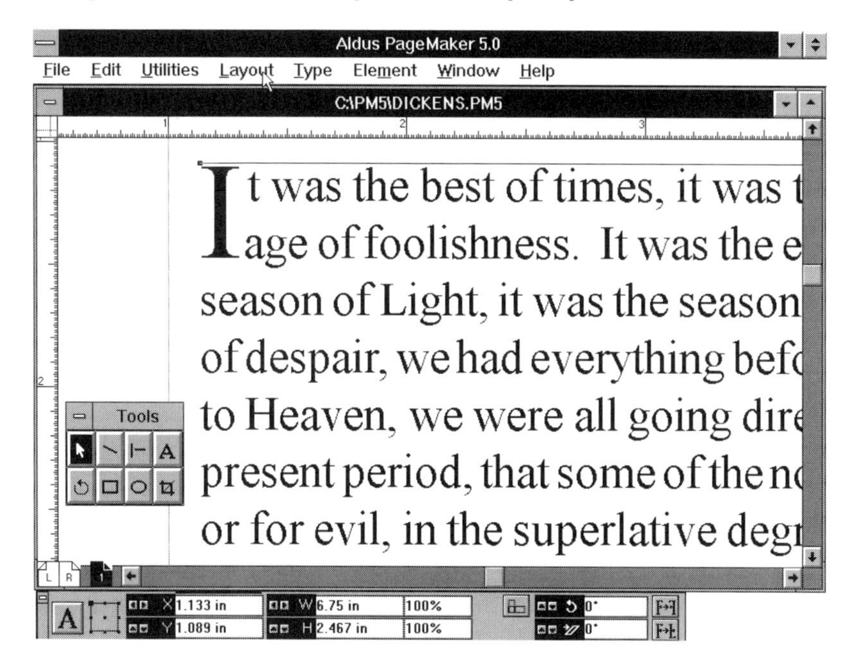

2. Open the **Utilities** menu and choose **Aldus Additions**. Select **Drop caps. . .** and the dialog will display the drop caps controls.
3. Choose how many lines of text you want the drop cap to extend through (two or three is standard). Click **OK**.

Once the command is carried out, the first letter of the selected paragraph will be enlarged and fit into the paragraph as a drop cap. You may also want to use the kerning facility to slightly space the drop cap from the text because PageMaker's default setting may appear tight or unattractive with some letter combinations. To add space, insert the cursor between the cap and the text and use the kerning function to add space between the cap and the paragraph.

TIP

Use drop caps sparingly at first. Used with discretion, drop caps can make your document appear elegant. Too many drop caps, however, particularly in short paragraphs, can be unattractive or can make text difficult to read.

CHECK YOURSELF

Using the **Text** tool, select the remaining paragraph from the file left open after the previous Check Yourself exercise. Go to the Utilities menu, choose **Aldus Additions** and then **Drop caps. . .** Then specify a drop cap that drops for two lines in the paragraph and click **OK**. What happens? Close the publication without saving changes.

▲ The first letter of the paragraph becomes larger and drops through the second line of text.

PageMaker's Hyphenation and Justification Controls

Hyphenation and justification are two more methods for making type fit better on the printed page. When setting type (either conventionally or within PageMaker), lines of text in which each line is composed of an equal number of characters and spaces rarely exist. As a result, methods of "equalizing" lines of text were created. One method is letterspacing, in which a line with too little text has extra spaces added between words and characters to make it fill the space better. Letterspacing is used to justify type where each line must touch both the left and right margins of the text block. If properly implemented, the letterspacing is usually subtle and unnoticeable.

PageMaker handles letterspacing automatically when you select the justification option. PageMaker also applies subtle letterspacing to type that is left, right, or center justified as well, in an attempt to make the edges of the lines of print appear less ragged. Note that this kind of letterspacing is different than that discussed in the last section when tracking was introduced. Using tracking to manually space letters for a decorative effect is different than the automatic letterspacing performed by PageMaker to space a line of justified text.

Of course, when working with justified type, the letterspacing solution is limited, especially in narrow paragraphs where too

PageMaker's Hyphenation and Justification Settings

much extra spacing is instantly noticeable to the eye—no matter how hard PageMaker tries to make it look good for you. A second solution, when justification is required, is hyphenation. This solution allows multisyllabic words to be broken in logical places at the end of lines, with the remaining part of the word being bumped to the next line of text. Without hyphenation, a narrow paragraph with one line composed of a single very long word, such as "succinylsulfathiazole," could only be letterspaced and might look ridiculous on the line by itself.

PageMaker automatically applies letterspacing and hyphenation to compensate for such problems, but its hyphenation function should be turned off for some kinds of documents where the hyphenation of words is unacceptable. For example, lines of poetry can be letterspaced, but hyphenating instantly destroys the meter of such writing and breaks the reader's concentration.

Specifying and Changing Hyphenation

You can specify hyphenation by selecting **Hyphenation. . .** from the **Type** menu. The dialog box appears as in Figure 8.11. If you choose to apply hyphenation to your document, three methods are available for PageMaker to use:

1. **Manual only**—PageMaker only hyphenates words that have a *discretionary* hyphen. A discretionary hyphen is one that the user enters when PageMaker indicates that a word needs to be hyphenated.

▼ ***Figure 8.11. The Hyphenation Dialog***

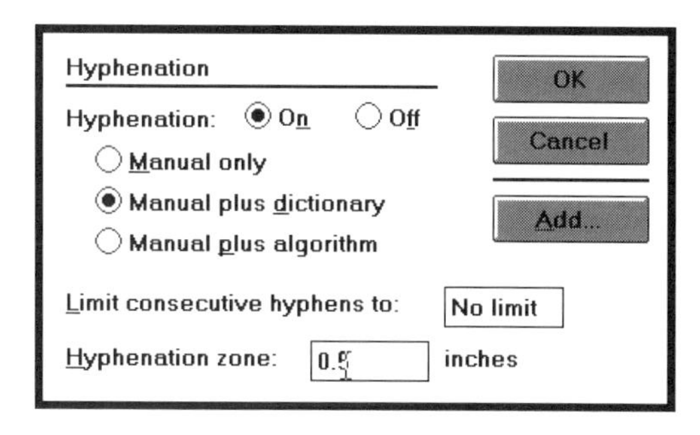

2. **Manual plus dictionary**—PageMaker maintains its own dictionary with hyphenation rules. If a word appears in PageMaker's dictionary but you wish to select different hyphenation for one particular occurrence of the word, you may place a discretionary hyphen. To change the hyphenation for all occurrences, enter it into the dictionary with your new hyphenation.
3. **Manual plus algorithm**—Allow words to be hyphenated at discretionary hyphens, dictionary hyphens, or by the hyphenation algorithm. This algorithm calculates breaks for words that don't appear in the dictionary.

The **Hyphenation zone:** setting controls when to apply hyphenation. If PageMaker reaches the end of a line and the last word in the line does not fit, PageMaker looks to see where the word began. If it began to the left of the hyphenation zone, then PageMaker will try to hyphenate it. If it began within the hyphenation zone, PageMaker will move the word to the next line. The smaller the hyphenation zone the more chance that hyphenation will occur.

Limit consecutive hyphens lets you control the unattractive "laddering" effect of having many consecutive lines with hyphens. You will usually specify no more than two hyphens in a row.

To apply hyphenation:

1. Make any changes to the hyphenation settings.
2. Select the text you want to hyphenate.
3. Turn hyphenation on.
4. To override the automatic hyphenation and instead insert a discretionary hyphen, move the insertion point to the place where you want the word to break and hit the **Ctrl+-** (hyphen) keys.

Adding Words to the Hyphenation Dictionary

Though PageMaker's hyphenation dictionary is extensive, inevitably you will want to add words. Clicking on **Add** in the **Hyphenation** dialog box brings up the dialog in Figure 8.12. Enter

▼ ***Figure 8.12. The Hyphenation Dictionary Dialog***

PageMaker's Hyphenation and Justification Settings

the new word using tildes (~) to indicate where you want the word broken. You can indicate priorities by using one, two, or three tildes. One tilde indicates the most preferable break point, two tildes the next, and three tildes the least preferable. You may also indicate if the word should be used exactly as typed, or with no case sensitivity. If, for instance, you enter "PageMaker" and choose **Exactly as typed**, then "pagemaker" and "PageMaker" will be considered two separate words for hyphenation purposes.

Justification Settings

The **Spacing** dialog box off of the **Paragraph...** dialog contains the settings for PageMaker's justification. Unless you are familiar with typesetting, we recommend you leave the settings as they come from PageMaker. Any adjustments to type spacing can be more easily made through the tracking and kerning controls.

CHECK YOURSELF

1. Open DICKENS.PM5. Resize (narrower) the text block until at least one line becomes hyphenated. Use the **Text** tool and locate the insertion point anywhere in the paragraph. Open the **Hyphenation** dialog box found under the **Type** menu. Click on "**Off**" to turn off automatic hyphenation. Click **OK**. What happens?
   ▲ The hyphenated word or words jump to the next line and no words remain hyphenated.

2. Open the **Add** dialog box found under the **Hyphenation** dialog box. Enter "Page~Mak~~er" (exactly as shown) in the **Word:** field and click on **Exactly as typed**. Click **OK** to save your entry into the dictionary.

Defining and Using PageMaker's Styles

Styles are used to apply several predefined text parameters to a block of text. Although type parameters can always be applied manually to change font, size, style, tracking, justification, and so on, styles are a much more expedient method for applying the same specifications to text in different parts of a document. Styles are particularly useful in long documents that use the same, multiple styles throughout. They are also useful when you have a predefined design used by the same company. For example, your company may use the same fonts, headline specifications, and colors throughout its publications. Properly defined, a single style can apply approximately a dozen parameters to a paragraph or document with one command.

A publication's styles are known collectively as a *style sheet* and are listed in the **Styles** palette. Style sheets can be copied to other PageMaker publications, so once you come up with a set of styles you can reuse them. For example, you may have one set of styles for newsletters, another for brochures, and another for training manuals. Each set of styles, or style sheet, can be imported into each new publication you make.

There are two parts to styles—defining them and applying them. We'll show you how to define them first.

Defining a New Style

PageMaker's **Define styles** dialog is the last item on the **Type** menu. This dialog allows you to define new styles or make

Defining and Using PageMaker's Styles

changes to existing ones. Your PageMaker styles can be as simple as defining a style made up from a font name and size to a complicated style that encompasses almost all of PageMaker's typographic commands in a single style.

Establishing new styles is like using the submenus from PageMaker's **Type** menu that we looked at in the last chapter—you use the dialog boxes that you normally use to control type specifications and save the parameters for each style. So, to make changes to a style, you use the standard **Type specs, Paragraph, Indents/tabs,** and **Hyphenation** dialog boxes that you have already learned. You can also base a new style on an existing one. This latter capability allows you to take an existing style, make minor (or major) changes, and create a new style without starting over from scratch. The true power of styles cannot be communicated in words—you need to try them.

To define a new style within PageMaker:

1. Open the **Type** menu and choose **Define styles. . . .** Click on **New** to open the dialog shown in Figure 8.13.
2. Name the style. (Use a name that means something. Instead of Style 1, consider naming it Main Headline or Body Copy.)
3. If the new style will be based on an existing one, select the old one from the pop-up menu. By basing a new style on a related existing one, you can save yourself the time required to define a new one from scratch, particularly if the style is a complex one.

▼ ***Figure 8.13. The Style Dialog with the New Button Held Down***

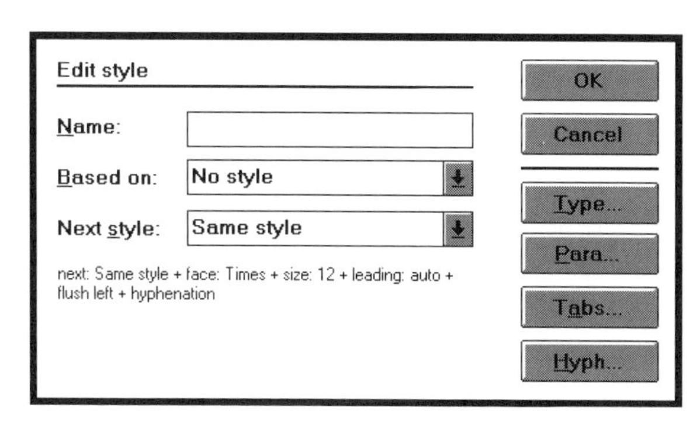

4. If you always want this style to be followed in the next paragraph by a particular style, choose it from the pop-up menu.
5. As shown in Figure 8.14, click one at a time on the **Type. . .**, **Para. . .**, **Tabs. . .**, and **Hyph. . .** buttons to set parameters for each one. These buttons bring up dialogs identical to the ones accessible from the **Type** menu. When you have finished making changes, click **OK** to put the dialog away. (If you don't need to make changes to any of the four dialogs, you do not need to open them during this process.)
6. Click **OK** to put the **New** dialog box away. When you arrive back at the **Define styles** dialog box, you will see the effects of your changes at the bottom of the box. Although the description of the style may appear cryptic, it can be deciphered to check your work.
7. Click **OK** to close the **Define styles** dialog box.

Applying Styles to Text

Once styles are defined, they can be applied directly to text by selecting text with the **Pointer** tool and then using the **Style** menu found under the **Type** pull-down menu. You can also select the text and then choose a style from the **Styles** palette.

If you later edit a style, all text that has been applied to the style will be automatically modified to reflect your changes. For example, if you applied a style to a paragraph that was set up to be bold text and then you edit the style to replace the bold with italic, when

▼ *Figure 8.14. The Edit Style Dialog*

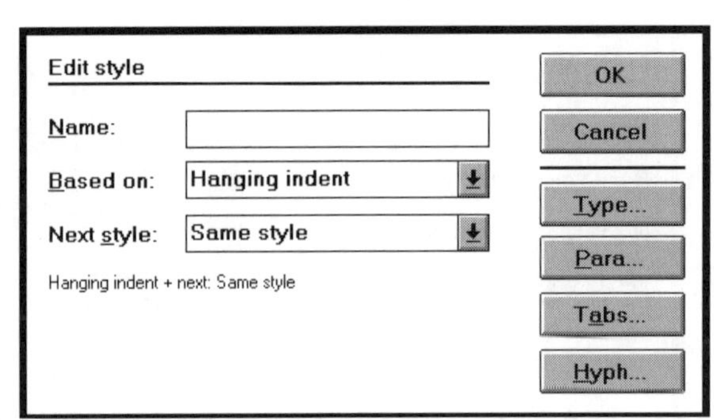

you save the modifications to your style, the paragraph will be modified to reflect the style change. This is one of the most powerful aspects of styles—a single modification to a style can effect change throughout an entire document containing multiple text blocks and pages. In the case of a long and complicated document, to perform the same chore manually would take considerably longer to select and reformat the text—and you'd be more likely to miss one of the headlines or text blocks you need to change.

Defining and Using PageMaker's Styles

CHECK YOURSELF

1. Use the same text block used in the last Check Yourself. Select **Define styles...** from the **Type** menu. Then click **New...** so that the **Edit style** dialog box opens. Define a style with italic text by clicking on the **Type** button and then checking the **Italic** box in the **Type specifications** dialog. Click **OK**. Then click on the **Paragraph** button. Choose **Justified** from the **Alignment** pop-up and click **OK** to close the dialog. In the **Edit style** dialog box, assign the name "Justified Itals." Click **OK** to put the dialog away. Now, select the text and apply the style just defined by using the **Style** menu under the **Type** menu. What happens?
   ▲ The new style is applied to the text. It becomes fully justified italic text.

2. Select the style **Normal** from the **Style** command in the **Style** menu. What happens?
   ▲ The Normal style is applied to the text.

Meet PageMaker's Typographic Preferences

Preference menus were introduced in Chapter 6. Now that we've looked at some of PageMaker's advanced typographic capabilities, we'll take a closer look at typographic preferences. This group of preferences allows you to define how PageMaker sets type, handles leading, and a number of other features. In this section, you will learn how to use some of the more immediately useful settings to make your work go faster and achieve better typesetting results.

Superscript and Subscript

Superscript and subscript type is used primarily for numbers and equations as shown in Figure 8.15. PageMaker allows you to define your preferences for both superscript and subscript. If you use these functions often, you will want to change the defaults because they are not usually optimum as set at the "factory."

To change either the subscript or superscript settings:

1. Open the **Options** dialog box from the **Type** dialog.
2. The size of the super- or subscript character is set by changing the value in the **Super/subscript size:** field. By setting this value to 50%, the superscripted or subscripted character will be made 50% of the size of the "regular" characters next to it.
3. Choose a **Superscript position:** and **Subscript position:**. The position is expressed as a percentage of the point size. The superscript is shifted up from the baseline and the subscript is shifted down from the baseline.
4. Specify whether you want the baseline for the super/subscript to be shifted up or down.
5. Click **OK** to close the **Options** dialog box, then **OK** again to close **Type specs**.

Setting Auto Leading

As you learned earlier in the chapter, leading is the space between lines of text. It can be set manually, or PageMaker will automatically determine the best value for it depending on the type size

▼ ***Figure 8.15. Example of Superscript and Subscript***

Superscript^{5}

Subscript$_{6}$

specified. Unfortunately, for many applications, PageMaker's automatic leading is a little too loose, meaning that it applies slightly too much leading. You can change the default leading value in the **Typographic Preference** box. The default setting is 20% of the size of the type size. So, 20-point type is automatically set in 24-point lines, which is fine for many applications. But, if you work with text-intensive documents such as books, where you need to accommodate as much copy on a page as possible while still maintaining readability, try setting the default to 18%. This will maintain readability but will fit more copy without resorting to manual leading controls.

Defining and Using PageMaker's Styles

To change the auto leading:

1. Open the **Spacing** dialog from the **Paragraph** dialog box off of the **Type** menu.
2. Change the value in the **Autoleading:** field.

Auto Kerning

We saw earlier in this chapter that kerning is the process of fitting two characters together so that clumsy combinations such as LT fit better with each other. PageMaker will handle most of this chore for you (you may still want to manually kern large headlines) with its auto kerning feature. This feature automatically kerns type as you enter it to make it more readable. It is turned on through the **Spacing** dialog box. The default setting, which works fine, is used to automatically kern type above 12 points in size. Type smaller than this size is too small to notice kerning problems usually, and kerning it slows down screen redraws.

Small Caps

In the last chapter you saw how to create small caps from the **Type specs** dialog box and **Control** palette. You can change the relative size of your small caps through the **Options** dialog box found in the **Type specs** dialog. The default setting is 70% of the size of normal caps. Consider changing this value to 60% to make this style more noticeable.

CHECK YOURSELF

1. In a new text block, type **E=MC2.** Select the "**2**" and click on the **Superscript** style in the **Control** palette to superscript it. What happens?
   - ▲ Unless someone else has already modified the preferences, the "2" moves above the rest of the equation, but remains the same size.
2. In the **Options** dialog box off of the **Type Specs** dialog box, change the **Superscript position:** to 33% and click **OK**. What happens?
   - ▲ The equation now appears as E=MC^2.

QUICK COMMAND SUMMARY

Shortcut Keys	*Commands*	*Procedures*
(Type menu)		
Alt T→L	Leading	Adjusts leading values
Alt T→R	Track	Changes type tracking
Alt T→W	Width	Changes horizontal width of type
Alt T		
Ctrl T→O→L	Baseline shift	Moves a group of letters up or down
Ctrl H	Hyphenation	Changes hyphenation
Ctrl 3	Define styles	Adds new styles or edits existing ones
Alt T→S	Styles	Selects a style to use

PRACTICE WHAT YOU'VE LEARNED

What You Do	*What You'll See*
1. Open a letter-sized PageMaker publication and enter the following text:	1. A new PageMaker publication is created and the type is entered.

What You Do	*What You'll See*
"This is an example of a major headline as used in an ad to catch the reader's eye. Headlines must be short and easy to read."	
2. Use the **Leading** menu under the **Type** menu to set the leading to **Auto**. After selecting the text you just typed, change the font size to 36 points. The text should flow onto several lines. Justify the text using the **Control** palette alignment controls (Remember to access the **Paragraph** view of the **Control** palette by clicking on the **Paragraph** button.)	2. The text becomes larger, flows onto several lines, and is centered in the text block.
3. Change the leading from Auto to 25 points by entering a value in to the **Leading**: field of the **Control** palette.	3. The lines of text overlap each partially.
4. Use the nudge buttons on the **Control** palette to change the leading to 36 points.	4. The text leading is increased so that the lines no longer touch.
5. Go to the **Leading** submenu from the **Type** menu and change the leading to 38 points. Using the **Set width...** submenu, change the type's width to 80%.	5. The characters become thinner and the characters are narrower; the text takes up less space on the page.

What You Do	*What You'll See*
6. Use the **Track** control on the **Control** palette to set the tracking to "Normal."	6. The characters move closer together.
7. Select the second line of type. Shift the type vertically (up) by entering a value of 11 in the **Baseline shift:** field (from the **Type** dialog, select **Type specs. . ., Options. . .**).	7. Only the second line of type is affected. It moves up vertically to overlap the first line slightly.
8. Use the **Control** palette to return the Baseline shift to 0.	8. The baseline shift is undone and the text appears as it did in Exercise 6 again.
9. Delete the text block by selecting the **Pointer** tool, clicking anywhere in the text block, and hitting the **Delete** key. Place the file DICKENS2.WP5 you created in Chapter 5 at the top of your publication. Remove the tab at the beginning of each of the two paragraphs by moving the insertion point to the first word of the paragraph and hitting the **Backspace** key. Insert a blank line between the two paragraphs.	9. The text block containing the headline is deleted from the layout. The text contained in the file DICKENS2.WP5 is imported.
10. Use the **Text** tool to place an insertion point anywhere in the first paragraph. Use the **Drop cap** function in the **Aldus Additions** submenu off of the **Utilities** menu to create a drop cap that extends for two lines.	10. The initial character of each paragraph is greatly enlarged and subsequently "drops" through the first 2 lines of text.

What You Do	*What You'll See*
11. Open the **Hyphenation** dialog from the **Type** menu. Turn hyphenation on (if it's not already on). Set **Limit consecutive hyphens:** to 2 instead of Unlimited. Set the **Hyphenation zone:** to .5".	11. The dialog box opens.
12. Select **Add. . .** from the **Hyphenation** dialog box and add "work~~~station." Click **As all lowercase,** then **OK** to add it to the dictionary. Click **OK** to exit the **Hyphenation** dialog.	12. A dialog box opens, the new entry is added, and the dialog box is closed.
13. Open the **Define styles** dialog box found under the **Type** menu. Click on the **New. . .** button to open the **Edit style** dialog box.	13. The **Define styles** dialog box opens. Once **New** is clicked, the **Edit style** dialog is opened.
14. Open the **Type specifications** dialog by clicking on the **Type** button. Choose **Italics** and set **Width** to 70%. Click **Ok.**	14. The **Type** dialog opens and changes are made to it. Clicking OK puts the dialog away and returns you to the **Edit style** dialog.
15. Open the **Paragraph specifications** dialog box by clicking on the **Para. . .** button. Enter .5 into the **First indents:** field. Click **OK**.	15. The **Paragraph** dialog opens and changes are made. Clicking **OK** returns you to the **Edit style** dialog.

What You Do	*What You'll See*
16. Name the new style "Test" and click **OK**. Click **OK** again to save the new style and put the dialog away.	16. A name is entered and by clicking **OK**, the dialog is put away and the underlying Styles dialog becomes visible. Clicking **OK** again puts this dialog away as well.
17. Place the insertion point anywhere in the second paragraph. Go to the **Window** menu and click on the **Styles** palette to bring the Styles palette on-screen. Click on **Test** from the **Styles** palette.	17. The second paragraph of text is assigned the new style. The text becomes narrower because of the 70% horizontal scale applied. The type is in Italics.
18. Delete the text block. Type your name on the page. Make your name 36 points in size.	18. The text block is deleted and a new one is created with your name typed into it. The type becomes larger once the new point size is selected.
19. Select the text with the **Text** tool and choose **Small Caps** from the **Case:** menu in the **Type specifications** dialog box under the **Type** menu.	19. The selected text becomes small caps once the style is applied to it.
20. With your name still highlighted, go to **Type specs. . .** and then **Options. . . .** Set the **Small caps size:** field to 25%. Click **OK**.	20. The **Type specs** dialog box opens, changes are made and it's put away. The new drop caps settings change the text used for your name dramatically. The large caps remain unchanged, but the small caps become much smaller.

What You Do	*What You'll See*
21. Exit PageMaker and do not save changes.	21. PageMaker returns you to Windows.

In this chapter, you have learned to work with a number of PageMaker's advanced typographic controls. You have also learned how to speed document assembly and improve type cosmetics. In the next chapter, you will learn the basics of working with graphics inside of PageMaker.

Working with Graphics

A page layout program would be little more than a typesetting tool without the ability to import graphics created with other programs or captured through scanning. Fortunately, PageMaker not only handles graphics with aplomb, but it's also adept at importing and manipulating photos and illustrations. In addition, once a graphic has been imported into a publication, PageMaker can track changes made to it in the originating program and automatically update PageMaker's copy. In this chapter you will learn how to:

- **Import and place graphics in PageMaker documents**
- **Modify graphics in PageMaker**
- **Keep track of graphics revisions with** Links. . .
- **Wrap text around graphics**
- **Use the Library palette**

Importing Graphics in PageMaker for Windows

As with importing text (covered in Chapter 5), PageMaker imports graphics using the **Place...** command found in the **File** menu. The graphics you import into your PageMaker publications will most likely have originated in a graphics program. They may be photos that were scanned into your PC and then modified using *image retouching* programs. Or perhaps they were created from scratch in a *paint* or *drawing* program. They may even have originated on videotape and been captured using a *frame grabber.*

For PageMaker to import an image, the graphic must be saved in a format compatible with PageMaker's image filters. The image filters are built-in routines that translate graphics so they can be displayed and manipulated by PageMaker. PageMaker can import pictures created by many popular graphics programs. Some of the image file formats supported are: .BMP, .CGM, .DXF, .GIF, .EPS, .PCX, .PIC, .TIF, and .WPG. These extensions are created on the end of the filename when an image file is saved in a graphics product, like an illustration program or draw program. Graphics products can save in one or more file formats, though not all of them can save in the preceding formats. Before creating a graphic for use with PageMaker for Windows, make sure it can be saved in one of the preceding formats by the originating program. (Refer to the product manuals for information on the appropriate file formats to use.)

Graphics saved in noncompatible formats must be converted to a compatible format before importing, otherwise PageMaker will either display the file's name in the import dialog as grayed out or give you an error message when you attempt to import it. If the format is unknown by PageMaker, the file's name may not show when you use the **Place...** command to import the file. This means you need to save the file in another format that PageMaker can use before you can import it into your page layout.

If your graphics program cannot save in a PageMaker compatible format, an alternative is to purchase a *translation* program. A

Importing Graphics in PageMaker for Windows

translation program's single purpose is to convert graphics from one format to another. A number of them are available, such as *HiJaak* from Inset Systems, which are capable of converting among scores of different graphic formats.

Importing and placing an image is very similar to importing text.

To place a compatible image into a PageMaker document:

1. Open the **File** menu and choose **Place....** Use the dialog options to locate the image file.
2. Click the correct filename to select it and then click **OK** to import the picture. The cursor will change into a loaded graphics icon as in Figure 9.1.
3. Position the graphics icon where you would like the image to appear (you can easily move it around later). Hold down the left mouse button and drag the mouse. A rectangular frame will open up as the mouse is dragged.
4. When the frame is the size you want, release the mouse button and the image will be imported into the frame.
5. If the file is small, it will appear instantly (depending on the speed of your PC's CPU and hard disk). A large file will take more time to load.

Depending on the kind of image imported and the settings in your **Preferences** dialog box, PageMaker may display the image in either high- or normal-resolution mode. High-resolution display of images allows you to see exactly how the image looks with other elements in your page layout. However, in the case of a large color image, it may take a long time to redraw the page containing the image and slow down the design process. For that reason, you may want normal resolution turned on to avoid waiting for the screen to redraw as you move through your publication and make changes. If you are making only text changes on a document with a large number of images, you can use the **Preferences** dialog to

▼ ***Figure 9.1. The Loaded Graphics Icon***

have the images gray out. This setting replaces your images with only gray boxes but allows you to navigate around the publication very quickly. Then, when you have everything as desired, you can change the settings and view the image file as it will actually appear.

CHECK YOURSELF

1. Create a new letter-sized PageMaker document. Check that **Graphics** is set to normal in the **Preferences** dialog box. Use **Place...** to import the file SMLTABLE.TIF. This file is copied to your hard disk by PageMaker during installation. It is located in the directory C:\PM5\TUTORIAL\LESSON2.
2. Once the cursor changes into a loaded icon, move it into the middle of your publication and drag a box about 2" square. Release the mouse button to bring in the image. Leave this document open for the next Check Yourself.

Modifying Graphics in PageMaker

Once a graphic is imported into an PageMaker document, it can be modified or duplicated. Duplication is easy: With the **Pointer** tool selected, click on the graphic. Now use the **Copy** command from the **Edit** menu to make a copy. The **Paste** command from the same menu is used to put the copy wherever you want in your publication. The imported image just becomes another object on the desktop and can be acted on with most of the object commands you've learned to this point.

The chameleonlike Control palette puts on another face when a graphic object is selected. Figure 9.2 shows the palette and all of its associated graphics tools. The Control palette will prove to be extremely useful as we explore image manipulation.

Modifying Graphics in PageMaker

▼ *Figure 9.2. The Control Palette in Graphics Mode*

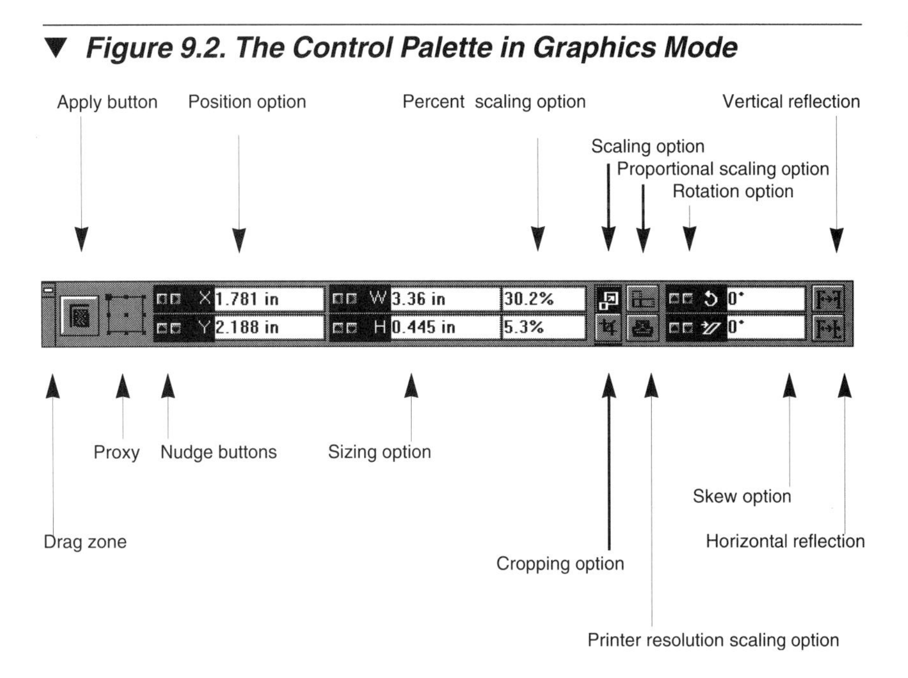

Moving and Resizing Graphics

Once a graphic has been imported into PageMaker you can modify it in a number of ways to fit your current publication. Often the picture will need to be moved or resized because it is too large or too small. Or it may be that you want to use only a portion of an image. PageMaker provides the tools to help you deal with these problems.

In Chapter 3 we saw how to move objects once they were created. Moving graphics is exactly the same. Use the Pointer tool to move the cursor anywhere in the graphic. Hold down the left mouse button and the cursor will change into a four-headed arrow. Drag the graphic to its new location and let go of the mouse button.

Graphics are resized the same way as any other object: Grab a handle and drag it until the object is the correct size. With graphic objects, however, there is one more consideration: the original scale. Every graphic has an original scale or ratio of its height to its width. When you import a picture you place it in a frame of arbitrary dimensions. The image is stretched in one or both directions to fit the frame you specify and it is unlikely that the image will maintain its original scale. The table imported in the last Check Yourself may end up looking like a coffee table for a basset hound if it is stretched horizontally or turn into a daddy longlegs if pulled vertically. Figure 9.3 shows both these possibilities. When you go to modify the size of an image, you run into this same problem again. Luckily, PageMaker has anticipated this problem and provided the Proportional-scaling option on the Control palette to cope with it. Figure 9.4 shows the Proportional-scaling option turned on and turned off. When turned on, this option modifies one dimension of the image to return it to its original scale. The position of the Proxy's reference point determines whether the vertical or horizontal dimension will be changed. If the reference point is anywhere on either of the vertical sides, then the vertical dimension is changed to achieve the correct scale. If the reference point is in the middle of either horizontal side, then the horizontal dimension is modified.

▼ ***Figure 9.3. The Table, out of Proportion***

Modifying Graphics in PageMaker

▼ *Figure 9.4. The Proportional-Scaling Button*

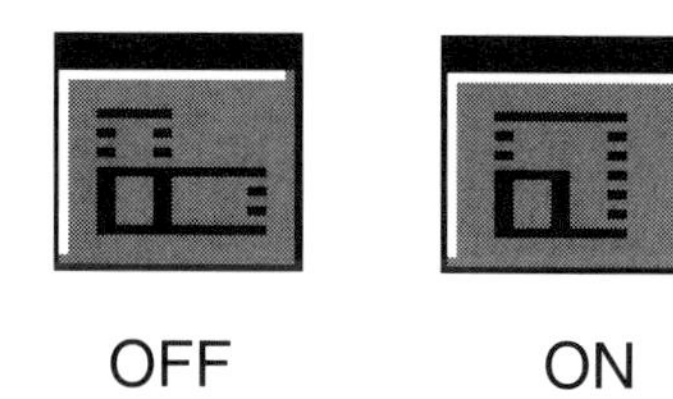

If you have imported a graphic and want to return it to its original proportions, first select the object and make sure the reference point on the **Proxy** is set correctly. Now click on the **Proportional-scaling** button. The object should jump to its original scale.

To maintain the proportions of an image as you resize it, first click on the **Proportional-scaling** option so the icon resembles two boxes. Now when you resize the object, PageMaker will automatically move both dimensions to keep the object in proportion.

In Chapter 3 we saw how to enter exact dimensions of arithmetic formulas into the **Position** and **Sizing** option fields to modify objects. The same procedures apply to graphics. Precise resizing is a simple matter of entering the requested new size in the option fields. You can even enter different percentages for each box. For example, you can make a photo of a tall person appear short by leaving the **Width Percent-scaling** option at 100%, but entering 70% in the **Height Percent-scaling** option.

Resizing Black-and-White Images

Resizing black-and-white images that are to be printed presents one more problem. Monochrome bit-mapped images are composed of a series of small dots. Both your screen and your printer present these images as a series of dots, but the resolution of the two is different. When a bit-mapped image is resized, the pattern of dots is affected and may not be optimal for the printer you are using, though the image appears fine on your screen. Symptoms of this problem are printed images that look washed out or mottled. To correct this problem, click on the **Printer resolution scale** option before resizing a monochrome graphic. PageMaker will then restrict the size of the object to exact multiples of your printer's resolution. This assures you of a clean printed image.

CHECK YOURSELF

1. Using the picture imported during the last Check Yourself (SMLTABLE.TIF), stretch the picture horizontally. What happens?
   ▲ The table becomes very long and very low.
2. Undo the horizontal stretch and pull it vertically. What do you see?
   ▲ The table appears very tall.
3. Use the **Pointer** tool to click on the image and select it. Click on the **Proportional-scaling** option on the **Control** palette. What happens?
   ▲ The table assumes normal proportions.
4. Leave the publication open for the next Check Yourself.

Cropping Images

Cropping is the process of removing unimportant information from the edges of a graphic so that the reader sees only what's important. In conventional page layout, this is accomplished manually by trimming off the edges of a photo that contain unimportant detail, leaving only what is important. For example, if you have a photo of two people standing next to each other, but you only want to show the person on the left, you can trim (crop) the other person out of the image.

Cropping is accomplished within PageMaker by resizing the frame around the graphic and moving the image around as necessary. To accomplish the removal of the second person in the example inside PageMaker, you would simply use the **Cropping** tool to make that side of the picture box smaller, effectively hiding the second person.

Modifying Graphics in PageMaker

To crop an image:

1. Click on the image you want to crop.
2. Click on the **Cropping** tool on the **Toolbox** palette or the **Control** palette. The cursor turns into a cropping icon.
3. Position the **Cropping** tool so that one of the handles on the graphic's frame shows through the center of the tool.
4. Drag the handle to resize the frame. Notice that the image itself is not resized. Release the mouse button when the frame is the desired size.
5. If the position of the image within the frame needs to be adjusted, move the **Cropping** tool into the image and hold down the left mouse button. The icon changes into a hand.
6. Hold down the left mouse button and drag the hand. The hand moves the image around within the frame. When positioned correctly, release the mouse button.

TIP

Large images that require substantial cropping may be easier to work with if you crop them within the application you used to create them. Thus, when the file is saved, it will be smaller. This saves memory and the printing of the image will go much faster when using PageMaker.

Rotating, Reflecting, and Skewing Images

We looked at the object transformations of rotating, reflecting, and skewing in Chapter 4 when they were applied to rectangles and ellipses. Because graphics are treated much like any other objects, you apply these same transformations to pictures.

To apply any transformation, first use the **Pointer** tool to select a graphic. You can rotate the graphic using either the **Rotation** tool from the **Toolbox** palette or the **Rotation** option on the **Control** palette. The **Reflecting** buttons will flip the image either horizontally or vertically. Finally, the **Skewing** option slants an image to one side or the other. To undo any of these, select **Remove transformation** from the **Element** menu.

These controls, combined with the **Copy** and **Paste** functions, can be used to achieve some eye-catching effects in your publications. Like all effects, however, they are best used judiciously as it is to easy to overdo it.

Adding Borders to Graphics

Often you will want to place a border around pictures. PageMaker provides a convenient means for accomplishing this: the **Box it** function under **Aldus Additions**, found in the **Utilities** menu. **Box it** automatically places a rectangular border around any selected object. This border is an object in its own right; you can use any of the line tools to change its weight or style.

What PageMaker is actually doing is drawing a rectangle, which is slightly larger than the graphic, behind your graphic. The overhang of the rectangle is what appears as the border. You can select how far from the edge of the graphic the border appears by entering a value in the **Extends** field. By default the outside edge of the border is 5 points from the outside edge of the graphic. To leave more white space around a graphic, increase this value. To bring the border closer to the graphic, decrease the value.

CHECK YOURSELF

1. Using the open publication from the last Check Yourself exercise, use the **Cropping** tool to resize the frame so that the frame just touches the edge of the table. What do you see?
   ▲ The frame gets smaller and closer to the table.

2. Use the **Control** palette to locate the point of rotation at the center of the table image. Rotate the image 90 degrees. What happens?
   ▲ The table is turned 90 degrees.

3. Go to the **Line** submenu from the **Element** menu and select the 4-point double line. Click on the table picture to select it and use the **Box it** function in **Aldus Additions** to add a frame around the picture. Leave the spacing at the default 5 points. What happens?
   ▲ The frame you selected appears around the table as a border.

The Image Controls

The Image Controls

If you are working with a monochrome scanned image or one created with a compatible paint program, the **Image control** dialog box from the **Element** menu allows you to make changes to the image. When the graphic is selected, **Image control. . .** becomes active (not grayed out in the menu bar) indicating that it can be used to modify the image. The **Image control** dialog is shown in Figure 9.5.

The **Lightness** control adjusts the overall brightness of an image. This slider works the same way as the horizontal and vertical scroll bars. Use the arrows to either increase or decrease the brightness a bit at a time or else drag the scroll box to make changes more quickly. Positive numbers increase the brightness of the image; negative numbers decrease the brightness.

The second slider is **Contrast. Contrast** adjusts the difference between light and dark regions. The higher that **Contrast** is set, the more light and dark regions will stand out from each other. However, high contrast tends to make subtle gray shades disappear, because everything becomes either black or white. Again, positive numbers increase the contrast while negative numbers decrease it.

▼ ***Figure 9.5. The Image Control Dialog***

Image control
Lightness: 0 %
Contrast: 50 %
OK
Cancel
Printing parameters
Screen patterns:
Default
Screen angle: DFLT degrees
Screen frequency: DFLT lines per inch

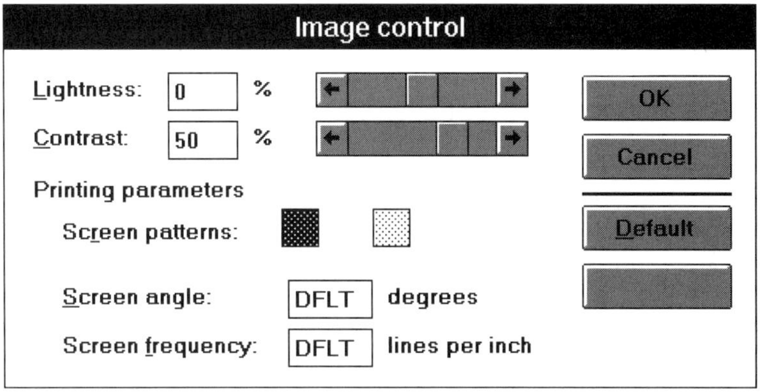

Screen Settings

Images are broken down by PageMaker into patterns of dots to facilitate printing them on offset lithographic presses, which are incapable of printing solid grays and colors. This is accomplished by laying a *screen* over the image. The holes in the screen let the image show through; the finer the screen, the more holes and the higher the resolution. PageMaker allows you to assign different screen resolutions or *frequencies* for the printing process. This means that the dots that make up the image are larger or smaller depending on how fine a screen is used. Fine screens create the smallest dots, but papers such as newsprint cannot print such small dots without the dots running together. So, for newsprint and other lower-quality printing requirements, a coarser screen is used for reproducing the image.

You can also replace the dots of the screens with lines that can be varied in thickness as well as angle. This is another of the options under the **Image control** dialog box. Unless you are already an expert in the use of screens and lines, ask your printer what to use. If you use lines in your image specifications, ask your printer for a proof so that you can see what it will look like in print. A proof is a special reproduction made from your art at the print shop or at a service bureau that shows what the printed document will look like.

Links—Keeping Track of Image Changes

Often graphics need to be updated or modified in other programs before they are ready to go to print. A photo may need enhancement to sharpen the detail in an image retouching program such as Aldus PhotoStyler. A graphic may require additional components to be added inside an illustration program such as Aldus Freehand. When changes are made to graphics that have already been imported into a PageMaker page layout, you can simply reimport them and replace the obsolete version in the document, or you can let PageMaker automatically handle the job for you. Once a graphic is placed into a PageMaker layout, PageMaker tracks the image to see whether it gets updated by another program. If it does, PageMaker's **Links...** function can be set up to automatically import the new version while retaining most of the settings you have already prescribed for the image. Using the automatic update feature, instead of reimporting the image using **Place. . .**, is advantageous because the resizing, rotation, Image control changes, and other parameters will remain as already specified for the image. This saves you the task of making changes to the settings all over again after the updated graphic is reimported.

Links—Keeping Track of Image Changes

The Links Command

PageMaker's **Links...** command is found under the **File** menu. A dialog as shown in Figure 9.6 opens when you select the command. This dialog box displays the name of each graphic file placed in your PageMaker publication, on which page it's located, a status character, and the file type.

Clicking on any of the files listed displays that file's status more fully in the **Status:** field below the file list window. If a file has not been modified and PageMaker knows where it's located, the **Status:** field indicates that the item is up to date. If the picture has been modified, a dash appears before its name and the **Status:** field

▼ ***Figure 9.6 The Links Dialog Box***

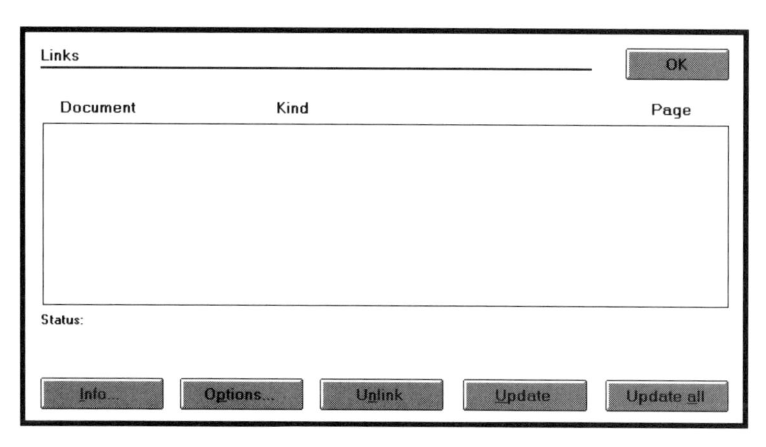

reports that the linked file has been modified. A picture that has been deleted, moved to another place on disk, or put in another directory on disk shows up with a question mark before it, and **Status:** reports that it cannot be located.

You can use the **Links...** feature to manually "update" graphics that have been modified. When PageMaker indicates that a graphic has been modified, clicking on Update will replace the old version of the graphic in your publication with the newer one.

To manually update a graphic:

1. Open the **Utilities** menu and choose **Links....** Review the status of graphics in your document by clicking on their names and reading the status reports as they come up.
2. Select a graphic to update by clicking on its name and then clicking the **Update** button. PageMaker will reimport the updated graphic.
3. Click on **OK** to put the dialog box away.

Automatically Updating Graphics

PageMaker can be set up to automate the process of updating graphics each time you open a document containing images. You can set up PageMaker's tracking and updating of graphics in three ways:

- ▲ Reimport modified graphic files only when you request the update
- ▲ Reimport graphic files automatically when the document is opened
- ▲ Reimport graphic files automatically after telling you that a file has been modified and asking whether you want to replace it.

The third method is the best one for most purposes. It allows you to control the picture import process while still taking advantage of the automation possible using the **Links...** command. To select this or other auto picture import preferences, open the **Options** dialog in the **Links** dialog box. (This should be done upon opening a new publication, before importing any graphics.) From the **Options** dialog, click on **Update automatically** and **Alert be-**

fore updating. Click **OK** to put the box away to save your preferences. The next time you open a PageMaker document containing a modified graphic, PageMaker will prompt you whether to replace the existing graphic with a newer version.

Links—Keeping Track of Image Changes

Wrapping Text around Graphics

PageMaker allows you to set up graphics or other objects so that text automatically wraps around them. If you are new to design, you may have no experience working with text wrap, which is also called *wraparound* or *runaround* by designers. Quite simply, a text wrap is where the edge of an object defines the edge of the text as shown in Figure 9.7. The **Text wrap** dialog is shown in Figure 9.8.

Text wrap can be a powerful design element to make the text a more "active" element in the design. One of the reasons that Text wrap is a standard tool in modern page layout programs is that at one time, typesetters had to assemble text wrap by hand—and it

▼ ***Figure 9.7. Example of Text Wrap***

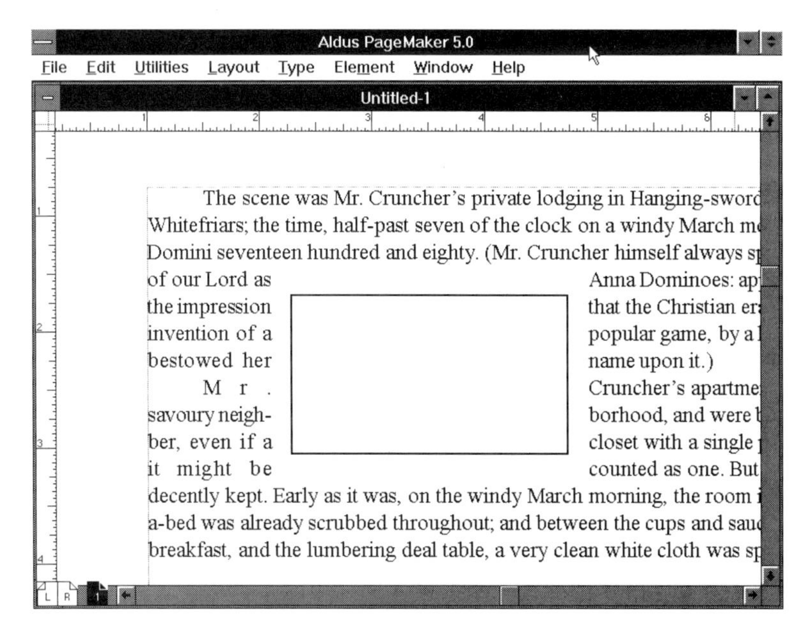

▼ *Figure 9.8. The Text Wrap Dialog*

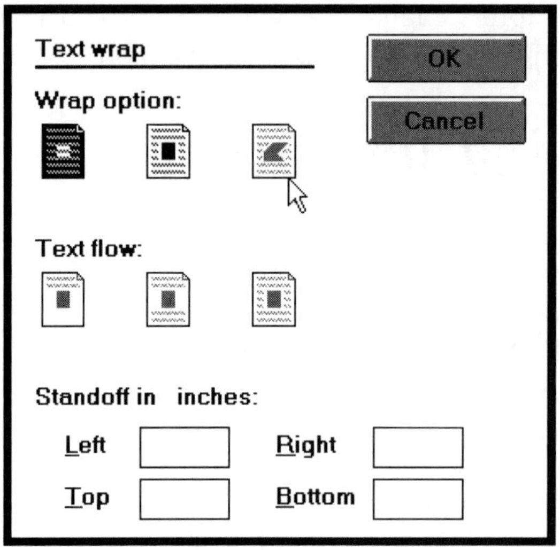

was expensive to do that. Now, sophisticated designs with text wrap are no sweat, thanks to products like PageMaker. With the power of the computer, this formerly time- and budget-intensive effect is easy.

To implement Text wrap:

1. Select an object to wrap the text around.
2. Choose **Text wrap. . .** from the **Element** drop-down menu.
3. Choose the type of **Text wrap** you want to use and set the distance parameters in the box that tell PageMaker how close to the object you want the text to wrap. Click **OK.** Experiment with different distance settings to get the look you want.

PageMaker has three text wrap modes. They are:

▲ *None*—Text flows over the graphic.
▲ *Normal*—Text runs around an object at a distance set by the measurements set in **Standoff** in the **Text wrap** dialog box.
▲ *Custom*—Rather than follow the default text wrap frame you can specify how the text is to wrap around the graphic.

Once the text wrap mode is chosen, you can select how you want text to flow. The options are:

Wrapping Text around Graphics

- *Column-break*—Text flow stops at the top of the graphic and then continues at the start of the next column (or the next page if there is only one column).
- *Jump over*—Text stops above the graphic and continues below it, leaving white space on both sides of the object.
- *Wrap-all*—Text flows around all sides of the object.

Custom Text Wrap

Although regular shaped objects lend themselves to the built-in text wrap, irregular or rounded objects may benefit from having the text wrap customized. Figure 9.9 shows an ellipse before, with the normal text wrap, and after, with the wrap customized. The latter makes the object look more integrated into the publication.

To customize Text wrap:

- Click on the object that you want to wrap.
- Open up the **Text wrap** dialog box from the **Element** menu and select **Normal** text wrap and the text flow option.
- A dotted line will appear around the object, as in Figure 9.10, to indicate the current text wrap *boundary*.

▼ Figure 9.9. Text Wrap around an Ellipse

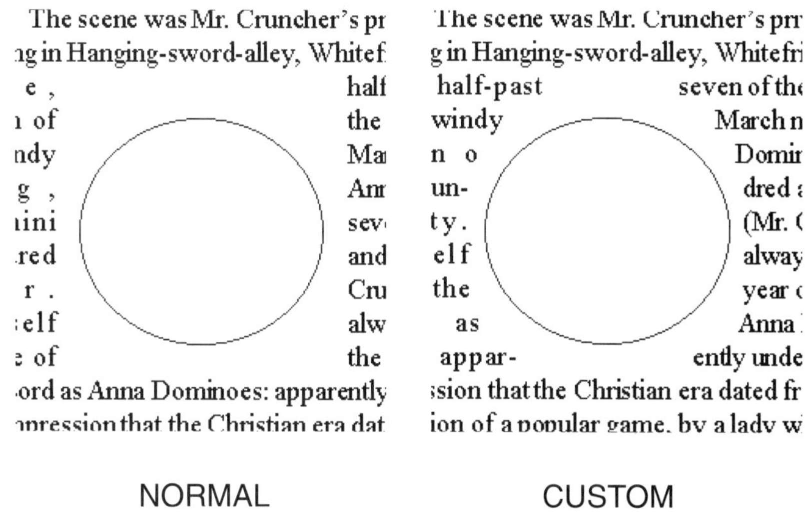

NORMAL

CUSTOM

Figure 9.10. The Object Boundary

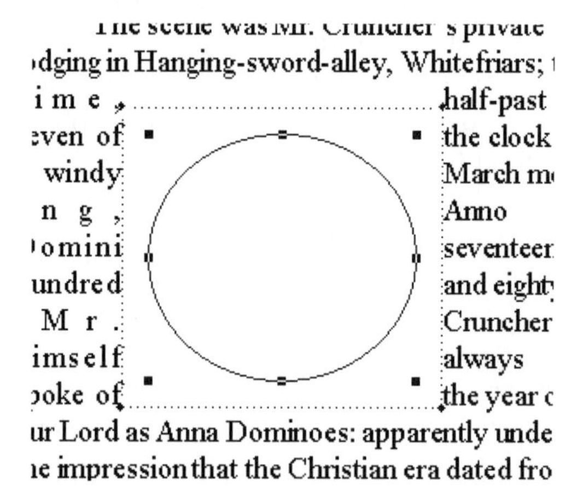

- ▲ Click anywhere on the boundary and a new handle will appear. You can use this handle, or any existing handles, to drag the boundary into a new shape.
- ▲ Use the new handle or any existing handle to drag the boundary to the desired shape. To drag the boundary, point at one of the handles and hold the left mouse button down. As you move the mouse you will see that part of the boundary moves with you. Figure 9.11 shows a boundary being fit around an ellipse.

▼ *Figure 9.11. Modifying the Boundary*

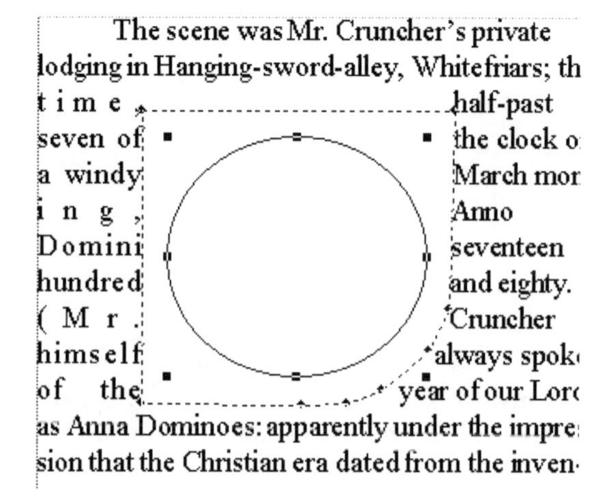

▲ For curved or complex objects, define a number of new handles spaced close together. By dragging each one a small amount, the boundary can be made to match even the most unusual shape.

QUICK COMMAND SUMMARY

Shortcut Keys	*Commands*	*Procedures*
(File menu)		
Ctrl D	Place. . .	Imports a graphic from a non-PageMaker file
Shft Ctrl D	Links. . .	Track imported graphics
(Element menu)		
Alt E→W	Text wrap	Flow text around a graphic
Alt E→I	Image control	Change graphics settings

PRACTICE WHAT YOU'VE LEARNED

What You Do	*What You'll See*
1. Open a new PageMaker publication. Move the **Control** palette to the bottom of the screen. Go to **Preferences. . x.** and set **Graphics** to **High resolution.**	1. A new publication is opened.
2. Place the file C:\PM5\TUTORIAL\LESSON2\BIGTABLE.TIF in the middle of the first page.	2. A color graphic of the edge of a table appears in the publication.
3. Go to **Preferences. . .** again and set **Graphics** to **Normal.**	3. The picture loses many of its details.

What You Do	*What You'll See*
4. Use the **Cropping** tool to eliminate most of the table leg from the picture. Click on **Scaling** option and then the **Proportional-scaling** option to bring the graphic back to its original proportions.	4. The picture becomes smaller. When Proportional-scaling is turned on, the picture assumes normal proportions.
5. Skew the image 45 degrees by using the **Skewing** option on the **Control** palette.	5. The picture is slanted to the right.
6. Set the reference point in the **Proxy** to the middle of the image and use the **Control** palette's **Rotation** option to turn the image 30 degrees.	6. The whole picture turns.
7. Go to the element menu and select **Remove transformation.**	7. The image is straight again.
8. Open the **Element** menu and select **Line.** Choose the 6-point dashed line style. Use **Box it** in **Aldus Additions** to draw a border around the picture.	8. A thick, dashed border surrounds the image.
9. Open the **File** menu and select **Links. . .** Click on "BIGTABLE.TIF." Click **OK** to close the dialog.	9. The Status: field shows that the image is current.
10. Click on the border of the image to select it. Hit the delete key.	10. The border is deleted but the picture remains.

What You Do	***What You'll See***
11. Click on the table picture. Hit the delete key.	11. The table picture is deleted.
12. Place DICKENS.WP5 at the top of your open publication. Set the **View** to **Actual Size** and use the scroll bars to adjust the publication so you can see the first few lines.	12. Text fills up about one-third of the page.
13. Click on the **Ellipse** tool and draw a circle (or close to it) in the center of the text so there are two or three lines above and below the circle.	13. A circle appears near the top of the page. Text flows over the ellipse.
14. Select **Text wrap...** from the **Element** menu. Choose **Normal** wrap and **Wrap-all** text flow.	14. Text flows around the circle. Surrounding the circle is a rectangular dashed line.
15. Select the **Pointer** tool and click on the circle.	15. When the Pointer is first selected, the dashed line disappears. When you click on the circle it reappears.
16. Click four or five times on the dotted line around the circle to create new handles.	16. New handles appear as small, rectangles on the dashed boundary.
17. Drag the handles to move the boundary closer to the circle and to follow the curvature of the circle.	17. As the boundary is moved, text moves closer to the circle.

What You Do	*What You'll See*
18. Use the nudge buttons next to the **X Position** option to move the circle an inch to the left.	18. As the circle moves, the text realigns itself. Some pops over from the left side of the circle to the right.
19. Close the publication and do not save changes.	19. PageMaker returns you to the Windows desktop.

In this chapter you have learned how to import and manipulate graphics created in other programs. In the next chapter, things definitely get colorful. You will learn how to define colors and apply them to objects contained in PageMaker page layouts. So put on your atist's cap, and let's go.

Working with Color

So far we have been dealing almost entirely with black and white. In this chapter we liven up the scene by exploring some of the extensive color capabilities built into PageMaker. PageMaker offers sophisticated control of color and allows you to choose colors in a number of different ways. Color control is also very convenient in PageMaker—a color palette is available that provides instant control of color applied to type or objects. This chapter introduces PageMaker's color functions and shows you how to use them on the desktop to add color to your page layouts. In this chapter you will learn how to:

- **Use PageMaker's basic color tools**
- **Define colors in PageMaker**
- **Meet the color libraries supported by PageMaker**
- **Add colors to text, borders, and objects**
- **Use color tints**
- **Control layers in documents**

PageMaker Color Basics

Designing in color is one of the most exciting and creative aspects of assembling documents on the desktop. Unfortunately, documents containing color can also be the most problematic to take into print. Color printing is complex even for professionals who have worked in the industry for years. When you begin creating documents containing color on the desktop, you must learn about production issues such as trapping and registration that used to be handled conventionally by your print shop.

However, there are also significant advantages to creating your own color documents on the desktop: You have complete control of the design and production of your work and fewer outside services are required to finish projects. This saves you both time and money because instead of waiting for and paying for print shop services such as *stripping* (readying documents for press), you can handle the entire procedure yourself. Keep in mind, however, that mistakes you make assembling color documents may make it into print. If a serious mistake gets printed, it may require a complete reprint of the job to correct it. A mistake that the print shop catches before print may cost so much to fix that the time and money savings you would otherwise realize from desktop design and production are more than completely negated.

Before Taking a Sophisticated Color Document into Print

Before you begin a desktop design for a multicolor project, such as a brochure, direct mailer, catalog, or annual report, discuss the job with your print shop. First, locate a print shop that frequently works with desktop-created jobs that also has facilities for taking your file and running it out to film with an imagesetter. (Imagesetting and imagesetters are discussed briefly in the next chapter.) Some things aren't yet practical or efficient to do on the desktop, but that doesn't mean that PageMaker will stop you from attempting these operations. Your print shop, however, can caution you about applying unprintable effects or attempting to place large color photo images that would be better handled conventionally.

TIP

If you plan to produce color publications using PageMaker, start simple and work upward in complexity. Start out with two-color documents where colors don't touch each other and work from there.

Objects, Fills, and Borders

In Chapter 3 you saw how to create objects such as rectangles and ellipses. When you create the object, you see its outline on your screen. This outline of the object is called its *border.* The inside of an object is known as its *fill.* By default, an object's fill is set to **None,** so the object really does not consist of anything other than its outline. For you to be able to color the inside of an object, you have to define what the inside, or fill, actually is. You do this through the **Fill** submenu in the **Element** menu.

To define the fill of an object:

1. Use the **Pointer** tool to select the object.
2. Open the **Element** menu and click on the **Fill** submenu. The menu shown in Figure 10.1 appears.
3. Select any of the patterns in the menu to be the object's fill. When working with color, you will generally select a "solid" fill. This will make the object appear black until a color is chosen. The selection **Paper** can be used to make the inside of the object take on the color of the paper stock on which your publication is printed. The inside of the object is actually left blank so that the paper shows through the object.

Color Operations on the Desktop

Color operations on the PageMaker desktop are usually handled in order. There are three steps to using color in your designs:

▼ ***Figure 10.1. PageMaker's Fill Menu***

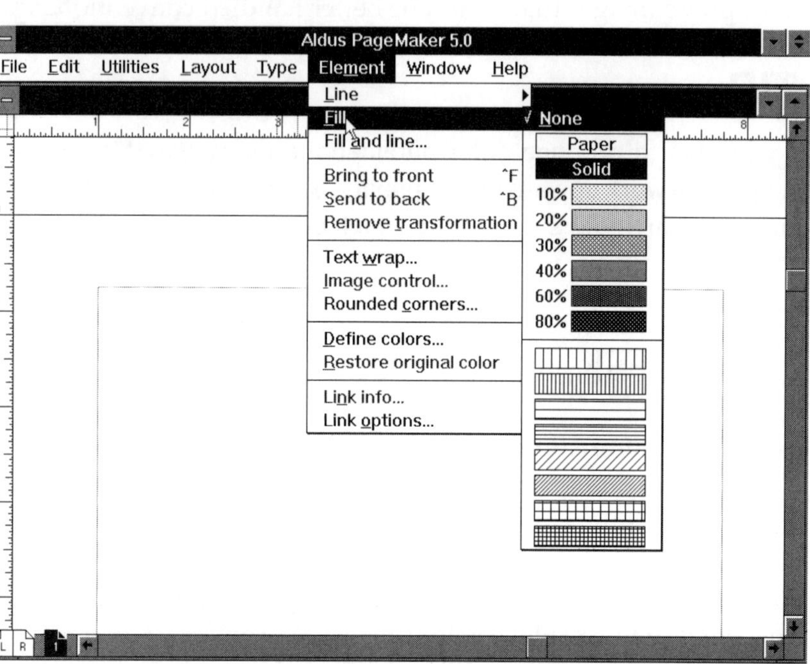

1. Define a color you plan to use in PageMaker's **Define colors** dialog box.
2. Select the part of an object to which you will apply the color.
3. Use the **Colors** palette to apply the colors to the correct part of the object.

Colors are separately applied to the inside, or fill, of an object and to its outside edge. If you color the outside edge of an object (its *border*), this is a different operation than filling the background. The border and background can have two different colors, or one can be colored and the other left black or transparent.

In addition to these two coloring functions, the third component that you can color is the text contained in a text block. Type can be colored either through the use of the **Text** tool and the **Colors** palette or by changing the color attribute in the **Type specs** dialog box.

CHECK YOURSELF

1. What are the three steps for applying color to PageMaker objects?
   - ▲ Define a color, select the element in an object where color will be applied, and then apply the color.
2. What three elements can have color applied to them in PageMaker?
   - ▲ Type, border, and fill.

Defining Colors

PageMaker allows you to define colors that you want to add to your document. In addition, several colors are already defined at the "factory." Colors are defined within the **Define colors** dialog box found under the **Element** menu. When you choose the **Define colors. . .** command, you will open the **Define colors** dialog box, shown in Figure 10.2, which looks similar to the **Define styles** dialog you learned about in Chapter 8. But instead of style names, the dialog box contains a list of colors that are already defined in PageMaker. If you are working on a color monitor with a color card, the colors will be represented by their name and color.

▼ ***Figure 10.2. The Define Colors Dialog***

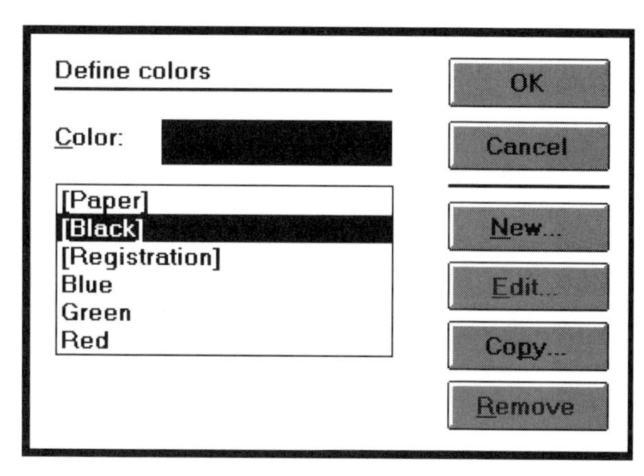

At this point, you can define a **New** color, **Edit** an existing one, **Delete** a color, or Copy colors defined in another PageMaker document. If you click **New,** or **Edit,** PageMaker opens the **Edit color** dialog box, where you can define new colors.

To define a new color:

1. Open the **Element** menu and choose **Define colors. . . .** When the dialog box opens, click **New** to open the **Edit color** dialog box shown in Figure 10.3.
2. From the **Edit color** dialog, choose the color library you want to use and then select the color from the scrollable menu. If you want to use color mixing, select the correct color model and use the sliders to create the color.
3. When you have achieved the correct color, click **OK** to close the box. From within the open **Edit color** dialog, click **OK** to retain your new color on the **Colors** palette, then click **OK** to close the **Define colors** dialog box.

▼ ***Figure 10.3. PageMaker's Edit Color Dialog***

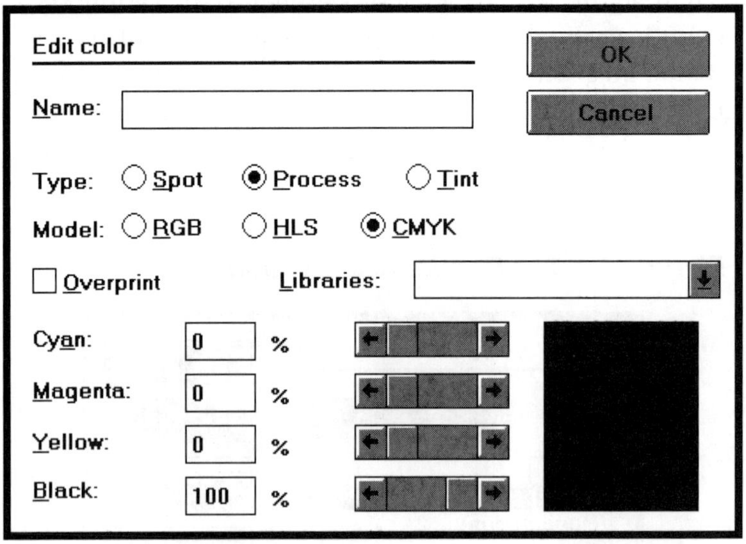

Color and Monitor Color Accuracy

It's important to keep in mind that the color you see on your monitor may have little relationship to the actual color you have selected when it is printed. Even if you are using a SuperVGA card capable of 256 colors or a 24-bit true-color card capable of almost 17 million colors, the rendering of the color on the monitor will still not be very accurate. Computer monitors are still inaccurate when reproducing blues and true white, because of the technology used in video displays. These problems with blue and white throw off the rest of the spectrum considerably. New (expensive) color calibration systems help but are not perfect either.

If you are choosing a color from one of PageMaker's color libraries (discussed next), choose colors from a swatch book purchased from an art supply store or ink manufacturer instead of making the selections on-screen. If you are using colors created from PageMaker's ink-mixing models such as CMYK and your job will finish on a printing press, have your printer make a color proof to see what the color will actually look like before going to print—otherwise you may be in for a big (and possibly unpleasant) surprise when you see the completed job.

PageMaker's Color Libraries

PageMaker ships with several color libraries from which you can choose color. You can either "mix" colors using the slider controls, or you can choose a color from the on-screen swatch books. The colors you choose will have a direct impact on your job. If your publication will print on a color printer attached to your PC, almost any color can be selected. But, if your job will finish on a printing press, choose your colors carefully because the number of colors you apply and the way you apply them will directly affect the cost of printing your project (as well as the aesthetics of the piece). The commercial color matching systems supported by PageMaker, including Dainippon, Pantone, Focoltone, and TruMatch, all have swatch books available for selecting and matching colors. The Pantone system is the most widely implemented system, but Focoltone and TruMatch, which were designed for specification on computers, may be the superior color systems and are beginning to gain favor with desktop designers.

CMYK, RGB, and HSL colors are mixed by moving sliders for each represented color. Although there are no swatch books to show you how to mix these colors, most art supply stores carry a color specifier chart for CMYK colors that allows you to rotate a wheel representing values for each of the cyan, magenta, yellow, and black colors to see the resulting color in a window on the chart.

WARNING

Before adding color to your project that will finish in a print shop, discuss your color selections with your printer. It is easy to design a job with 22 solid Pantone colors with PageMaker. Even if you could find a printer willing to print such a piece, it could be a disaster on press or so expensive it would make the design impractical. For that reason, the way colors are specified and the number of colors to use is something that should be discussed beforehand with your print shop. Again, if you will only be printing your document on your own desktop color printer, don't worry about it—though some printers may slow down if you use too many different color specifications.

PageMaker's Predefined Colors

When you open the **Define colors** dialog box, you will see that five colors already exist, which also appear on PageMaker's **Colors** palette. Besides red, green, blue, and black, there are two entries that require some explanation:

▲ **Registration** is not a color but an attribute that you apply to objects that you want to print on each of your separations. It is used to add names and guides to the various film layers as a way to track all the pieces.

▲ **Paper** refers to whatever color paper you are printing on. When you choose this color, PageMaker makes the selected object, and all layers below that object, transparent so that the paper shows through.You may edit this entry to simulate the color of the stock you are printing on, but the color will appear on-screen only as a reference; when you print, no color will be applied.

Defining Colors

CHECK YOURSELF

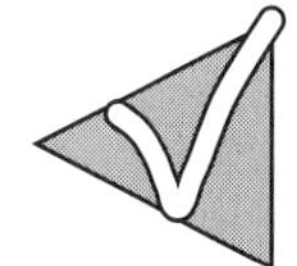

1. Go to the **Element** menu and open the **Define colors** dialog box. Select **New** to open the **Edit color** dialog box, then choose the Pantone system from the Libraries pop-up menu and select Pantone 305 from the "swatch book." Click **OK** and then click **OK** again in the **Edit color** and **Define colors** dialogs to save your selection. What color is Pantone 305?
   ▲ Pantone 305 is a turquoise blue.
2. What are the names of any three color libraries supported by PageMaker that have physical swatch books available for selecting colors?
   ▲ Pantone, Pantone Pro, Dainippon, Focoltone, and TruMatch are the color libraries supported by PageMaker.
3. Which is the most widely used color matching system?
   ▲ The Pantone system is the most widely used and is also the oldest color matching system.

Adding Color to Text, Borders, and Fills

As explained earlier in this chapter, color can be applied to text, borders, and object fills. Color can also be applied to lines. To apply color, PageMaker allows you to select colors from the **Colors** palette, the **Type specs** dialog box, and from the **Fill and line** dialog box in the **Element** menu. To apply a color, you must first define it through the **Define colors. . .** dialog explained in the last section. Once a color is defined, the most convenient way to apply it is with the **Colors** palette. The **Colors** palette displays all defined colors in addition to the predefined colors described in the previous section.

To apply colors with the Colors palette:

1. Open the **Colors** palette by choosing **Colors** palette from the **Window** menu.
2. Use the **Pointer** tool to select the object you want to color. If you want to color text, use the **Text** tool to select the text the same way you would to change the font or font size.
3. If the object you want to color is not text, you have a choice of coloring the fill or the border. To color only the fill, click on the **Fill** icon below the title bar of the **Colors** palette. To color only the border, click on the **Border** icon. If you want to color both, point at the down-arrow icon below the title bar and hold down the mouse button. The menu shown in Figure 10.4 will open. Still holding the button down, slide the arrow until it is over **Both** and release the button.
4. Click on the color selection to apply it to the selected portion of the object. The element (border, text, fill, or line) will change color on your monitor to reflect your selection.

▼ ***Figure 10.4. PageMaker's Colors Palette***

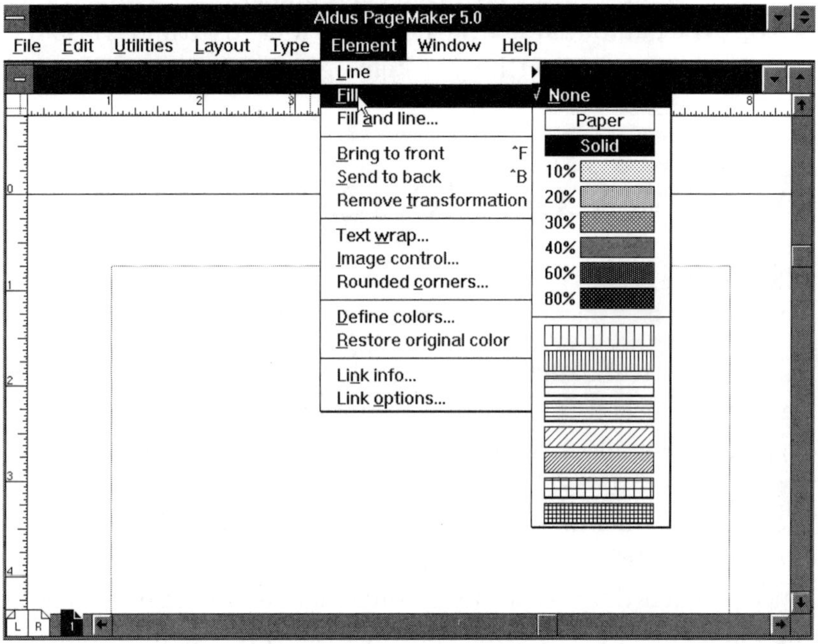

Once the color of an element is changed, you can still modify the object in any way you want through the usual methods. Of course, you can also change colors as many times as you want as well. This is a powerful tool for color design because, with a capable color monitor, monitor board, and calibration system, you can see your layout in full color, complete with color images. You can make changes until the design looks just right or you run out of time, whichever comes first.

Adding Color to Text, Borders, and Fills

TIP

When assembling a document that incorporates color and/or color images, there's a new way to get high-quality output to check your work. Many service bureaus (described in Chapter 11) offer color output through new color copiers made by Canon or Kodak. Using these high-quality photocopiers, which can reproduce documents through a computer attached to the copier, you can directly print your documents to paper as large as 11" by 17". Output costs between $3 and $10 per page in most shops.

Coloring Elements Through the Menus

As you have probably noticed as you have worked through exercises earlier in this book, color can be applied through the dialog boxes found under the Type and Element menus. Although this is somewhat slower than using the convenient Colors palette, if your color requirements are limited or your monitor is too small to accommodate another floating palette, you can apply color directly with the menus. In the same way that only defined colors can be applied through the Colors palette, only predefined colors will be available through the dialog boxes and menu selections. There are two ways to apply color without using the Colors palette:

1. If you are applying color to an object's fill or border, use **Fill and line. . .** from the **Element** menu. To do this, select the object that you want to apply color to and open the **Fill and line. . .** menu as seen in Figure 10.5. Click on whichever item you want to modify and select the color from the pop-up menu.

▼ ***Figure 10.5. Applying Color Through the Fill and Line Dialog***

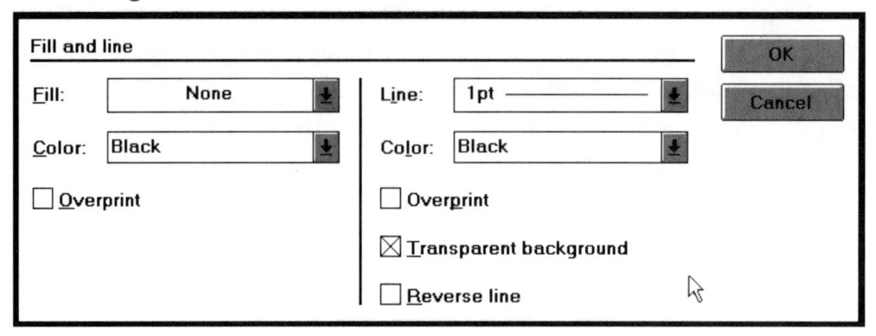

2. You can change text colors using the **Type specs** dialog box from the **Type** menu. To do this, select the text you want to apply color to with the **Pointer** tool and use the **Color:** menu found in the **Type specs** dialog box.

CHECK YOURSELF

1. In a new letter-sized PageMaker publication, type your name and make it 24 points in size. Then, with the **Colors** palette open, select your name with the **Text** tool and choose the color **Blue** from the palette by clicking on it. What happens?
   ▲ Your name is changed to blue.

2. Below your name, draw a rectangle and give it a solid fill. Click on the fill icon in the color palette and choose **Green** from the palette. What happens?
   ▲ The rectangle fills in with green.

3. Click on the rectangle with the **Pointer** tool to select it. Open up the **Line** dialog box in the **Element** menu and specify a 6-point frame. Now go to the **Colors** palette, click on the **Border** icon, then click on **Red.** What happens? (Leave the publication open for the next Check Yourself.)
   ▲ A wider border is added to the rectangle. It is red, not the standard black.

Applying Tints in PageMaker

Applying Tints in PageMaker

Sometimes you may want a lighter version of a color, but the shade is not directly available in a color matching system such as Pantone or Focoltone. There is a standard technique in the graphic arts for lightening solid colors that is supported by PageMaker. Instead of printing a solid color as specified in the swatch book, the color is broken down into tiny dots with a screen that allows some of the underlying paper to show through in print. The resulting color is lighter than the solid from which it is derived. This is called *tinting* (or *screening*) and can be easily applied inside PageMaker to almost any color.

The principle behind tinting is simple. By breaking the color into dots that allow some of the paper surrounding each dot to show through, the color appears lighter—just as if white had been added to it (the paper provides the white). Using smaller dots that allow more paper to show through creates a lighter color. Using larger dots that allow less paper to show through creates a darker color.

Tints are specified in percentages of the original color. A 10% tint creates a very light color that consists of 10% color and 90% white (paper color). A 90% tint produces a color that is 90% of the original color and 10% paper, creating a color that's almost as dark as the original color.

On-screen, PageMaker does not create dot patterns, so you won't be able to see the dots in your tinted colors until you print your document. On-screen, PageMaker mixes the "white" of the monitor with the specified color to create a rendering (or approximation) of the tinted color.

TIP

To learn more about tints and screens, study any daily newspaper that uses color. You will be able to see the screens (dots) easily because absorbent newsprint requires that large dots be used to make the screens. A magnifying glass will help if you have one.

Tints must be defined before you can use them, the same as any other color.

To define a tint:

1. Open the **Element** menu and choose **Define colors. . . .** Click on **New.**
2. Type a name in for the tint. This is the name that will also appear on the **Colors** palette, so you may want to give it something meaningful such as "50% Red."
3. For the **Type:** in the **Edit color** dialog box, click on **Tint.** The dialog box will change as seen in Figure 10.6.
4. Choose your **Base color**: from the drop-down menu. The color list will include any of the colors that you have already defined.
5. Next to **Tint:,** type in a percentage or use the slider to achieve the tint you desire. Remember, the color you see on your monitor will not be quite the same color you eventually will print. See the TIP below.
6. Click **OK** to save your selection, then **OK** again to close the dialog box.

The tint you have defined will appear on all your color lists and can be applied like any other color.

▼ ***Figure 10.6. The Tint Dialog***

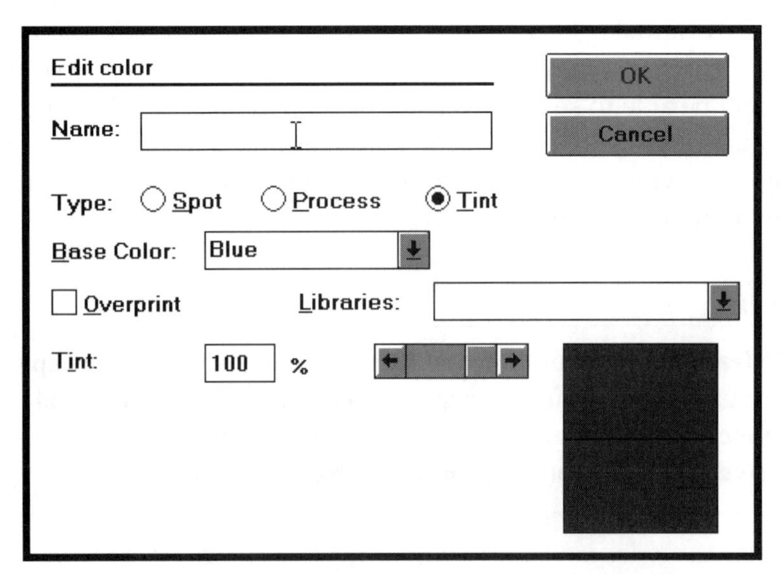

TIP

Pantone sells a color guide called the *Pantone Color Tint Selector* that shows what each of their colors look like with tints from 10% to 90%. This guide is expensive, but if you plan to print a lot of documents with tinted colors derived from solid Pantone colors, it is invaluable.

CHECK YOURSELF

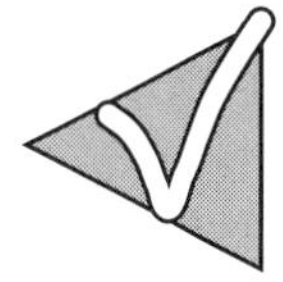

1. Use the publication from the last Check Yourself. Open the **Element** menu and click on **Define colors. . . .** Then choose **New. . .** to open the **Edit color** menu. Type in **50% Green** as the name, and select **Tint** as the type. Choose **Green** as the base color, then double-click on the tint percentage window and type in **25.** Notice that the color sample on the right of the dialog box changes to reflect the new settings. Click **OK** to save your new color, then exit the **Define colors** dialog box. Now click on the rectangle to select it, click on the **Fill** icon in the **Colors** palette, and, finally, find **25% Green** on the **Colors** palette and click on it. What happens?
   - ▲ The green assigned to the rectangle's fill changes to a pale green.

Layers and Layer Control

Though it's not immediately apparent from looking at a PageMaker layout on the desktop, objects in PageMaker documents exist in layers. To understand this, consider the possibility of looking at your layout sideways—you would be able to see that some objects exist on layers on top of other objects. This is called *Stacking Order* and refers to the way objects are in front (on top) or behind (on the bottom) of each layer. If you've worked with other page layout programs or drawing programs, then you are probably already familiar with the concept of layering. If not, we will explain it in this section. The reason layers are required is that

PageMaker objects may become opaque when they are filled with a color, so it is easy to add a shape in the layout that obscures another shape or text block. If all objects were transparent, then layers and layer control would not be required.

Figure 10.7 provides a simple example of layer control. It shows a large black box and a slightly smaller white box in PageMaker. When the black box is placed on top of the white box, it hides it completely. But, if you use PageMaker's layer control to send the black box behind the white box, then it only appears around the edges of the white box. At first this may seem confusing, but in this section's Check Yourself exercises, you will get to try it to better understand the concept.

To change an object's position on the layers, PageMaker provides a **Send to back** and a **Bring to front** command under the **Element** menu. By selecting an object or objects, you can send your selections behind other objects or bring them in front of other objects. Keep in mind that there are more layers than just a "front" or top layer and a "back" layer or bottom. You can pile objects on top of each other as deep as you need for a design.

▼ ***Figure 10.7. Layer Example with Boxes***

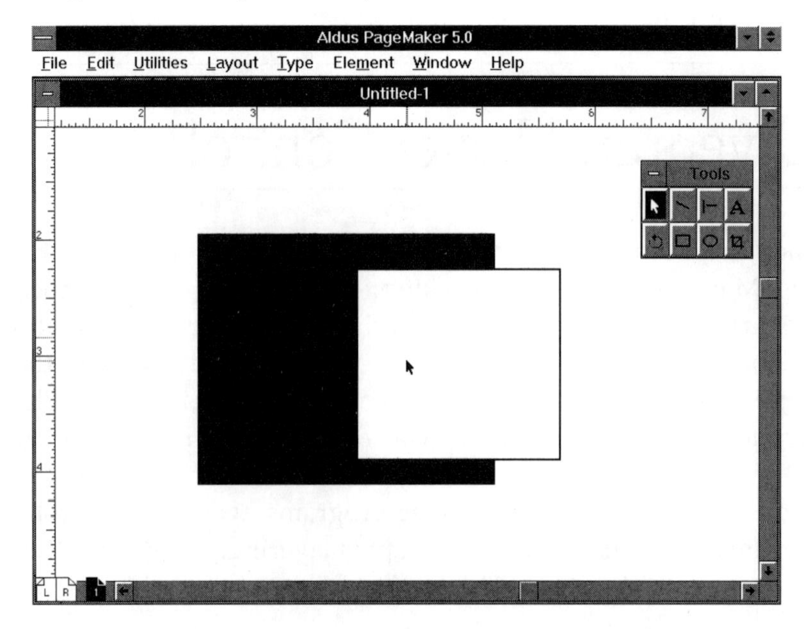

Layers and Layer Control

To reposition an object:

1. Select the object you want to move to an different layer. To move text, select the text block.
2. Choose **Bring to front** or **Send to back** from the **Element** menu. The object will be moved to the top layer (front) or the bottom layer (back) as appropriate.

Still confused? Think of layer control in terms of a hamburger on a bun with lettuce and tomato. If you look at an assembled hamburger from the top of the bun you can see the bun and a fringe of lettuce—you can't see through the bun to the meat or tomatoes unless they stick out the sides. To assemble the "layers" of a hamburger, you place the bottom of the bun into position, then, in order, put the meat, lettuce, and tomatoes in place, finally adding the top of the bun. Each element exists on its own layer, blocking the view of the other layers unless it is removed. PageMaker works the same way; each element exists on its own layer. To see the tomatoes, the top of the bun must be removed. Or, if you selected the tomatoes and use a **Bring to front** command (as in PageMaker), the tomatoes would suddenly appear on the top of the bun, creating a rather odd-looking hamburger. Though you'd never really do this, it gives you the idea.

When designing with PageMaker, particularly when you use color, the layers allow you to place objects in front or behind each other. For example, you can place type in a picture and position the type "in front" of the image so that it is not hidden by it. Keep in mind when working with objects, if you can't see it on your monitor because another object partially or completely blocks the view, the obstructed area will not print either. What you see on the screen is what you get.

CHECK YOURSELF

1. In a new letter-sized PageMaker document, create a 3" by 3" square, select a solid fill, and color the fill black. Then create a 2" by 2" square and fill it with blue. Place the small object on top of the large object. What happens?
   ▲ The blue object obscures the black object partially.

2. With the blue object still selected, choose **Send to back** from the **Element** menu. What happens?
   - ▲ The blue object is sent behind the black object and cannot be seen.
3. Select the black object and send it to the back layer with the **Send to back** command. Now, select the blue object and fill it with Paper instead of blue. What happens?
   - ▲ The blue object becomes white and you cannot see the black object.

QUICK COMMAND SUMMARY

Shortcut Keys	***Commands***	***Procedures***
(Window menu)		
Ctrl K	Colors palette	Shows the Colors palette
(Element menu)		
Alt E→D	Define colors...	Opens the Define colors dialog
Ctrl F	Bring to front	Moves the selected object to the front layer
Ctrl B	Send to back	Moves the selected object to the back layer

PRACTICE WHAT YOU'VE LEARNED

What You Do	***What You'll See***
1. Open a new letter-sized PageMaker publication.	1. A new window opens with a letter-sized document.
2. Open the **Define colors** dialog box by selecting it from the **Element** menu. Click the **New** button to open PageMaker's **Edit color** dialog box.	2. PageMaker's Define colors dialog box opens. When the New button is clicked, the Edit color dialog box opens.

What You Do	*What You'll See*
3. Select the Pantone Matching System from the pop-up menu. Choose the color **Pantone 190** by entering its number in the Pantone Number specification box above the sample swatch colors and pressing the **Enter** key. Click **OK** to return to the **Edit color** dialog.	3. The Pantone colors appear, and entering the color number scrolls the on-screen swatch book to the correct color. When OK is clicked, you are returned to the Define colors dialog box.
4. Click **New** again to define a second color.	4. Step 2 is repeated.
5. Choose **Pantone 291** and click **OK** to return to the **Edit color** dialog box.	5. Step 3 is repeated.
6. Click **OK** to close the box, then **OK** to exit **Define colors....** These two new colors will be added to PageMaker's **Colors** palette.	6. The Define colors dialog box is closed.
7. Enter the headline text **A Tale of Two Cities by Charles Dickens.** Set the type in **Times New Roman**, and scale the type to 70% using the **Set width...** command. Then increase the type's size to 36 point. Highlight the text with the **Text** tool and use the **Alignment** submenu under the **Type** menu, to center it.	7. The headline text is made narrower and larger. It is centered between the two margins.

What You Do	*What You'll See*
8. With the text still selected, use the **Colors** palette to color the type with **Pantone 291.**	8. The type color changes to a blue.
9. Select the **Rectangle** tool and draw a rectangle around your text. It should extend about 1" beyond the text on the top and bottom and be as wide as the margins. Select a solid fill and color it with **Pantone 190.**	9. The rectangle is colored lavender and blocks out the text.
10. With the rectangle selected, use the **Send to back** command to move it behind your headline text.	10. When the rectangle is moved to the back, the text is visible once again.
11. While the rectangle is still selected, use **Line. . .** from the **Element** menu to add a 6-point, triple line as a decorative border to the rectangle. Color it blue.	11. The outside edge of the text block is assigned a blue border.
12. Save your PageMaker document as MASTHEAD.	12. The **Save As** dialog box is used to save the document to disk.
13. Exit PageMaker without saving changes.	13. You are returned to the Windows desktop.

In this chapter you learned how to apply color and tint to objects on the PageMaker desktop. You also learned how to control layers so you can manipulate the view of type and objects on the layout. In the next chapter, you will learn to print PageMaker documents on a printer attached to your own computer. You will also learn how to have your PageMaker document's output on an imagesetter at high resolutions made suitable for reproduction at the print shop.

Printing PageMaker Documents

Now that you've explored all of PageMaker's basic functions and some of its advanced functions as well, it's time to learn how to print with PageMaker. Two kinds of printing are explained in this chapter: printing to a dot matrix or laser printer and printing to a high-resolution imagesetter. The latter option reproduces PageMaker documents on film at enough resolution that the document can be printed at a print shop. In this chapter you will learn how to:

- **Use PageMaker's Display Pub Info. . . command**
- **Set up documents for printing**
- **Print tiles of large documents**
- **Differentiate between straight output and PostScript output**
- **Understand desktop printing versus imagesetting**
- **Ready documents for imaging**
- **Prepare your files to bring to a service bureau for imaging**

The Display Pub Info. . . Command

When you prepare a document for printing, you should check to see what fonts you've used. Some fonts appear almost identical on-screen, but will look quite different when printed. If your document will be printed on another computer or if it will be output at a high resolution on an imagesetter (explained later in this chapter), you must make sure that the fonts you used in the document are available on the PC that drives the imagesetter. If they aren't, then the problem called *font substitution* occurs. If fonts are substituted, the machine chooses another font to replace the one that is missing. Rarely is this substitution acceptable, which usually means rerunning your document because the substituted font will mostly likely be slightly different in size. This reflows the text arbitrarily and creates other problems in the layout.

Fortunately, PageMaker includes a command that allows you to review the fonts used in your document. You can then use the Change. . . command to automatically replace undesirable fonts that may have been incorporated into your document accidentally. You may have thought that you had already manually replaced the occurrences of a particular font, but missed one used somewhere in your document. PageMaker lets you find these annoying problems.

The Display pub info. . . command opens the box shown in Figure 11.1. As you can see, there are three columns of data:

- The name of the font.
- Whether it appears in the current publication.
- Whether it is loaded on the system.

This information dialog is used to find fonts in your publication and on your system. To make use of this information, you also need to know which of the fonts is available on the target system. You can find this out by talking to the print shop you'll be using.

Once you have this information, the actual font substitution is accomplished using PageMaker's **Change** dialog box, which we briefly discussed in Chapter 5.

The Display Pub Info. . . Command

▼ ***Figure 11.1. The Pub Info Screen***

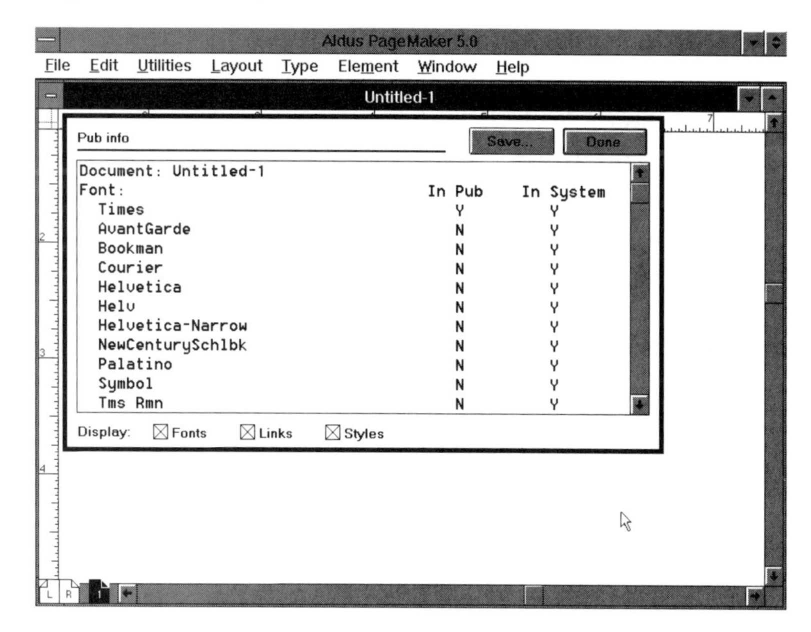

To use the dialog for font substitution:

1. Open your publication. Use the **Pointer** tool to select a story. Choose **Edit story** from the **Edit** menu (the **Change** dialog box is accessible *only* while in **Edit story).**
2. Open the **Utilities** menu and select **Change. . . .** When the dialog opens, click on **Attributes. . . .** The **Change attributes** dialog box in Figure 11.2 will appear.
3. Choose the font you want to find or replace with the **Font** menu under **Find.** Optional: Choose the size and/or style of

▼ ***Figure 11.2. The Change Attributes Dialog***

Change attributes
OK
Cancel

Find:
Para style: Any
Font: Any
Size: Any
Type style:
☒ Any ☐ Underline ☐ All caps
☐ Normal ☐ Strikethru ☐ Small caps
☐ Bold ☐ Reverse ☐ Superscript
☐ Italic ☐ Subscript

Change :
Para style: Any
Font: Any
Size: Any
Type style:
☒ Any ☐ Underline ☐ All caps
☐ Normal ☐ Strikethru ☐ Small caps
☐ Bold ☐ Reverse ☐ Superscript
☐ Italic ☐ Subscript

the font as well by clicking on any of the **Style** check boxes and/or selecting from the **Size** menu.

4. Choose the new font you want from the **Font** menu under **Change.** This font will replace whatever you have selected in the **Find** section. Choose the size and/or style of new font by clicking on the **Style** check boxes or using the **Size** menu. Click **OK.**
5. Click on either **Current publication** (the default) or **All publications** to select the scope of your search. If you select **Current publication,** you may choose to further limit your search to **Current story, All stories,** or **Selected text. All publications** will check every publication in the current book (we'll discuss books in the next chapter).
6. Click on the **Find** button and PageMaker will find the first occurrence of the font in the document. Once a match is found, you can either make the change manually by clicking the **Change** button, or replace all occurrences automatically by clicking **Change all**. If you clicked on the **Change** button, the specific occurrence of the font will be changed, and the **Find** button will be replaced by **Find next.**
7. To close this dialog, use the Windows **Close** command found in the dialog's **Control-menu** box.

CHECK YOURSELF

1. Enter the following text from *A Tale of Two Cities* in a new PageMaker document.

   The scene was Mr. Cruncher's private lodging in Hanging-sword-alley, Whitefriars; the time, half-past seven of the clock on a windy March morning, Anno Domini seventeen hundred and eighty. (Mr. Cruncher himself always spoke of the year of our Lord as Anna Dominoes: apparently under the impression that the Christian era dated from the invention of a popular game, by a lady who had bestowed her name upon it.)
   Mr. Cruncher's apartments were not in a savoury neighborhood, and were but two in number, even if a closet with a single pane of glass in it might be counted as one. But they were very decently kept. Early as it was, on the windy March morning, the room in which he lay a-bed was already scrubbed throughout; and between the cups and saucers arranged for

breakfast, and the lumbering deal table, a very clean white cloth was spread.

Select all of the text and export it in WordPerfect format. Name the file CRUNCHER.

2. Set the first paragraph as 14-point Italic Times New Roman. Set the second paragraph as 12-point Arial.
3. Open PageMaker's **Display pub info** in the **Additions** submenu. Look for Times New Roman and Arial fonts.
4. Use the **Pointer** tool and click anywhere in the text. Select **Edit story** from the **Edit** menu. Click at the beginning of the first paragraph to position the cursor. Choose **Change. . .** and then **Attributes.** In the **Font** box below **Find,** choose Times New Roman from the drop-down menu. Click on **Italic** in the **Type style** section.
5. In the **Change** section, choose **Arial** for the font. Click on the **Size** menu and select **12.** Then, click on **Normal** in the **Type style** section. Click **OK** and return to the **Change** dialog box. Make sure that **Current publication** and **Current story** are selected. Click **Find** then **Change.** Double-click the **Control-menu** box to close the **Change** dialog. Return to **Edit** layout. What do you see?

 ▲ The New Times Roman paragraph is selected when the Find button is clicked. When the Change command is clicked, it becomes 12-point Arial without Italics.

The Display Pub Info. . . Command

PostScript Output and Non-PostScript Output

When printing your files to a desktop printer, there are two kinds of output: PostScript and non-PostScript. PostScript is a "page description" language (developed by Adobe Systems) that tells a PostScript-compatible printer how to draw the contents of a page. PostScript issues commands to the printer such as , "Draw a .5 point line from point A to point B." This allows very flexible resizing of documents and resizing of type, because to change the size, new values are simply plugged into the page description and PostScript does the rest.

Non-PostScript printing sends a page description as a series of dots telling the printer, "Print a dot here, but don't print one there." This is a less elegant solution, because PageMaker objects print with more ragged edges than when PostScript output is sent to a PostScript printer. Unfortunately, most PostScript printers are more expensive than their non-PostScript counterparts; however, the superior output is well worth the added cost.

Which Kind of Printer Is Right for You?

If you plan to take your work into print via the imagesetter, you should use a PostScript printer for your own test output, even though the printer is a little more expensive. And though new page description languages are being developed by Microsoft and other notable companies, the fact remains that PostScript is the current standard in desktop publishing output. Because your documents will be imaged on a high-resolution printer driven with PostScript commands, test printing your documents on a non-PostScript printer may produce very different results than printing them on a PostScript printer. For that reason, a document that prints fine on an inexpensive ink jet printer or a non-PostScript laser printer, may come back from PostScript-based imagesetting full of problems and surprises.

If, on the other hand, your document will simply be photocopied, end in finished form on your computer's printer, or be printed at a quick printer's shop where quality is not much of an issue, then non-PostScript output should be adequate.

TrueType or Adobe Type Manager?

Another element that complicates the output issue for desktop publishers is the use of TrueType or Adobe Type Manager (ATM). These programs, when using compatible fonts, handle type much the way PostScript handles objects. (*Note:* You must use TrueType

PostScript Output and non-PostScript Output

fonts with TrueType and Adobe Type 1 fonts with Adobe Type Manager for the programs to have their intended effect in improving type output on your monitor.) Instead of a series of print-a-dot instructions, these programs tell the printer to draw a precision line to create the edges of type characters. This results in much cleaner-looking type that can be scaled (resized) by the programs automatically, just as PostScript can rescale lines and other page elements.

Again, both of these products are designed to draw a clean outline of fonts at almost any size (of course the outlines are automatically filled in by the printer). If you plan to finish documents on your printer, TrueType works just fine. However, if your documents will be imaged for print, most service bureaus who handle this kind of work use Adobe-compatible fonts, so TrueType will not be the optimum choice, even though TrueType and TrueType fonts are included with Windows. At this writing, for such work, you should use Adobe-compatible fonts and ATM to accurately render the fonts on your monitor. This situation will gradually ease as more and more service bureaus offer service for TrueType fonts—but for now the standard remains Adobe-compatible fonts and ATM at the service bureaus.

CHECK YOURSELF

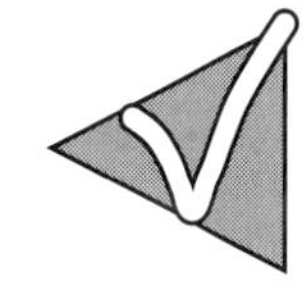

1. Is your printer PostScript-based or not?
   - ▲ Call your dealer if you're not sure. If you do need PostScript, some printers can be upgraded with a PostScript cartridge to allow it to run in PostScript mode.
2. Check your font collection. What fonts do you own that are TrueType compatible? Which do you own that are ATM compatible?
   - ▲ If you don't know, ask your dealer or a service bureau to help you find out.

Printing PageMaker Documents

Printing PageMaker documents is relatively easy. For basic letter-sized documents, you simply open the **File** menu, choose **Print...**, and click **OK.** PageMaker sends the file to your printer and that's all there is to it. Within the **Print** dialog box, you can specify the number of copies you would like, the range of pages to print (if you don't want to print the entire document), and if you are using a color printer, you can choose to print in color.

You can also choose to print a **Proof**, which prints all imported graphics as rectangles. This lets you get a quick look at the overall layout of the publication without having to endure the time it takes to print out graphics.

Print a Document

To print a document, you must make sure that a printer is selected and then set up the print parameters the way that you require for your document. Two dialog boxes directly control printing. The first is the **Print** dialog box found under the **File** menu and is shown in Figure 11.3. Depending on the type of printer you are using, different options may be available. It is within this dialog that you can set the range of pages you want to print (for a multipage document) and specify the number of copies to be made of each page.

The **Setup** dialog box shown in Figure 11.4 is accessed from the **Print** dialog box. Again, the options available here depend on the printer you have chosen. If this dialog looks vaguely familiar to you, that is because it is the same dialog you see when choosing **Setup. . .** from within the **Printers** dialog box from Windows' **Control Panel**.

Use this dialog to choose paper trays, select the orientation for paper passing through the printer, and other printer characteristics as appropriate.

▼ Figure 11.3. The Print Dialog

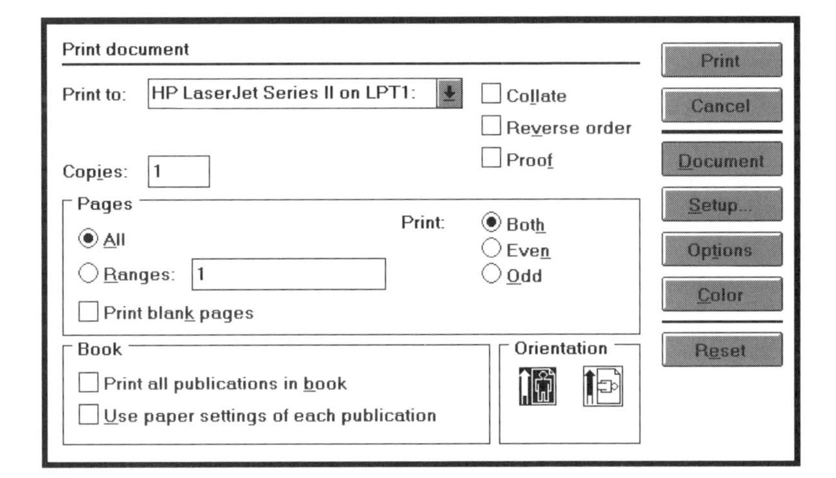

▼ Figure 11.4. PageMaker's Printer Setup Dialog

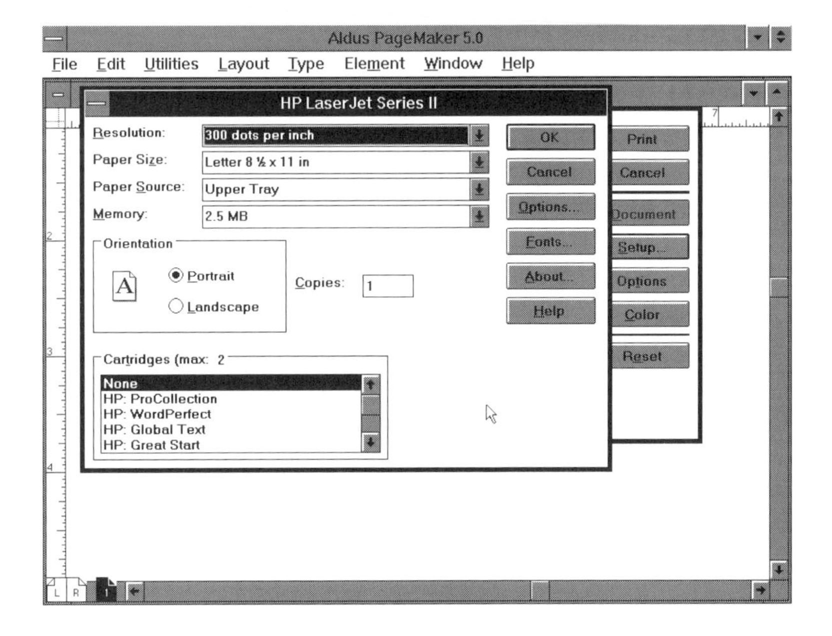

The Tiling Option Lets You Print Oversized Pages

If you are using a regular printer that handles only 8 1/2" by 11" paper, you can't fit larger documents onto one page of output. So, if you design an 11" by 17" poster, only the lower left of the document will print. PageMaker provides a way to work around this limitation. It will print the entire document in pieces—one section per page so that you can tape it back together to form a full-sized poster. Although this solution, called *tiling,* is not entirely elegant, the only alternative is to purchase a large format printer, which is expensive. If you are just proofing copies of the document, tiling should be an acceptable alternative.

To tile a document:

1. Open the **File** menu and choose **Print. . . .**
2. Select **Options. . . .** Click on the **Tile** check box. Choose either **Auto** or **Manual. Auto**, or automatic tiling, lets PageMaker determine the number of tiles to print after you have entered the desired overlap (the default is .65 inches). If you choose **Manual,** PageMaker will pause at each page and require you to position the zero point of the ruler where you want the upper left of the tile to begin.

Printing Thumbnails

The term *thumbnail* refers to a small drawing that shows the basic layout for a page or a document. By using thumbnails, the overall design of a publication can be viewed without having to print out a full sheet for each page. This helps the designer place design elements and make sequencing decisions. PageMaker allows you to print your publication as a series of thumbnail sketches with up to 100 thumbnails per page.

To print thumbnails:

1. Open the **File** menu and select **Print. . . .**

2. Click on **Options....** Choose **Thumbnails** and enter the number of thumbnails per page. Remember that the more thumbnails you specify, the smaller each one will be. More than 20 per page is very hard to see.
3. Click on the **Print** button to print the thumbnails.

Printing PostScript

As explained in the next section, you may want to print your file to disk as PostScript for imaging at a remote service bureau. To do this, open the **Print** dialog box and click the **Options** button. (You must have a PostScript compatible printer driver installed and selected to make this work.) The dialog shown in Figure 11.5 appears. Click on the **Write PostScript to File** and **EPS** options. Click on the box to the left of **Browse,** and fill in a filename for the Postscript publication. If you are not sure that the service bureau printer has all of the fonts needed for your publication, select **Include downloadable fonts.** This includes all of the needed fonts within the Postscript file. The file will be larger but ensures that you will not have font substitutions at print time. Finally, click on **Print** and the publication will be saved to disk as a file in the form of PostScript commands. Nothing will be output to your printer.

▼ ***Figure 11.5. Print PostScript File to Disk Option***

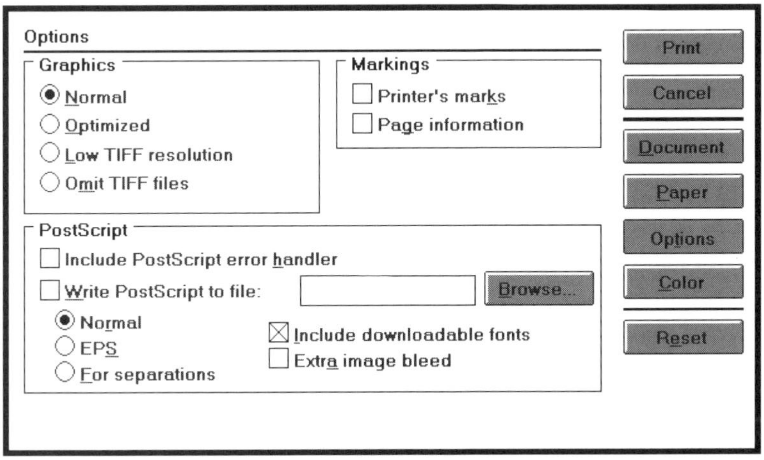

Keep in mind that PostScript files can be quite large, so make sure you have room on your hard drive, and avoid trying to save anything but the smallest document on a floppy disk. It probably won't have enough room and floppies take much longer to write to than a hard disk. If you save as PostScript and nothing seems to happen, remember that the process takes time—as much as half an hour for a large document with placed graphics. The flickering access light on your hard disk will tell you that the computer is still busy creating the file.

CHECK YOURSELF

1. With printer hooked up and turned on, start PageMaker and set up a new tabloid-sized document. Place the story CRUNCHER at the top of the publication. Place the story DICKENS at the bottom. Choose **Print. . .** from the **File** menu and click **OK.** What happens?
   - ▲ With Tiling turned off, only the lower left of the document prints.
2. Choose **Print. . .** again and then **Options.** Click on **Tile** and **Auto.** Now click on **Print.** What happens?
   - ▲ Four pages print out. Together they form the full tabloid-size publication.

Computer Printing Versus Imagesetting

For many kinds of projects, such as memos, reports, and forms, ordinary laser printing or ink jet output is adequate. But, if you design projects that will finish at the print shop instead of at the photocopier, higher resolution output will probably be required. To handle this chore, you will most likely work with a *service bureau.* A service bureau is (usually) a small company that owns a specialized piece of equipment called an *imagesetter,* which is a very high resolution laser printer. Most laser printers print at 300 dots per inch, but an imagesetter "images" up to 3,300 dots per inch, and it images on photographic paper or film rather than on the plain paper used in most desktop printers.

Computer Printing Versus Imagesetting

Where Can You Find Service Bureaus?

Service bureaus can be found in several places in the *Yellow Pages.* Look for them under *Typesetting, Desktop Publishing, Printing* (some print shops have in-house service bureaus), and *Color Separators.* If you work with other desktop publishers, they may be able to recommend a suitable imagesetter service bureau for your needs. The majority of service bureaus handle work created on the Apple Macintosh, but not all of them handle PC-based output. Although this is changing, you may need to call around to find a bureau that will accept PageMaker files directly from the PC. The good news is that your PageMaker for Windows files are directly translatable into PageMaker for the Macintosh files, so this really shouldn't be an issue for you. Thus, if you can't locate a company in town that offers direct PC-based imaging services at reasonable prices, another option is for you or the service bureau to convert your Windows-based files to Mac-compatible files.

TIP

If you absolutely can't find a bureau to accept your PageMaker for Windows files, save them as PostScript and have your bureau use the file on their Macintosh to set up and send the PostScript file to their imagesetter. Make sure that the bureau you choose understands how non-Macintosh PostScript files are converted to Macintosh files. It's easy to do, but not all bureaus understand the process.

What Should You Bring to a Service Bureau?

Almost nothing is more frustrating than driving across town with a file to be output at a service bureau, only to find that you are missing a key component that requires a trip back to the home or office so your document can be imaged. When taking PageMaker files to a service bureau, remember bring *all* of the following:

- ▲ The PageMaker-created page layout file in normal format or saved as a PostScript file (ask the bureaus what they prefer).
- ▲ A list of fonts, the name of the file to image, its page count and page size, and a list of placed graphics.
- ▲ A PostScript laser-printed proof of the file so that the service bureau can see what the output should look like.
- ▲ Your name, company, and phone number labeled on the disk in case there are problems.

When you get to the service bureau, discuss your output requirements with the imagesetter operator regarding image resolution and your choice of either photographic paper or slightly more expensive film for the output. The operator will let you know the best way to specify the output based on your printing requirements.

TIP

If you save your file as a PostScript file, it contains all the graphics and fonts imbedded in the file. You need not bring your graphic files or worry about the service bureau owning copies of the same fonts you used in the document. This is good news if you don't want to assemble a complex set of files. This is bad news if there is a problem with the output—because you will need to fix the file and resubmit it. If you let the service bureau have the files, they can often fix problems for you so you don't have to waste your time driving back and forth. (Of course, there is a charge for this service, but almost everything in life is a trade-off between time and money.)

Three Ways to Send a File to a Service Bureau

There are alternatives to driving to the bureau to image your PageMaker file, including:

Computer Printing Versus Imagesetting

1. Choose a service bureau that offers pickup and delivery. In most cities, larger bureaus offer this service and it's usually free or offered at a nominal fee unless your office is out of town.
2. Send your file by modem. Almost all bureaus accept files this way and may have a dedicated bulletin board system (usually on a Macintosh) for such needs. Use a fast modem—at least 2400 baud. 300 or 1200 baud is much too slow, particularly if scanned images are involved.
3. Use an overnight shipping service. If your bureau is distant (say in another city), use an overnight shipping service to send the job. Though it costs between $20 to $45 round-trip, consider this part of the project's budget.

What If It Won't Fit on a Floppy Disk?

If you plan to send a file to a bureau on floppy disk and the file is too large to fit (a common occurrence), here are three alternatives for transmitting large files in addition to using the modem transfer method we just mentioned:

1. Use compression software to make the file more compact. A variety of programs are available for this purpose, including some free and shareware programs. Make sure your service bureau has access to the same program so that they can restore your file.
2. Use a hard disk backup program to break the file into pieces to fit on multiple disks. Make sure your service bureau has access to the same program so that they can restore your file.
3. Purchase a tape backup drive, cartridge drive, optical drive, or other removable storage medium that handles large files. Again, this media must be readable by your service bureau, but most bureaus own several removable media devices for this purpose. Remember that color document files can take up a hundred megabytes of storage. Some type of transportable mass storage option is a definite requirement if you are going to be designing complex color documents with PageMaker—and since PageMaker is so capable in this regard, you will probably want to do just that.

CHECK YOURSELF

1. What are the two main differences between a laser printer and an imagesetter?
   - ▲ A laser printer prints at 300 dpi and prints to plain paper. An imagesetter images at 1,200 to 3,300 dpi and prints to photographic paper or film suitable for reproduction at a print shop.
2. If you save a PageMaker file as PostScript, do you need to bring files for the graphics placed in the document to the service bureau?
   - ▲ No, they are embedded into the PostScript file.

QUICK COMMAND SUMMARY

Shortcut Keys	*Commands*	*Procedures*
(Edit menu)		
Ctrl E	Story editor	Enter story editor mode
Ctrl 9	Change...	While in story editor, change fonts, attributes, styles
(File menu)		
Ctrl P	Print...	Controls printing of a publication

PRACTICE WHAT YOU'VE LEARNED

What You Do	*What You'll See*
1. Open a new PageMaker document.	1. A new window opens with a letter-sized document.
2. Import and place DICKENS.WP5 into it. Set the font to **Times New Roman** and make it **14 points** in size. Use the **Pointer** tool to click anywhere in the text.	2. The text from the previously created file is placed in the new publication.

What You Do	*What You'll See*
3. Go to **Edit story** mode. Use the **Change. . .** command to change the type from **14-point Times New Roman** to **12-point small caps**. Click **OK** when finished.	3. The type becomes 12-point small caps.
4. Use the **Change. . .** command to change the type to **14-point Arial.**	4. The type changes to 14-point Arial.
5. Use the **Change. . .** command to change the type to "normal" 8-point type. To do this, click on **Normal** in the **Type style** section under **Change.** Close the **Change** dialog box using the Windows **Close** command found in the dialog's **Control-menu** box and return to **Edit layout** mode.	5. The type becomes plain (no style) 8-point type that is barely readable on your monitor. The dialog is closed after Close is selected.
6. With a printer connected and ready, open the **Print** dialog box using the **Print. . .** command. Select **Options** and click on **Thumbnails.** Click on the **Print** button.	6. A miniature of the page is printed on your printer.
7. Exit PageMaker without saving changes and return to Windows.	7. PageMaker returns you to Windows.

WHAT IF IT DOESN'T WORK?

6. If you can't print to your printer, make sure it's connected, has paper, and is powered up. If you still can't print, make sure that it has been selected as your printer with the Windows Setup routine. You may need to load another printer driver from one of the Windows master disks. If you have problems, call your dealer for help.

In this chapter, you have learned how to print PageMaker documents of all sizes and how to produce high-resolution PageMaker documents at a service bureau. In the next chapter, you will learn to work with PageMaker's tools for streamlining the assembly of multiple-page layouts.

Organizing Large Projects

PageMaker provides tools for effectively handling the complexities of working with print projects up to several hundred pages. With PageMaker you can define default layouts, or *master pages*, link publications together to form *books,* create comprehensive indexes, and/or generate tables of contents. With these facilities, the process of designing and implementing a long project is dramatically shortened. In this chapter you will learn how to:

- **Link publications to form books**
- **Define and add text and graphics to master pages**
- **Add automatic page numbering to publications and books**
- **Create facing master pages**
- **Create indexes**
- **Use Styles to generate a table of contents**

Publications and Books

PageMaker refers to a single desktop publishing file as a *publication.* Often a publication stands alone, as in a one-page flyer or newsletter. Other times, the publication may be one part of a larger project, such as a book or a multipage pamphlet. It is convenient and more efficient to break up these large projects into smaller parts, such as chapters. All of the parts can be worked on simultaneously and later be consolidated to form the finished work.

Creating a Book

PageMaker has the ability to link separate publications together to form a *book.* Once the publications are *booked,* you have the option of treating the book as a single entity when you perform certain operations such as page numbering, indexing, or search and replace. Or, you can still treat each chapter as a separate publication to do editing work.

To link publications:

1. Open any of the publications you wish to link.
2. Open the **File** menu and select **Book. . . .** The dialog box shown in Figure 12.1 appears.
3. Double-click on the names of the publications that you want to become part of the book. As you pick publications (they can be anywhere on your disk), their names appear in the *book list* on the right of the dialog. The order of names on the list determines the order in which operations on the book will be performed. If you don't assemble the list in the correct order at first, you can later use the **Move up** and **Move down** buttons to rearrange entries.
4. Once you have selected all of the publications, choose one of the **Auto renumbering** styles:

   ▲ **None**—No renumbering. Each publication will retain whatever page numbering was assigned to it when it was written.

Publications and Books

▼ *Figure 12.1. The Book Dialog*

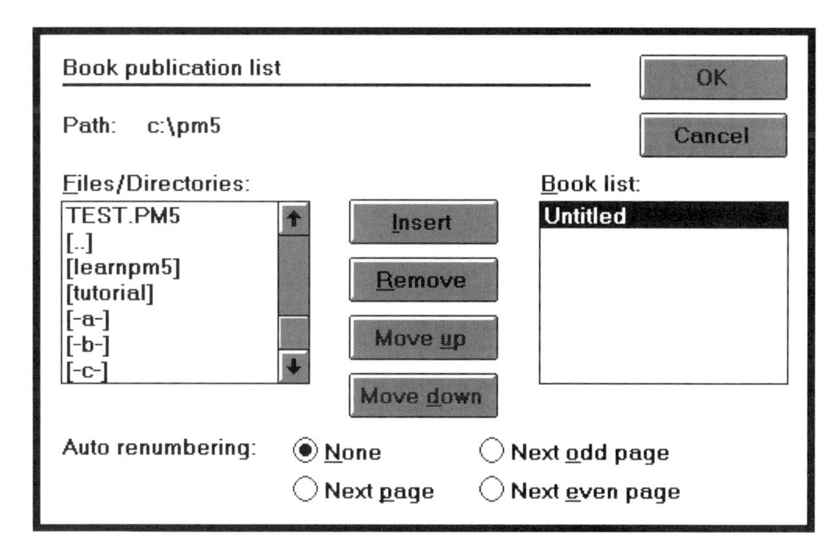

- ▲ **Next page**—Page numbering starts with the first page of the first publication and runs consecutively through all publications.
- ▲ **Next odd page**—Page numbering starts with the first publication. Each new publication is forced to start on an odd-numbered (right-hand) page. If necessary, PageMaker pads the document with a blank page.
- ▲ **Next even page**—Same as above except each publication is forced to begin on an even-numbered (left-hand) page.

Note: You can override the automatic renumbering by clicking on **Restart page numbering** in the **Page setup** dialog box of any of the publications on the book list. This will cause the page numbering for that publication to start with page 1.

5. Click on **OK** to close the dialog. To transfer the book list you have just built to all publications on the list, hold down the **Ctrl** (control) key and again choose **Book** from the **File** menu. PageMaker will indicate that it is passing the book list information on to all the linked publications.

Using Master Pages

When assembling documents consisting of multiple pages, you can save yourself time by using PageMaker's master pages. Master pages let you develop a template for your publication; elements that will appear on every page—such as page numbers, ruler guides, borders, or graphics—need only be defined once. They will then appear automatically each time you add a new page to your publication. Of course, you can reposition or delete them from any page if you wish. This automatic assembly using master pages speeds document production significantly. It is especially useful in documents such as manuals, which have a somewhat rigid format.

The difference between master pages and regular pages in your PageMaker document is that anything found on a master page is automatically applied to every page in your publication. For example, if you place a copy of your company's logo on a master page, it will appear on all pages of your document unless you explicitly exclude it. Another important difference between master pages and regular pages is that the master pages themselves don't print.

Single Master Pages or Facing Master Pages?

Two kinds of master pages are available to you in PageMaker. The first kind is a single page that allows you to define master templates for single-page documents or documents that do not have facing pages.

The second kind of master pages are those that are defined for documents with facing pages. **Facing pages** is an option only if you have checked **Double-sided** in the **New** or **Page setup** dialogs. With **Facing pages**, two pages face each other so that you can work on two pages side-by-side just like the two open pages you are looking at now in this book. Using facing pages master page allows you to set up a two-page spread with elements that jump from one page to the other, which is not possible with a single master page.

Creating a Master Page

Using Master Pages

When you set up a publication in the **New** dialog box, PageMaker automatically creates one or two master pages. They appear as the page icons located on the far left of your desktop and are labeled "L" and "R," as shown in Figure 12.2.

To add elements to a master page, use any and all of PageMaker's tools just as you would on regular pages. You can add type for a page heading, logos, and other graphics. You can also set up default graphics boxes that you plan to use throughout your document. That way, no matter how long your document is, you need only draw the boxes once whether designing a 16-page brochure or a 450-page book.

To add elements to a master page:

1. Click on the left master page icon. The master page will then become the current page and its icon will be highlighted.
2. Add elements or make changes to the master page as if the page was an actual PageMaker document.
3. To put the page away (and save your changes), click on any other page icon.

▼ ***Figure 12.2. The Master Pages***

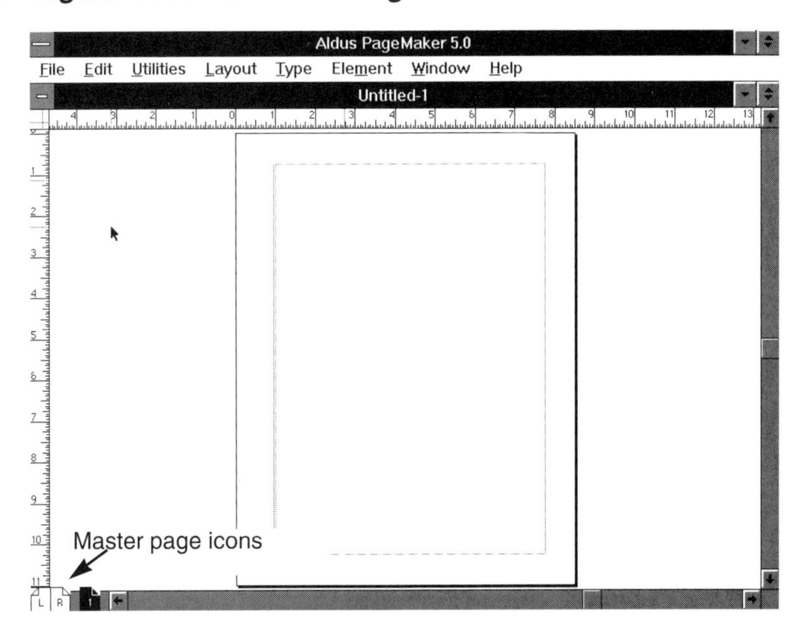

Adding Automatic Page Numbering to Master Pages

You can add page numbering to master pages by placing *page-number markers* on the master pages. Pages created from this master page will automatically be numbered. This method is superior to manually adding page numbers one at a time. Using automatic numbering, the page-number sequence is correctly modified each time you add or delete pages. Plus, in a long document, adding page numbering manually wastes time that could be better used for some more creative aspect of the design process.

If your publications are destined to become part of a book, they all must have page numbering defined. Even if you have set **Auto renumbering** in the **Book** dialog box, the numbers will only print for those publications that have page numbering assigned on their master pages.

To add automatic page numbering to a master page:

1. Click on the master page icon.
2. Use the **Text** tool and position an insertion point where you want the page number to appear. The font and size of the printed page numbers will be whatever is current at the time you define the page-number markers.
3. Press **Ctrl Shift 3** to create a page-number marker.
4. The marker will appear on the master page as either "RM" or "LM."

TIP

Although every design rule is meant to be broken, you will usually want to size your page numbers about one-third smaller than the text that will be placed on the page so that they are less noticeable (unless the page numbers are being used as a design element for some reason). Setting page numbers as Italics works well in most documents, and the thinner lines that make up an Italic typeface further lighten the page number to make it less noticeable.

Selecting a Page-Number Format

Using Master Pages

In Chapter 2 we breezed by the **Page numbering** dialog box found in the **New** dialog of the **File** menu; now we'll return to it. The dialog appears as in Figure 12.3. As you can see, there are a wide variety of formats. Clicking on one of the selections darkens the circle at its left. Clicking on the **OK** button will save your selections and return you to the Windows prompt. Your selection affects only the current publication. Other publications, even within the same book, can have different formats.

Frequently, a long document is composed of several sections with different page numbering schemes for each section. For example, this book contains title pages and other front matter that use a different page numbering scheme than the rest of the book. Each section can easily be assigned its own numbering format: roman numerals, arabic, or even a combination a prefix and a number, such as in an appendix.

To add a prefix to page numbering:

1. Click on the master page icon for the publication.
2. Type in the desired prefix before the page-number marker on each master page.
3. Open the **File** menu, choose **Page setup. . .**, then select **Numbers. . . .**
4. Type the page-number prefix in the **TOC and index prefix:** field.
5. Click **OK** to save the new prefix.

▼ ***Figure 12.3 The Page Numbering Dialog Box***

Page numbering

OK

Cancel

Style: ◉ Arabic numeral 1, 2, 3, ...

○ Upper Roman I, II, III, ...

○ Lower Roman i, ii, iii, ...

○ Upper alphabetic A, B, C, ... AA, BB, CC, ...

○ Lower alphabetic a, b, c, ... aa, bb, cc, ...

TOC and index prefix:

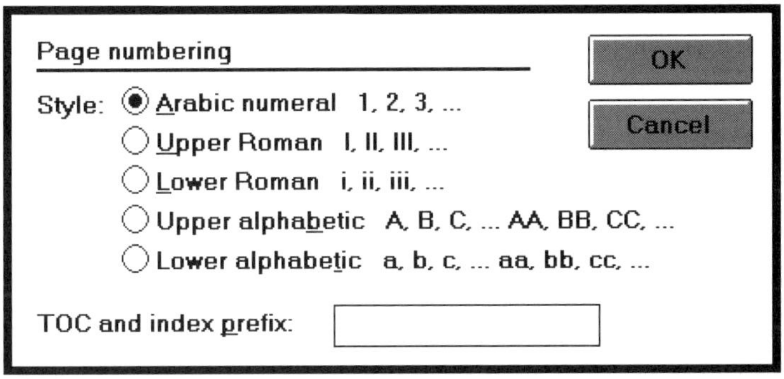

CHECK YOURSELF

1. Create a new four-page letter-sized publication in PageMaker and open the master page by clicking on its icon at the bottom left of your desktop. Enter your name near the top left margin of the right-hand master page. Now click on the page icon for page 1. What do you see?
   ▲ Your name now appears in the upper left of page 1.
2. Click on the master page icon again. Go to the bottom of the left page. Select the **Text** tool and position an insertion point below the bottom margin and use the space bar to move it about halfway across the page. Press **Ctrl Shift 3.** Do the same thing for the right-hand page. What do you see?
   ▲ The letters "RM" appear below the right-hand margin and "LM" below the left margin of the master page.
3. Click on the page icon for page 2 and go to the bottom of the page. What do you see?
   ▲ The automatic page number shows that the page is now numbered 2.
4. Exit PageMaker without saving.
   ▲ You are returned to the Windows desktop.

Indexing a Publication or a Book

There is no way of getting around it: Indexing is one of the most tedious tasks associated with producing a book. At the same time, a book with no index or a poor index is invariably a frustrating experience for the reader. PageMaker takes much of the pain out of generating indexes by supplying tools to help construct everything from a simple keyword index to an in-depth directory of your book. Whatever type of index you intend to use, the concepts are the same.

An entry in an index is composed of two parts: the topic and the reference, which points to a page number or a cross-reference to another topic. Topics can be nested up to three deep as seen in Figure 12.4. When you define an index entry, an *index marker* is

▼ ***Figure 12.4. Nested Topics***

Story editor 35-41
    display font 37
    displaying
        nonprinting characters 363
        style names 59, 363
    editing text in 190

Indexing a Publication or a Book

placed in your text just before the text you indexed. The marker is anchored to the position on the page and moves as you add and delete text from your story. The marker is not, however, attached to the original text; if you delete the text from the page, the marker will remain. The marker itself is only visible while in **Edit story** mode; it cannot be viewed in **Layout** mode.

To index a single term:

1. Highlight the word or phrase you want indexed.
2. Click on **Index entry...** from the **Utilities** menu to open up the dialog shown in Figure 12.5. You can also use the shortcut keys **Ctrl ;** to get to the **Index entry** dialog box after highlighting the text.
3. The text you highlighted appears under **Topic.** If you want this text to be indexed under a different topic, backspace over your text, type in the new topic, and click on **OK** to add this to the index.

You'll notice that three fields appear below **Topic** in the **Index entry** dialog box. Recall that PageMaker allows indexes up to three levels. When you first highlight text and move to the **Index entry** dialog, your text is placed on the first line of the topic field. This corresponds to the first level of topics. To move a topic down a level, click on the arrow icon between **Topic** and **Sort.** The text will be moved down to the second level. Click once more and your topic will drop to the third level. You can now use the mouse to click on the empty fields on the first and second levels and enter new topics.

Once you define a topic, it can be recalled to index other entries. In the **Index entry** dialog, click on the **Topic** button and you are brought to the **Select topic** dialog shown in Figure 12.6. Clicking on the arrow next to **Topic section** drops down a menu of

▼ ***Figure 12.5. The Index Entry Dialog Box***

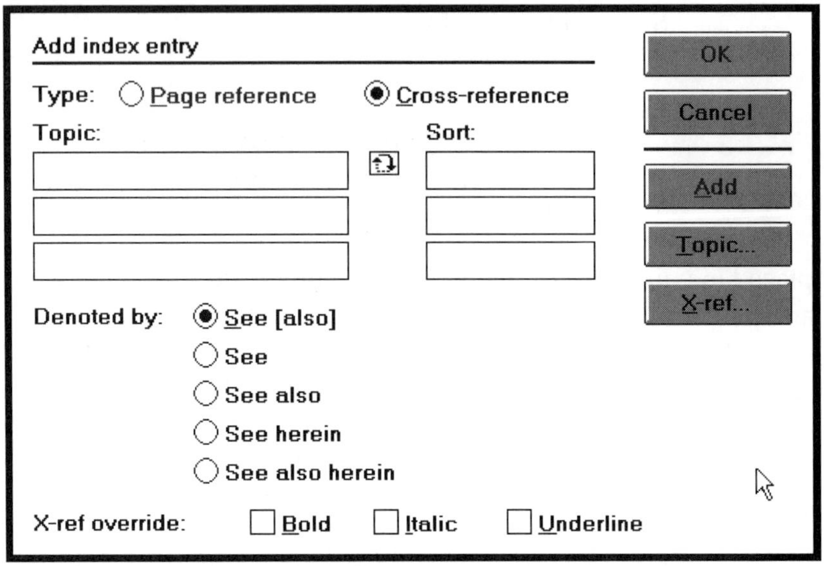

the alphabet. Selecting a letter brings up a listing of all the topics starting with that letter. Click on a topic and it will appear in the fields in the upper half of the dialog box.

▼ ***Figure 12.6. The Select Topic Dialog***

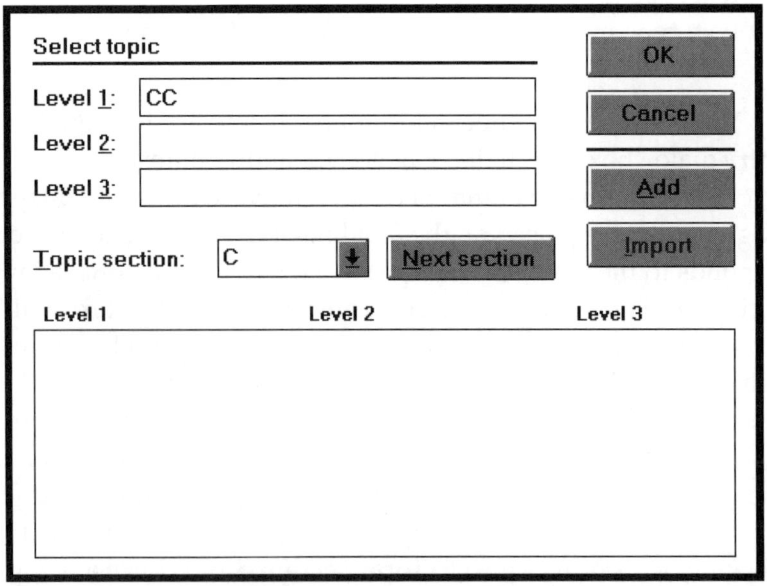

Indexing a Publication or a Book

If you want each occurrence of a particular word or phrase to appear in the index, you can achieve this *keyword* indexing through the **Change** dialog box in the **Utilities** menu.

To perform keyword indexing:

1. Go to beginning of your publication.
2. Open the **Utilities** menu and select **Change. . . .**
3. Type the word or phrase you want indexed in the **Find what:** field.
4. In the **Change to:** field enter "^;" (caret 1 semicolon).
5. If you want to index only occurrences in your current publication, click on **Current publication.** If you want all instances throughout the book to be indexed, click on **All publications.**
6. Click on **Change all** to index all entries of the word or phrase.

Generating the Index

After all the index entries have been specified, you need to actually compile and generate the index. From the **Utilities** menu, select **Create index**. PageMaker asks if you want to overwrite the previous index, if there is one. PageMaker will run through all publications on the book list, repaginate publications, compile index entries for each publication, reconcile duplicate entries, alphabetize the entries, and finally produce the index as a new story. The index will appear on-screen, and you then select **Close** from the **Control-menu** box. If the index has never before been generated, a dialog box will pop up and tell you that the story has not been placed. Click on the **Place** button and you'll be returned to the Layout view window with a loaded text icon containing the index. Go to the last page in your publication or book and place the index as you would any other text. If you have previously generated and placed the index, PageMaker will automatically update it.

Because an index requires accurate pagination, generation or regeneration of an index should be the last operation you perform on a book. If you generate an index and then add or delete text, your old index will most likely be inaccurate. Even worse than no index is one that has incorrect page numbers.

Table of Contents

Like an index, a table of contents is painful to do but essential to a book. Fortunately, PageMaker makes the process somewhat less difficult for all but the most complex documents.

The most effective strategy is to decide beforehand what will go into the table of contents. A reasonable choice is chapter titles, headings, and subheadings. Using the **Style** dialog box, a style is defined for each of these paragraphs that automatically adds the text to the table of contents each time the style is used.

To use styles for tables of contents:

1. Select **Define styles...** from the **Type** menu.
2. Click on **New** in the initial dialog box. Name the new style something descriptive such as "CHAPTER HEADING."
3. Click on **Para...** to review the paragraph options.
4. Click on **Include in table of contents.**
5. Click on **OK to close the dialog.**

Now, whenever the new style is applied to text, that text will automatically be included when you generate a table of contents. To actually generate the table of contents, use the **Utilities** menu and select **Create TOC**. By default, page numbers appear at the right-hand margin preceded by a row of dots known as a *dot leader*. Like the index, the table of contents will be generated as a story and can be placed anywhere in the book.

PageMaker's Change Command

PageMaker provides a powerful search and replace function that allows you to search for text based on word content, font, style, and font size. This facility is called **Change...** and is found under the **Utilities** menu only while in **Edit story** mode.

The **Change...** command works like the Find/Replace command found in most word processors with the additional power of supporting searches based on font and style information, which only the most powerful microcomputer-based word processors can handle. This command's power is based in its ability to initiate a search at almost any level of detail. It is equally adept at a search for only one component, such as a single word found in one story regardless of font and case (capitalization) or a search across an entire book for a sentence set in a particular font and style that should be replaced with a new sentence in a different font and style.

PageMaker's Change Command

Searching and Replacing Text

Change... allows you to quickly search for a single word, phrase, or sentence. Once found, you can either make manual changes to the text or automatically replace it with a new string of text. As shown in Figure 12.7, when you first open the **Change** dialog box, it looks much like the kind of dialog you would expect in an ordinary word processor's Find... command.

To search and replace text:

1. Open the **Change** dialog box by selecting the **Change...** command under the **Edit** pull-down menu. Enter the text for which to search in the **Find what:** field. If you want the command to replace the **Find what** text with a new word, phrase, or sentence, enter the replacement information in the **Change to:** field.

▼ ***Figure 12.7. The Change Dialog***

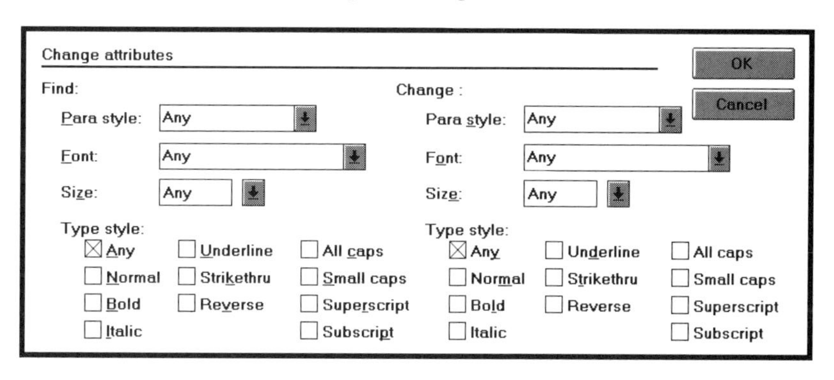

2. Set the scope of your search. By default, **Current publication** is checked. You then can choose to search either the **Current story** in the publication (the default) or **All stories.** Alternatively, clicking on **All publications** searches all stories in all publications linked via the current book list. When **Whole word** is selected, PageMaker will only find occurrences where it can match the entire word with a space on each side. If **Whole word** is not selected, PageMaker will match your text with matches inside of longer words or phrases. Last, when **Match case** is selected, PageMaker matches exact punctuation and case. If not selected, PageMaker matches words and phrases regardless of capitalization.
3. To start the search, click the **Find** button. If no matches are found, PageMaker beeps (on most machines). If a match is found, the **Change** buttons become active. You can make the change, change and find the next occurrence, change all occurrences in the entire document (**Change All**), or skip and find the next occurrence (**Find next**).

TIP

Beware of using the Change All button, particularly in a long document where it's difficult to track exactly what gets changed and what doesn't. For example, if you change all occurrences of a phrase using Change All, you may introduce a rash of hard to find errors that only a careful proofreading session will detect.

Using the Attribute Controls in a Search

The attribute controls are used to add font, font size, and style restrictions to your search. By clicking on the **Attribute** button, a second dialog box opens up as seen in Figure 12.8. These options are not in operation until you check the associated check boxes or fill in the fields to activate the **Para style, Font, Size,** and **Type style** controls for both the **Find what** and **Change to** portions of the dialog.

Searching and Replacing Text

▼ *Figure 12.8 The Attribute Dialog Box*

Change attributes

OK

Cancel

Find:
Para style: Any
Font: Any
Size: Any
Type style:
☒ Any ☐ Underline ☐ All caps
☐ Normal ☐ Strikethru ☐ Small caps
☐ Bold ☐ Reverse ☐ Superscript
☐ Italic ☐ Subscript

Change :
Para style: Any
Font: Any
Size: Any
Type style:
☒ Any ☐ Underline ☐ All caps
☐ Normal ☐ Strikethru ☐ Small caps
☐ Bold ☐ Reverse ☐ Superscript
☐ Italic ☐ Subscript

In addition to finding fonts and styles, you can also combine a search for text and text strings at the same time. The **Change attributes** dialog requires that you carefully adjust *all* of the settings. This process adds power to PageMaker's search and replace capability, because it allows you to specify very precise sets of parameters for the search and replacement criteria.

To set attribute controls:

1. Open the **Change** dialog box and click on the **Attributes** button. This will open the dialog box to reveal the attribute controls.
2. Choose the individual attributes you want to use in your search for **Para style, Font, Size,** and **Type style** by clicking on the check boxes, filling in the fields, or selecting from the drop-down menus. When you are done, click on **OK** to close the dialog box.
3. Click **Find** to initiate the search. Remember to adjust the scope of your search as described in the last section.
4. To close this box, double-click the Windows **Control-menu** box.

TIP

You don't need to search for text with the Change dialog. You can use the Para style, Font, Size, and Type style controls without any text entered to change only those specifications wherever they are found, regardless of the text with which they are associated. To skip the text search, leave the Find what: **field empty on the main** Change. . . **screen.**

Mix and Match

One of the most useful aspects of PageMaker's **Change** dialog is that you can mix and match controls to hone your search parameters right down to a single word used repetitively in a long document that has a specific style applied. For example, you can search for all occurrences of your company's name set as Times New Roman with the **Find what** half of the dialog. Then you can set the dialog to change the text to 14-point Bold Arial. You need only set the controls of the dialog to perform a search and replace operation that meets your criteria exactly.

QUICK COMMAND SUMMARY

Shortcut Keys	*Commands*	*Procedures*
Ctrl E		Toggles between Layout and story editor mode
Ctrl Shift 3		Automatic page numbering
(File menu)		
Alt F→B	Book	Links publications to form a book

PRACTICE WHAT YOU'VE LEARNED

What You Do	*What You'll See*
1. Create a new four-page, letter-sized document in PageMaker with the **Facing pages** option turned off.	1. A new window opens with a letter-sized document.
2. Open the master page by clicking on its icon.	2. The master page appears.
3. In the new master page, type **A Tale of Two Cities** in a small font and place it in the upper left-hand corner.	3. The text appears above the left margin.

What You Do	*What You'll See*
4. At the bottom of the page, enter **Ctrl Shift 3** to add page numbering to the publication.	4. The page-number marker appears at the bottom of the master page.
5. Click on the icon for page 1. Place DICKENS2.WP5 on page 1.	5. The text from DICK-ENS.WP5 is flowed onto page 1.
6. Click on the icon for page 2. Place CRUNCHER.WP5 on page 2.	6. The text from CRUNCH-ER.WP5 appears on page 2.
7. Go back to page 1. Use the **Text** tool and double-click on the word **king** in the first sentence of the second paragraph to highlight it.	7. The word king is highlighted.
8. Select **Index Entry...** from the **Utilities** menu. The word king appears on the top line. Click on the arrows icon between **Sort** and **Topic** to move king to the second line. Type **rulers** on the first line. Click **OK** to close the dialog.	8. King is moved to the second line, and rulers is typed in the first field.
9. Repeat step 9 for the word **queen** in the same sentence.	9. Queen is moved to the second line, and rulers is typed in the first field.
10. Select **Create index** from the **Utilities** menu. Click on **OK** to generate the index. When the index has been created, go to page 4 and place the loaded text icon.	10. After Create index is run, the load text icon appears. When the icon is moved to page 3 and the text placed, the index appears. There is only one topic, rulers, with two topics below it, king and queen.

What You Do	***What You'll See***
11. Go to page 2 and highlight **Whitefriars** in the first sentence of the first paragraph. Press **Ctrl ;** to open the **Index entry** dialog. Click **OK** to add this entry to the index and close the dialog box.	11. Whitefriars is added as an index entry.
12. Select **Create index**, then click on **OK** to update the index.	12. After the index is generated, you are moved to page 3. The index has been updated and the entry for Whitefriars appears.
13. Return to page 1. Use the **Text** tool and click on the first page to position the insertion point. Press **Ctrl E** to toggle into story mode.	13. The program shifts into Edit story mode.
14. Select **Change...** from the **Utilities** menu.	14. The Change dialog box opens.
15. Click on the **Attributes** button. Now click on **Normal** in the **Find what**: section and **Small caps** in the **Change:** section. Click **OK** to save and close the **Attributes** dialog box.	15. The Normal box in the **Find:** section is checked, as is the **Small caps** box in the **Change:** section.
16. Check that the scope of the search is set to **Current Publication** or **Current Story** and click on **Change All**. Remember, fonts are not visible in story edit mode.	16. The scope of the search should be set to **Current publication** and **Current story.**

What You Do	*What You'll See*
17. Use **Ctrl E** to toggle back into **Layout** mode and examine page 1. Now go to page 2 and look at it.	17. All of page 1 has been reset in small caps. Page 2 is unaffected because it is a separate story and the scope of the change was set to **Current story.**
18. Switch into **Edit story** mode and select the **Change** dialog. Click on **Attributes.** Make sure **Normal** is still checked in the **Type style** section of **Find what:** Change the **Type style** of the **Change:** section to **All caps.** Click **OK** to close the dialog. Change the scope of the search from **Current story** to **All stories.** Click on **Change all**.	18. The check boxes in the **Attributes** dialog are changed.
19. Double-click on the **Control-Menu** box to close the dialog. Go back to **Layout** mode and examine pages 1 through 4.	19. Page 1 is not changed because the **Find** criteria specified normal text and page was formatted with small caps. Page 2 is changed to all caps as is the index, which is treated the same as any other story.
20. Exit PageMaker without saving.	20. You are returned to the Windows desktop.

In this chapter you learned how to link publications to form a book and how to use PageMaker's master pages to speed the assembly of multipage documents. You have also revisited the Change command and seen how it can be a powerful tool to make changes to lengthy projects. In the next chapter you will put all of the lessons together to produce a small newsletter.

Putting It All Together

In this chapter, you will have an opportunity to put your newly gained PageMaker skills to work. You will create a simple newsletter that combines a number of the PageMaker operations you have learned in the book. The material for creating the newsletter was assembled in the previous chapters and should already be saved on your hard disk. If you skipped any chapters, each time one of the newsletter components is introduced we will indicate in which chapter it was created so that you can go back and assemble the required file. In this chapter you will learn how to:

- **Assemble guides for a publication**
- **Import multiple files and place them**
- **Mix text and graphic objects on a page**
- **Add decorative lines to enhance a publication**
- **Save the publication as a template**

About This Chapter

This chapter will be different to work through than the previous 12 chapters. Because you will assemble a complete newsletter from start to finish, the chapter will take you step by step through the enter process while you work hands-on with the computer. The familiar Practice What You've Learned section will be omitted and the chapter includes only one Check Yourself exercise.

Setting Up

The newsletter will be assembled as a single-sided, letter-sized document.

To begin the project, set up your document as follows:

1. Open a new letter-sized PageMaker document with the **Double-Sided** option turned off in the **New** dialog. Set the margins to be .5" on the right, left, and bottom edges of the document. Set the top margin at 2.5" Set the document up for three columns with a gutter between columns of 0.2".
2. With the new document open, make sure that the guides and rulers are showing. Choose **Snap to guides** from the **Guides and rulers** submenu of the **Layout** menu if it's not already selected. The **Toolbox, Control,** and **Colors** palettes should all be opened. Move these to get them out of the way as shown in Figure 13.1.

With these steps complete, you are now ready to lay out the newsletter. The next task is to define where the *masthead* will go. (The masthead is a newspaper's name located at the top of page 1. Familiar mastheads include those of *The New York Times* or *The Wall Street Journal.*) The masthead area is usually separated from the *body copy* by some design element. (Body copy is the text that makes up the news section of the newspaper. Unlike the masthead, which never changes, the entire body copy area changes every day in a daily newspaper.)

▼ ***Figure 13.1. Document Setup for Newsletter***

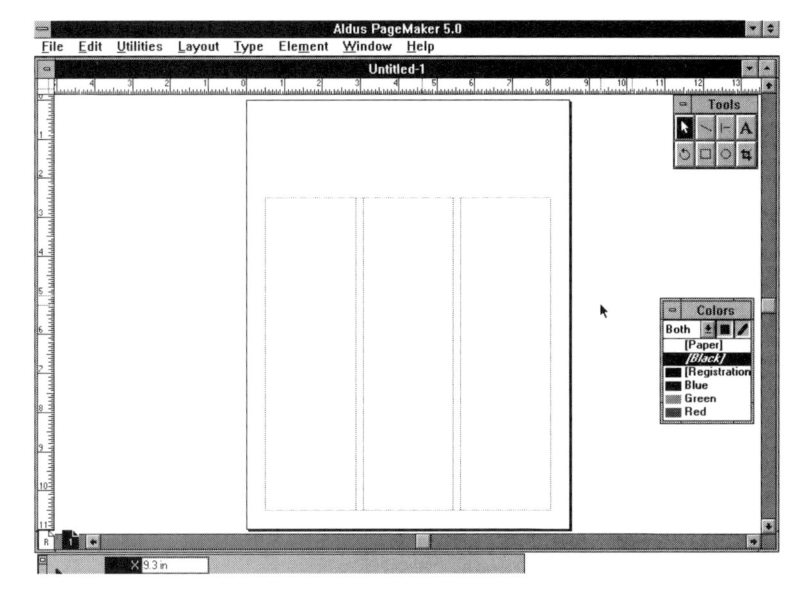

Setting Up

Assembling the Masthead

A color masthead was created in the Practice What You've Learned exercises in Chapter 10. You saved it in a file named MASTHEAD. The top margin was deliberately set to become the bottom of the masthead area. Before placing the masthead, add a ruler guide under the margin guide to delineate the top of the body copy area from the masthead area.

▲ Pull a ruler guide from the horizontal ruler bar (at the top of the PageMaker window) and position it 1/4" below the margin guide. Use the rulers to get the position right.

Now, as you can see, the document is divided into two distinct areas—the masthead area and the body copy area. There are also three zones outside the side and bottom margins that will be left blank because they are too close to the edge of the paper.

Place the Masthead

Next we need to import and place the masthead created in Chapter 10, which was saved as a PageMaker document. So, instead of using the **Place. . .** command, we will bring the masthead into the publication by copying it from the PageMaker document MASTHEAD.

To make the copy:

1. Open the PageMaker document MASTHEAD. The masthead is really composed of two objects: a rectangle and a text block. Click on the rectangle to select it. Now, hold down the **Shift** key and click on the text block to select both objects.
2. Choose **Copy** from the **Edit** menu. Then close the MASTHEAD document. (You will not be prompted to save changes because you didn't make any.)
3. Click on the newsletter document (or choose it from the **Window** menu) to make the window active if it is not active already. Choose **Paste** from the **Edit** menu to paste the objects copied from the MASTHEAD document into the newsletter layout.
4. Using the **Pointer** tool, select both objects and drag them until the left and bottom edges snap to the left and top margin guides. (You want the bottom of the text block to touch the top of the margin guide as shown in Figure 13.2)
5. Using the **Pointer** tool, adjust the right edge of the rectangle until it snaps to the right margin guide. Do the same for the right edge of the text block. This effectively centers the masthead.
6. Use PageMaker's **Save As. . .** command to save your file. Name it NEWSLTR.

Once the masthead is in place, you have completed the first phase of the project. The next step is to assemble the material for the body copy and place it within the newsletter.

Assembling the Masthead

▼ ***Figure 13.2. The Bottom of the Masthead Should Touch the Margin Guide***

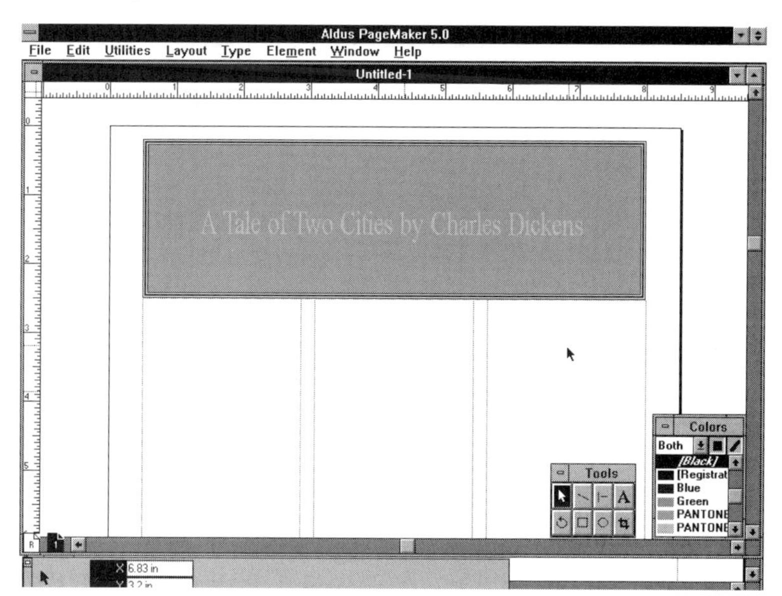

Add a Headline to the Layout

Just like big city newspapers, your newsletter needs a major headline. To help you place the text block in the correct place in the layout, we'll add a guide to show where the bottom edge of the text block should go.

To add the ruler guide:

1. Pull a ruler guide from the top ruler and position it 1/4" below the guide that was added to show where the masthead area ended and the body copy began. (Figure 13.3 shows where the new guide should go.)
2. Next, select the **Text** tool and position the insertion point at the left margin of the left column just below the guide you just placed. Enter the text **Uncertainty Grips London and Paris.** The text will occupy two lines in the column.
3. Using the **Pointer** tool, click on the lower right corner of the text block and stretch it all the way across to the right margin of your publication.

▼ *Figure 13.3. New Ruler Guide Placement*

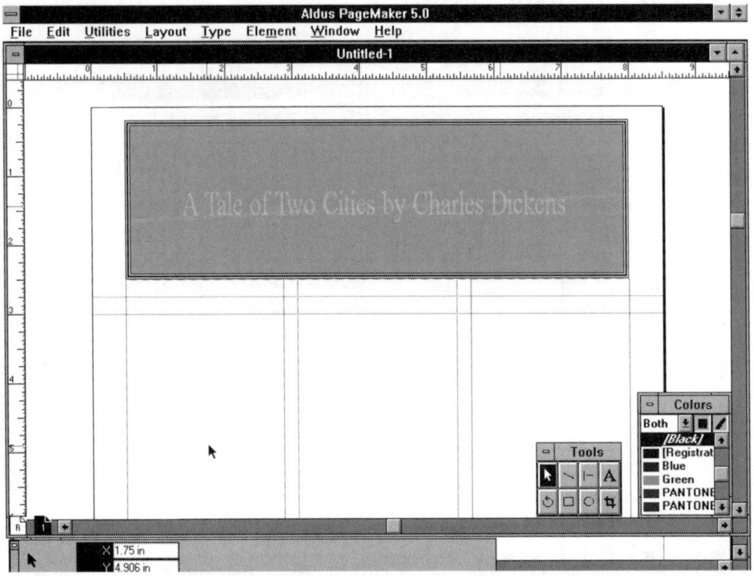

4. Then, to make it fit the space, change the font to **30-point Times New Roman** and choose **Bold** as the style. Use the **Width...** command explained in Chapter 8 to extend the type to better fit the space. 120% of the original width should work.
5. With the type still selected, select **Blue** from the **Colors** palette.
6. Use the **Pointer** tool to click on the headline and position it right up against the guide you dropped below the masthead.

You now have the first part of the news section of the newsletter complete. Next we'll reserve space for a graphic in the newsletter.

Using a Graphic Placeholder

Often you will know that you want to use a graphic in a publication, but you will not have the final artwork when you start doing the layout. The solution is to place a rectangle the size of the graphic you want in the layout and use it as a *placeholder* to reserve the necessary space. To align the placeholder, you will add two ruler guides to the layout as well.

Using a Graphic Placeholder

To reserve space for a graphic:

1. Add two ruler guides to the layout by pulling them from the vertical ruler (the ruler on the left side of the window). Position both of them between the guides between the columns as shown in Figure 13.4. To place them exactly in the center of each gutter, use the rulers. Place an additional guide at the bottom of the text block that contains the headline. You will need to go to the **Guides and rulers** submenu and select **Lock guides** to prevent the guides from being moved by the next step.
2. Create a square using the **Rectangle** tool. The box should measure approximately 4" by 4". Use the **Control** palette to make the sides equal. Position the box between the three guidelines.
3. Add a 1-point border to the picture box if one has not been added automatically based on PageMaker's **Line.**

You have now reserved space for a graphic in the layout. It's time to add the story text.

▼ ***Figure 13.4. Guides for Picture Box***

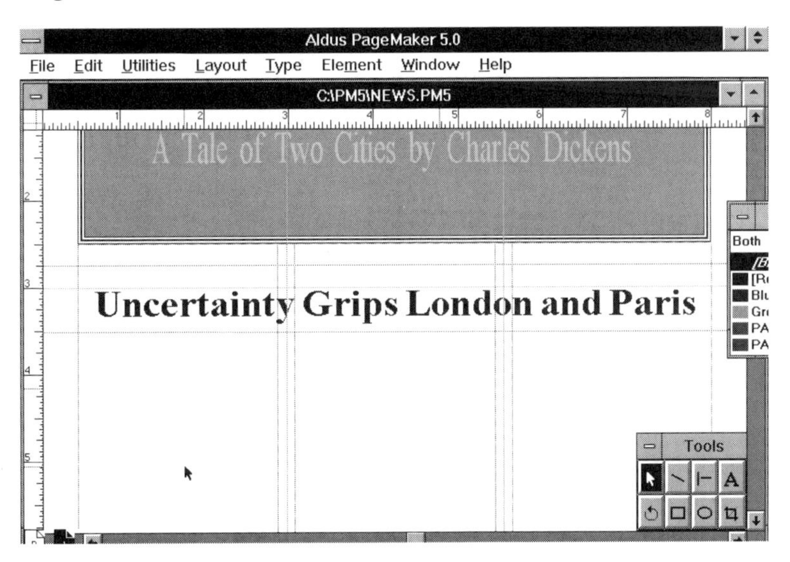

Adding Text to the Newsletter

You will add two existing stories to the layout to create the "news." The first story was created in Chapter 5 and is called DICKENS2.WP5. The second story was created in Chapter 11 and is called CRUNCHER.WP5. You will format the stories as you go and one paragraph from CRUNCHER will be deleted to make it fit the layout. After the stories have been imported, you will reformat them and add decorative touches, such as drop caps, using PageMaker's automatic drop cap feature. A headline will be added to the second story.

To import the text:

1. Check that **Autoflow** is turned off in the **Layout** menu.
2. Choose **Place** from the **File** menu. Select DICKENS2.WP5.
3. When the loaded text icon appears, position it at the top left of the left column and flow the text. It will not all fit in one column. The bottom windowshade handle will have an arrow in it.
4. Before flowing the rest of the text in the second column, we will reformat it. Use the **Text** tool to place the insertion point anywhere in the text. Choose **Select all** from the **Edit** menu. Go to the **Type** menu and select the **14-point Times New Roman** font with 19 points of leading. Set the alignment to justify.
5. Now use the **Pointer** tool and adjust the bottom windowshade to align with the dotted line near the bottom of the column. Click on the windowshade handle. The pointer becomes a loaded text icon.
6. Move the load text icon to the top of the middle column and click to flow the text. Use the Pointer tool to line up the text block with the left column. You are done with the first story.
7. Select **Place** from the **File** menu again. Import the story CRUNCHER.WP5 and place it in the right-hand column.
8. Set the story in **14-point Times New Roman** with 19-point leading and justification.
9. Add to the top of the story CRUNCHER, a subhead in 14-point Times New Roman: **A Private Dwelling in Whitefriars.**
10. Reformat the subhead you just entered as left-justified type and assign the style **Bold** to it.

11. Remove any paragraph indents assigned to both stories. (If there are none, skip this step.)
12. Make sure that the lines of text line up through the three columns and the layout looks like the one shown in Figure 13.5.

Adding Text to the Newsletter

Two Decorative Touches

The text is now all placed and formatted to fit the layout. It's time to add a couple of decorative touches to spruce up the design a little. First you will add drop caps to the layout, and then several lines will be added to visually enhance and define the newsletter.

Add Drop Caps

As you remember from Chapter 8, drop caps can be added by PageMaker. For the newsletter project, you will add them to the text portions of both stories. The "lead" story, which was import-

▼ ***Figure 13.5. Layout with Placed Text***

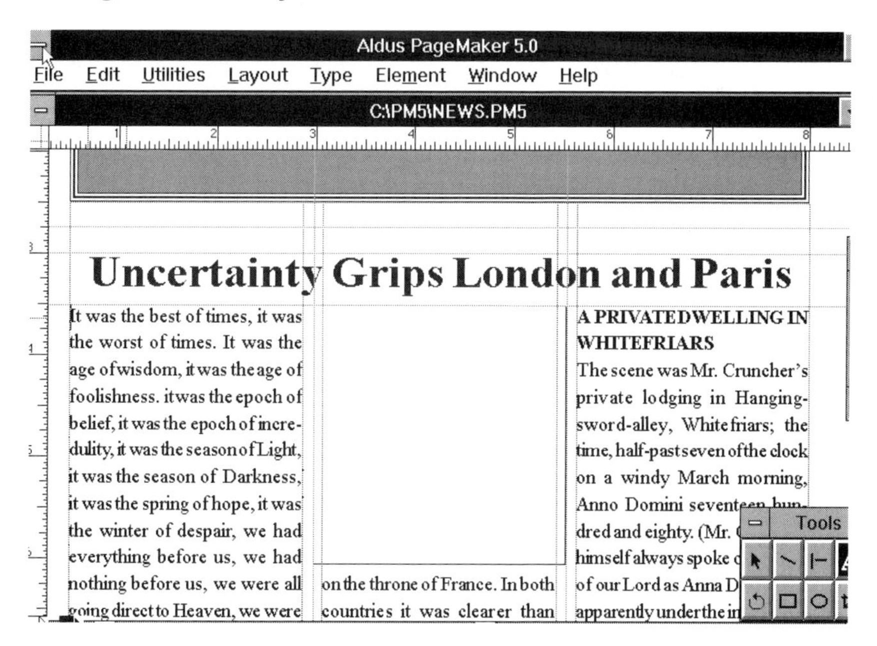

ed from the file DICKENS2.WP5, should contain two paragraphs, both of which will be assigned a drop cap. The story that originated as CRUNCHER.WP5 should also contain two paragraphs.

To add the drop caps:

1. Use the **Text** tool to place the insertion point anywhere in the first story. Go to the **Additions** submenu of **Utilities** and select **Drop cap....** Specify two lines for the size and click **OK.**
2. Add drop caps for the second paragraph of this story and the text of the second story.

The layout should now look like the one shown in Figure 13.6.

Add Rules (Lines) to the Layout

The last element in the layout process is to add three rules to the layout to improve its appearance. The first rule will be added between the masthead and the body of the layout. The second two rules will be added between the columns of text.

▼ ***Figure 13.6. The Nearly Finished Newsletter***

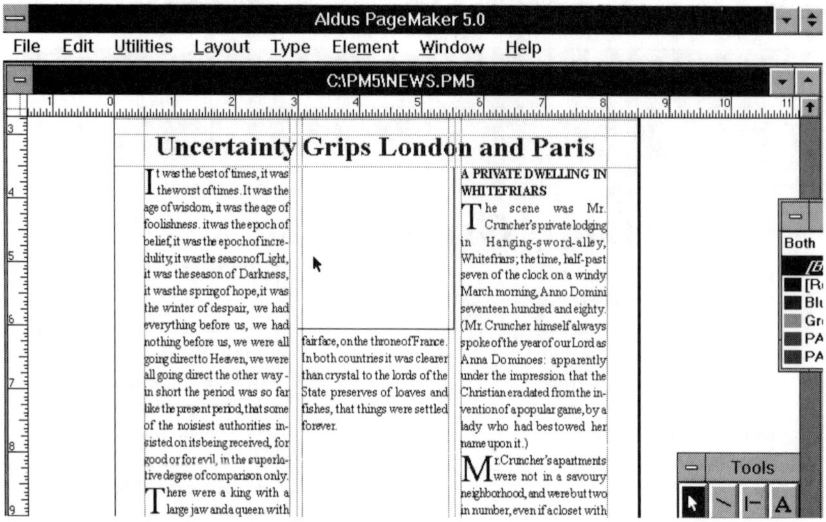

Two Decorative Touches

To add the rules:

1. Add a line halfway between the masthead and the body copy as shown in Figure 13.7. Make this rule 4 points wide, and make it a double line by choosing this style from the **Line** submenu. The edges of the line should touch the right and left margins as shown. Use the rulers to precisely place the rule vertically.
2. Add two rules between the text columns as shown. Each rule should begin just below the rectangle and extend to the bottom margin guide. Make each rule .5 points wide.

The newsletter project is now complete. It should look like the example shown in Figure 13.8.

Well Done!

If you have made it through the layout of the newsletter, congratulations! You have just assembled your first complete page layout using PageMaker for Windows—and you are ready to start de-

▼ ***Figure 13.7. Adding a Line to the Masthead***

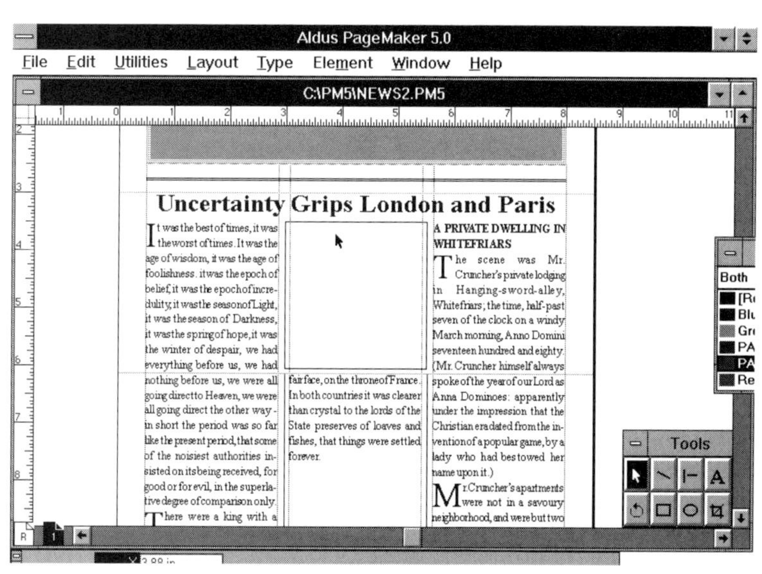

▼ ***Fugure 13.8. The Completed Newsletter***

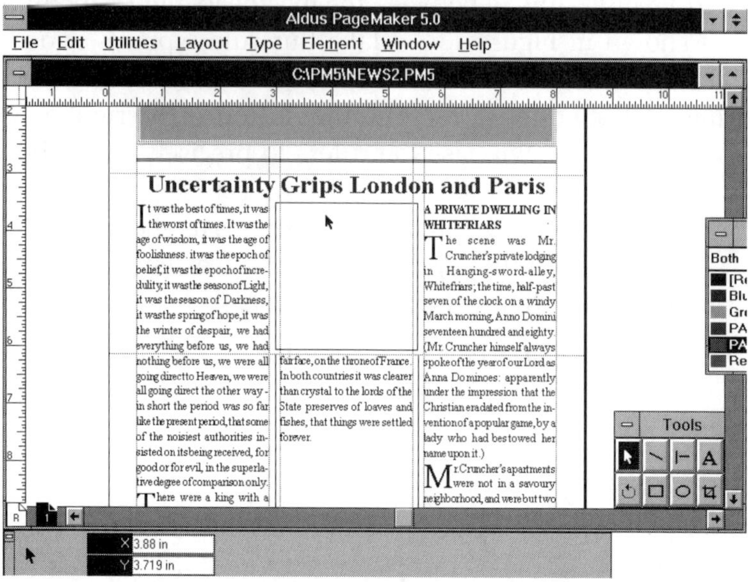

signing your own publications for the real world. You might want to take this opportunity to add more colors to the layout or print it as described in Chapter 11. But first, remember to save your work to your hard disk. Never forget to save your work.

This almost wraps up the lessons in the Self-Teaching Guide, but there's one more function that we would like to show you. PageMaker allows you to save the "infrastructure" of your publication for use later in another document. These saved structures are called templates and are explained in the next section.

Creating and Using Templates

Depending on the kind of documents you create using PageMaker, you may use much of the material over and over, making changes only to text and pictures while leaving the underlying format largely intact. This is especially true if you will create publications like magazines, books, or newsletters.

Unfortunately, if you open a document and modify it to be a new document, it's very easy to accidentally save the new

Creating and Using Templates

document over the old one—and your first work will be lost. Since this isn't always desirable, use PageMaker's template feature so that this problem can be avoided.

When you create a document that will be modified into other similar documents later, you can save it as a special kind of file that prevents accidental overwriting. This special document, a template, is saved with a .PT5 extension instead of the .PM5 extension assigned to regular PageMaker documents. A PageMaker template includes all of the original document and you can modify it any way you like, but when you use the Save... command, a Save As dialog box appears with no filename selected. Entering a new filename (for the new document) prevents accidental erasure of the original document used to create the template.

To create a template:

1. Save the document normally to create a regular PageMaker file.
2. Choose **Save As...** and enter a new name for the template. For example, you might save the newsletter as NEWSTEM. Click the **Template** button within the dialog, then click **OK.** You will notice that the extension for a saved template appears different than normal PageMaker documents.

To use a template:

▲ Open the template like any other PageMaker document. When you go to save your work, the blank name field reminds you to give the file a new name. The newly saved, renamed file will be a regular PageMaker document.

CHECK YOURSELF

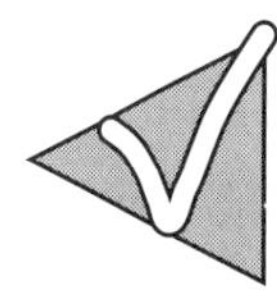

After saving your newsletter normally, save it as NEWSTEM and click the **Template** button within the **Save As** dialog box. Close the document and open NEWSTEM. Choose **Save. . .** from the **File** menu. What happens?

▲ Instead of saving the document normally, the Save As dialog box opens with no filename in the field, even though NEWSTEM has a name.

Glossary

Adobe Type Manager Adobe Type Manager is a program that renders fonts on-screen so they appear smooth in any size. Fonts are created as outlines in Adobe Type Manager (also known as ATM). ATM can render any compatible font smoothly in any point size.

Alignment Placing objects so that the edges, tops, bottoms, or sides of the objects are lined up.

Application A specific software program designed to perform a specific function. PageMaker for Windows is an application program designed to develop professional page layouts for reproduction.

ASCII An acronym for *American Standard Code for Information Interchange,* a standard coding system for representing text in computer systems. Text converted to ASCII format is almost universally readable by word processors, communication programs, and page layout programs—though almost no formatting information is included in an ASCII file, only characters and numbers.

Attribute A setting that lets you describe how a command or object will appear within PageMaker, often specified in dialog menus. Attributes are also referred to as *specifications* or *preferences.*

Background In PageMaker, all objects (except lines) contain a *background*, which contains a color or is transparent. The background is the inside of the object and does not include the frame or the text in a text block.

Bitmapped Graphic Dot structures in a computer's memory that represent images dot by dot. For the purposes of this book, a bitmap is a black-and-white image using one bit per pixel or dot.

Body Copy The bulk of the text contained in an ad, brochure, or direct mail piece. Where the headlines catch attention, the body copy reinforces the headline message and adds detail. Most body copy is set in a readable font ranging in size from 9 to 14 points.

Border The outside edge of any PageMaker object (except lines) is an entity that can be independently adjusted. A border in PageMaker can be adjusted for width, color, and style.

Buffer An area of computer memory used for temporary storage of data. (See *Paste Buffer*)

CMYK An acronym for cyan, magenta, yellow, and key, where key represents black. CMYK is the four-color process ink model used to render color images in print. CMY refers to a similar color model, but without black.

Contrast Used to describe differences in brightness or colors. High contrast describes an image with great differences in brightness and/or color. In a low-contrast image most brightness and/or color levels appear similar to one another in value.

Crop Photos are *cropped* to select only the area that is desired for print.

Crop Marks Marks that show where a photo crop should occur. Crop marks are becoming synonymous with the phrase "trim marks" that show where excess paper will be trimmed away, even if a photo is not involved.

Cyan A blue used as one of the process colors, which appears as a bright, medium blue to the eye.

Default Most computer hardware and software have *defaults* set for a variety of functions. These are the settings most likely to be used by someone not interested or knowledgeable enough to make changes. For example, the default font used by Windows programs is "System"—a font that's easy to read and will neither offend nor excite anyone—hence it is assigned as the default. In color publishing there are many default settings, some of which should never be adjusted unless you are a person of experience. Others can be readily adjusted with no ill effects. In this book, we point out when default settings are best left alone and when they can be modified freely.

Desktop The working area within PageMaker is called the *desktop,* because the page layout is made to resemble working on a conventional drafting table or desk.

DOS The acronym for the operating system used on IBM-PCs and compatible personal computers and the underlying system required to run Windows (and PageMaker). DOS stands for disk-based operating system.

Double-Click Clicking twice in rapid succession; it is used to open programs within Windows and to choose items within certain kinds of windows and dialogs.

Download To transfer a file, either by modem or directly by network or cable link from a remote computer, the file is *downloaded* to your computer.

DPI Stands for dots per inch, a measurement of resolution. More dots per inch equals higher resolution.

Drag Items are moved by clicking once and holding down the left button of the mouse. By holding down on the mouse while moving the item, it is dragged or moved to a new location.

Drop Caps Capital letters are sometimes enlarged and placed inside the top left corner of a paragraph as a decorative effect. This is a *drop cap*. PageMaker has a facility for automatically creating drop caps.

Drop-down Menu A menu you invoke from the top menu bar in a Windows program or within PageMaker. By clicking on or touching one of the menu items in the top bar, another menu of choices is displayed or "drops down" from the top.

EPS or *EPSF* EPS stands for Encapsulated PostScript—a file format for storing a PostScript description of a page or image. EPS files may consist of English-like words and binary or hexidecimal data. Also called EPSF by some.

Export To take a portion of a PageMaker document, such as a page or text, and translate it into another format that can be stored on disk separately and read by another program.

Facing Pages When two pages face each other in a layout (like the two you are reading now) they are said to be *facing pages*. The attributes of these pages are often designed to work with each other as a single design because both pages are seen at one time.

Fill A color, gray, or texture used to *fill* an area in an illustration or other image.

Film Transparent media covered with light-sensitive emulsion. Film in graphic arts is like the kind you use in your camera, but it is thicker and sold in sheets. Color film is rarely used in printing applications. Most graphic art film is designed to become transparent or remain black with no grays in between. This allows better transfer of dot structures for lithographic reproduction.

Film Processor Once film or RC (resin-coated) paper is imaged, it's passed through a *film processor* that automatically develops it. A film processor is a standard component of imagesetter installations.

Filter Used by PageMaker to strip out word processing codes from text and replace them with PageMaker codes.

Floating Palette Small windows that can be moved around the PageMaker desktop that contain information or controls are called *floating palettes*.

Focoltone Color System A color system designed to compete with the Pantone Matching System (PMS). The central feature of Focoltone is its compatibility with computer-specified color. Its colors can be specified as either solid spot colors or as process colors.

Font The complete set of characters, with a specific size, weight, and attribute, in a typeface. The term font is often used interchangeably with the term *typeface* in desktop publishing circles, even though this is not technically accurate.

Graduated Blend Even transitions in colors from one value to another.

Grayed A selection on a PageMaker menu that is not available because of the current selection or status of the system is grayed.

Grayscale Black-and-white continuous tone images are scanned into the PC as *grayscales* made up of 4, 16, 64, or 256 grays.

Group Individual objects can be assembled into a single object by grouping them.

Gutter The area where two pages of a book are connected to the spine is called the *gutter.* Gutters require extra paper so that contents of the left and right pages will align properly. Elements "jumping gutters" (images that continue from left to right on two pages) can be problematic when the job is assembled at the bindery because they have to be matched perfectly.

Hairline A very thin line (.5 point or less width) used in a design.

Halftone To print black-and-white images, the continuous tone must be broken down into dots. This is done conventionally by photographically converting the image through screens. The resulting dots are called *halftone dots.* The entire screened image is known as a *halftone.*

Headline Usually a single sentence or a few words of type that is larger and bolder than the rest of the text. Headlines are used to catch attention, convey a major message, or to balance a design on a page.

Horizontal Scale The characters that make up type can be made narrower or wider to fit a layout better or as a decorative effect. This is making an adjustment to their *horizontal scale.*

HSB HSB is an acronym for hue, saturation, and brightness—One of many models for describing and representing color supported by PageMaker.

HSL HSL is an acronym for hue, saturation, and luminance—one of many models for describing and representing color. HSL is not supported by PageMaker.

Hue One of the primary dimensions of color, along with saturation and brightness. Hue is the aspect of color that distinguishes it from other colors; for example, "peach" is a different hue than "pink."

Icon A small graphic intended to represent a tool or file type in Windows or PageMaker.

Imagesetter Devices that convert PostScript code into a rasterized format for high-resolution output on film or paper. Imagesetters are used to convert page layout files into film for print. In most of this book, the word "imagesetter" is used to refer to the complete imaging system, made up of a computer, a RIP processor, the imagesetter, and a film processor.

Import To bring a file from outside of PageMaker into the page layout.

Justify To align text within a text block.

Kerning Individual pairs of letters sometimes require the space between them to be adjusted to improve the readability of a line of type. This process is called *kerning.*

Key Part of the cyan, magenta, yellow, and key (CMYK) color model; *key* is another name for black.

Landscape Orientation Horizontal orientation of a document, so it is wider than it is tall.

Layer When working within PageMaker, images and design elements may be kept on separate *layers.* This makes it easy to get to an object that may have other objects in front of it.

Leading The space between lines of type is referred to as the *leading* because strips of lead were once used for this purpose. Increasing leading (spacing) between lines of type make it more readable. Decreasing leading allows more type to fit in a given space.

Line Art Art that is made up of lines and solids with no grays or colors. It can be the basis of color art created on the PC and used by a print shop as a guide for adding colors to a job.

Linear Fill A color, gray, or textured fill used to paint an area from one point to another with a mathematical gradation of texture or color between the two points.

Magenta *Magenta* is one of the four process colors. It looks like a bright purple-shifted pink.

Margin Guides When a new PageMaker document is created, guides are specified for the margin. This is usually where type and other objects stop so that they don't print unattractively close to the edge of the page.

Master Page PageMaker provides a *master page* function to speed layout assembly time. Objects placed on a master page appear on all subsequent pages unless explicitly excluded.

Modem Hardware devices used to transmit information from one computer to another over telephone lines. In desktop publishing, they are used to send files to a service bureau.

Object Elements placed within a PageMaker page layout are objects. These may consist of rectangles, ovals, lines, and text boxes.

Palette A selection of colors. Palettes are frequently created for groups of frequently used colors. By creating a standard palette in a publishing program, commonly used colors don't need to be specified each time a new document is started.

Pantone Matching System (PMS) A patented process for defining colors. Pantone colors (called PMS colors) can be specified from a swatch book and then closely duplicated by a print shop from books that explain how to mix colors to match the numbered inks in the swatch book. PMS colors can also be specified in many applications as screen color, although the resulting color may not match its spot counterpart exactly.

Paragraph Indent The first line of a paragraph is often indented to where the characters begin farther to the right than subsequent lines. A *paragraph indent* is used to visually separate one paragraph from the ones preceding and following it.

Pasteboard An area of space is provided around the edge of each page in a PageMaker page layout for temporarily placing objects on the desktop before pasting them into the page layout. The pasteboard is also useful for allowing items too large for the page to spill onto the pasteboard until they can be repositioned. The size of the pasteboard can be adjusted within the Application Preferences dialog.

Paste Buffer PageMaker uses a *paste buffer* for temporarily storing information to be copied to other areas of the document after using the Cut or Copy command.

Path The MS-DOS location (drive/directory/subdirectory) of a file.

Pica A unit of measurement used by printers, that will often be a measurement option in desktop publishing programs, though not often used by designers. There are 6 picas to an inch. A pica is also equal to about 12 points.

Plates Press images are transferred to paper by metal or plastic press *plates.* Metal plates are superior to plastic. Quality color publishing jobs are never printed with plastic plates.

Point A measurement used in the graphic arts to specify type sizes, line weights (widths), trapping values, and paper weights. There are 72.27 points to an inch, but most page layout programs measure a point as an even 1/72 inch. In measuring paper thickness, a point is 1/1000 of an inch.

Pointer Tool This tool is used within PageMaker documents to reposition and recess objects. It can also be used to place guides within the page layout and to select objects for manipulation by commands found under PageMaker's pull-down menus.

Pop-up Menu A set of choices that pop up within a dialog box.

Portrait Orientation Vertical orientation of a document, so the document is taller than it is wide.

PostScript A page description language developed by Adobe Systems and used to describe type and visual elements so they can be output on devices with PostScript interpreters. PostScript instructions are highly portable across a wide range of computer platforms and output devices.

Preferences Settings In a software product with as much functionality as PageMaker for Windows, instead of setting up each and every document, *preference settings* can be adjusted to eliminate a lengthy configuration session for each new document.

Prepress The process of getting a job ready for print is called *prepress.* In the case of Windows publishing, this begins with readying a page layout for output at the service bureau. It ends when the job is on press being printed. In traditional publishing, prepress involves processes like camera work, stripping, and platemaking. Many of these functions are now automated by computers and special software. Prepress is sometimes called preparation or prep.

Process Blue See *Cyan.*

Process Color *Process color* is a system of breaking down and reproducing all visible colors (in theory) in print. The process colors are cyan, magenta, yellow, and black.

Process Red See *Magenta.*

Registration Marks Marks added to color jobs at the imagesetter to show the printer exactly where each color film layer should be positioned in relationship to other layers.

Resolution How much detail is displayed on a monitor or a printer, normally specified in dots per inch (dpi) for printers and horizontal by vertical dots for monitors. The more dots the higher the resolution.

Reverse White type on a black or dark-colored background.

RGB RGB, or red-green-blue, is the standard color model for color monitors and color televisions. It is based on the use of red, green, and blue electron guns that cause phosphor on a monitor's screen to glow. Different amounts of output from each gun mix together to create different colors.

RIP An acronym for raster image processor; used to rasterize PageMaker output into a format that can be imaged on film or paper within the imagesetter.

Ruler Guides Lines that can be added to a page layout to simplify or verify alignment and placement of objects. They are added to PageMaker documents manually by "pulling" them from the rulers when the rulers and guides are showing.

Sans Serif Type Type that lacks decorative capping at the end of character lines and elements is said to be sans serif *type* because these caps are called serifs.

Scale To increase or decrease the size of an image.

Screen When a color is broken into dots it is said to be *screened.* Screens are used to lighten colors because around each dot of color white paper shows through. The smaller the color dot, the more white is allowed to show. This creates a lighter color.

Screen Color A color made up from screens of two or more of the four process colors.

Screen Tint Solid colors such as Pantone colors or solid process colors can be lightened by screening them; the resulting color is called a *screen tint* or simply a *tint.* For example, magenta printed as a 40% tint appears as a medium pink. The ink coverage for a screen tint is less than 100% and thus simulates shading or a lighter color.

Serif Type Type with decorative end caps at the ends of each character's body elements and lines.

Service Bureau or *SB* A company that provides publishing services to desktop publishers. A typical service bureau sells time on an imagesetter by the page or minute. Other service bureaus may include proofing, scanning, advice, and problem-solving as part of their services.

Shift-Click Multiple elements can be selected or deselected using the *Shift-Click* procedure. To use this procedure, the Shift key is held down while clicking on elements with the mouse.

Spot Color Color that doesn't use process color separation, but instead consists of solid-colored type and design elements, is said to be *spot color*.

Strip or *Stripping* The process of converting a mechanical into plate-ready film is the process of *stripping*. This involves taping together various pieces of film so they can be made into a printing plate. The people who handle the jobs are strippers.

Styles In longer documents, rather than individually reformatting each block of text, a *style* can be defined that applies any number of parameters to the text in one action. Styles are defined using the Define styles... command found under the Type menu and applied from the Style submenu also under the Type menu.

Templates A guide that is used to base one item on the design of another. Once a document is saved as a template, it can be opened and used to create a new document based on the one saved as a template. To avoid erasing the template accidentally, a new name must be specified before the file can be saved.

Text Wrap Formally a complex manual type procedure, PageMaker will automatically wrap type around objects, images, or other type using the settings found in the Text wrap dialog.

Thumbnails *Thumbnails* are miniature renderings of a page layout. Typically measuring larger than a human thumbnail, these tiny sketches are used to evolve designs with headlines, copy, and actual photos and illustrations. By creating the layout in a small format, drawing time is reduced and elements simplified. This way, the overall design is easy to see without the clutter of headlines, illustrations, and multiple colors. PageMaker for Windows can directly print thumbnail representations of a layout by selecting them as an option within the Print dialog.

Tiling When a document is too large to print on the selected printer, PageMaker can break it into pieces small enough to print and the document can then be assembled into a complete document again. These pieces are called Tiles and this option is selected in the Print dialog.

Trap Assembled where one color touches another to guard against ordinary and acceptable shift of registration on press. When two colors trap, their edges overlap slightly.

Trim Marks Marks that show where excess paper should be shorn away from the side of a printed sheet. They can be added automatically by most page layout programs. Trim marks are also called crop marks by some designers.

Trim Size The size of the final printed product after the final trim is made.

True Color True Color refers to a full-color representation. True Color is a term used in the PC world; it is called full color in the Mac world. It is also described as 24-bit color or 32-bit color.

TrueType TrueType is a font outline technology developed jointly by Microsoft Corporation and Apple Computers. Microsoft is now including TrueType and TrueType fonts with Windows. TrueType uses a mathematical description of each character to render the outline of it, just as Adobe Type Manager does. Because these outlines are simply math formulas, to make the font larger or smaller (scale it), TrueType simply plugs in new numbers for the new size.

TruMatch TruMatch is a patented system for specifying process colors that allows each color to be specified in one-percent increments.

Undo Found under the Edit menu, the Undo command is used to reverse the last operation performed.

WYSIWYG An acronym for *What You See Is What You Get*. It is a central idea behind the Windows visual display. If something is true WYSIWYG, what you see on the screen is identical to what you will see in print.

Index